Disability Intimacy

Disability Intimacy

Essays on Love, Care, and Desire

Edited by Alice Wong

VINTAGE BOOKS
A Division of Penguin Random House LLC
New York

A VINTAGE BOOKS ORIGINAL 2024

Introduction and compilation copyright © 2024 by Alice Wong

Library of Congress Cataloging-in-Publication Data
Names: Wong, Alice, [date] editor.
Title: Disability intimacy : essays on love, care, and desire /
edited by Alice Wong.
Description: First edition. | New York : Vintage Books,
a division of Penguin Random House, LLC, 2024.
Identifiers: LCCN 2023016059 (print) | LCCN 2023016060 (ebook)
Subjects: LCSH: People with disabilities—Sexual behavior. | People with
disabilities—Social conditions. | Disabilities—Social aspects.
Classification: LCC HQ30.5 .D57 2020 (print) | LCC HQ30.5 (ebook) |
DDC 306.7087—dc23
LC record available at https://lccn.loc.gov/2023016059
LC ebook record available at https://lccn.loc.gov/2023016060

Vintage Books Trade Paperback ISBN: 978-0-593-46973-6
eBook ISBN: 978-0-593-46974-3

Editor photograph © Eddie Hernandez Photography
Book design by Steven Walker

vintagebooks.com

Printed in the United States of America
10 9 8 7 6 5 4 3 2 1

For me. I love you very much. You deserve everything you desire.

Contents

PART II: PLEASURE AND DESIRE

PART III: CREATIVITY AND POWER

PART IV: EVERYTHING AND EVERYWHERE

Introduction

Alice Wong

Having a progressive neuromuscular disability means expecting the unexpected and knowing my body will become weaker with a timeline and mind of its own. In June 2022, my body rang alarm bells. My ability to swallow slowly diminished, becoming more difficult. I adapted for a while by eating only soft foods and liquids and tilting my head down to prevent choking. I was losing weight and my nutrition was declining, but I still thought I could manage despite being unable to swallow completely and regurgitating half a sip of latte or a bite of yogurt or peanut butter. I loved coffee and was unwilling to let go of a life of flavor and pleasure. Coughing and not eating for several days in a row, I felt bad but didn't realize the danger I was in.

After several days, something shifted. I texted my sister who was out of town for work and asked if she could come back the next day and take me to the ER. My friend Steve dropped off some pudding after learning I'd stopped eating and asked if I should go immediately, but I wanted to wait for my sister. My older parents did not have the stamina to stay with me in the ER, since a visit could take twenty-four hours or longer depending on waiting time. In the pit of my growling, empty stomach I knew another turning point in my disability was approaching fast. Its gravitational pull was impossible to deny.

I ended up developing aspiration pneumonia, which was compounded by a collapsed lung, unbeknownst to me. I spent four weeks in the ICU that summer and almost died more than once. When I was discharged, I left with a fundamentally altered body tethered to a feeding tube and tracheostomy with a ventilator. I could no longer speak or eat and had numerous medical needs requiring additional significant care. It was the most harrowing time of my life, and it continued well after I got home.

Death is an intimate partner of mine. I know its motions and shadowy presence. The relationship I have to death, dying, and suffering is inextricably linked to how I want to live.

My recovery has been slow and continues to this day. In the last two years I have been soothed by waves of love and care from my friends and family. As I adjusted to a new body and intensive healthcare needs, friends and acquaintances stepped up, offering support, resources, and time. Being high-risk, I self-isolated during the fall and winter with multiple viruses and the interminable COVID pandemic in full effect. Paid caregivers came in and out of my home every day, and I had to reduce my exposure by declining indoor gatherings with friends and visits to my favorite places such as museums, cafés, and bakeries. Instead, I sent silly cat memes and GIFs, shared snarky and bitchy comments, praised and celebrated with my friends via texts, emails, and Zoom sessions. Waves of love kept me afloat, despite feeling adrift from shore. I was lonely, but I wasn't alone.

My memoir, *Year of the Tiger: An Activist's Life*, debuted in fall of that year and I also began work editing the anthology you are reading right now. Slowing down and resting is radical, but I also felt an urgency to work. I wanted to create this book with my editorial team at Vintage, Anna Kaufman and Ellie Pritchett; our conversations were generative and gave me something to look forward to, adding much-needed variety to my mundane and time-consuming daily care routine. Wrangling these magnificent cats, the contributors for *Disability Intimacy*, and reading and editing their work was a joy. Creating something was a critical lifeline just like the breaths of air from my ventilator and the liquid nutrition flowing into my feeding tube. I consider this book as my latest labor of love and am grateful to be able to offer it to the world.

Disability Intimacy is divided into four sections: Love and Care; Pleasure and Desire; Creativity and Power; and Everything and Everywhere. There are original essays, reprinted pieces, and poetry on the nuances and complexities of intimacy. As with my first anthology, *Disability Visibility*, it is difficult to categorize a collection of wide-ranging work by such dazzling contributors. Referencing Wallace Stevens's poem "Thirteen Ways of Looking at a Blackbird," this book presents forty ways of looking at intimacy, among them: Nicole Schroeder on the love and kinship between disabled people; Sami Schalk on pleasure activism; Travis Chi Wing Lau on seeing himself reflected in a series of portraits; Moya Bailey on Black disabled doulas; Robin Wilson-Beattie on BDSM; Gracen Brilmyer on access intimacy in archival work; Ada Hubrig on their cat Rosasharon; Elliot Kukla on being a disabled parent; Marie E. S. Flores on becoming a disabled parent; Mia Mingus on disabled heartbreak; Leah Lakshmi Piepzna-Samarasinha on longing; Tee Franklin on finding disabled queer love; Sarah Young Bear-Brown on the intimacy of beadwork and the wisdom from her ancestors; Pelenakeke Brown on the intimacy of performance; Sejal A. Shah on writing love letters; Khadijah Queen on the illusion and intimacy of care; Ashley Volion and Akemi Nishida on reclaiming intimacy based on crip wisdom; Syrus Marcus Ware on love and activism; Gabrielle Peters on living in isolation and online community organizing; Melissa Hung on friendship; Maria Town on marriage equality and why disabled love is beautiful; the Redwoods on the intimacy of many people living in one body sharing a life together; and much more. Poetry is an intimacy with language, and I hope you also enjoy works by John Lee Clark, Ashna Ali, Cyrée Jarelle Johnson, and Ellen Samuels. This is a small sample of disabled brilliance that will provoke and seduce, inviting you to reexamine what intimacy can be.

When I started working on this book, I googled "disability intimacy" and the search results were disappointing and pathetic. "Ewwwwww," I muttered to myself. Under the People Also Ask section, questions such as "Can people with disabilities find love?" are what I considered basic AF. Articles on stereotypes, stigmas, sexuality, asexuality, sexual abuse, and sexual dysfunction abounded. Stories about and by disabled people on "what it's like" to date, have sex, or be in a relationship abounded. Intimacy is more than sex or romantic love. Intimacy is an ever-expanding universe composed of a myriad of heavenly bodies. Intimacy is about relationships within a person's self, with others, with communities, with nature, and beyond.

Disability Intimacy will blow your mind, leaving you shook and open to the possibilities around us. Each piece in this anthology is unique, but one theme that runs throughout is *tenderness*, an expression of all the labor and care the contributors put into their stories. I delicately gathered and edited this book with sensitivity, knowing how many people put their trust in me. Being thoughtful, intentional, and generous are acts of intimacy we can give to one another.

I am not an expert on intimacy, nor am I here to define the concept to you. Since tenderness is a major theme in *Disability Intimacy*, it is only right for me to share a vulnerable part of myself that I have never written about or publicly discussed before. True story: I have never been in a romantic relationship or gone on a date. Not once, and I am a fifty-year-old grown-ass woman! The disclosure comes with a mixture of internalized shame and a wish to keep parts of my life private. However, this book prompted me to reflect on the many intimacies of my life and what I wish for the future. My heart is full of rich and deep relationships. I am loved and I am not loved at the same time.

Not everyone needs romance or sex, but I personally want the entire dim sum cart of intimacy. I want to experience every unctuous, savory, sweet, crispy, chewy, spicy, and sour bite, filling my body with warmth and pleasure. My appetite is insatiable; I want the smoldering, undeniable attraction built on mutual respect and admiration like the one between Captain Wentworth and Anne Elliot in Jane Austen's *Persuasion*. I want to be seen and to have a lover who will be my sous chef in all things and vice versa. Our love will be a spark that burns slowly and completely. This person will write me hot, irresistible letters and make me laugh; will pick up ice cream for me; will buy groceries, binge-watch TV, and host amazing dinner parties with me. Downright filthy texts and facial expressions will be our sexual banter. We will be our own two-member book club where we talk passionately about books while sipping champagne and eating fancy potato chips. When I meet that person, I will disarm him with my charm, wit, intellect, and copious modesty.

Given the events of the past few years, I question whether this will ever happen for me and am reconciled to this reality. I struggle to see myself as desirable and can only imagine how the world perceives me. I'm not waiting for someone to sweep me off my feet, but I am ready in a nanosecond. In the meantime, I will continue to fantasize, lust, and be slutty all by myself. My dreams, cravings, and aspirations will sustain my body and soul for now.

Intimacy comes in many forms, and you are deserving of it, whatever it looks like or means to you. Reading the words on these pages creates a dialogue, an intimate act bringing us together across space and time. May *Disability Intimacy* set your spirit on fire and send you on a voyage of self-discovery, destination unknown. My journey continues, and I thank you for being a part of it.

I am but one small shiitake mushroom connected to a vast mycelial network with other disabled fungi, loving and caring for one another. We are not alone.

Disability Intimacy

I Promise You

John Lee Clark

there's nothing in my face. There is nothing in yours. What we have are called heads. They are nothing unless we kiss. Lips are wonderful. They are full of mechanoreceptors. In the Old World we all used to kiss and kiss. It was then that we did have faces. We had noses and cheeks and foreheads and soft downy hair. In the New World we stopped kissing. Those who were already here stopped. Those who came stopped. Now there are only four people who have heads that are also faces. They are an artist and three children for whom I have a face other than my hands.

PART I

Love and Care

Unspooling

Nicole Lee Schroeder

Disabled love is a different kind of love. It's neither born from blood ties nor proximity. It doesn't hold to the same rules as romantic, platonic, or familial love. It comes from a shared desire for a better world. It sustains us in moments when we don't love ourselves, and it offers a tether to cling to as we cycle through grief and readjustment. It's not performative or draining. These days, I weave disabled love into my life like a practiced artisan. I spin threads of love from late-night phone calls, Zoom get-togethers, and disparate Twitter threads. Hand over hand, I wind up scraps of wisdom from those who've come before me. I weave line after line, watching as patterns spring into existence, crafted from the instructions they have patiently and lovingly written down. I tamp down row after row, interlacing the love I have for me, the love I have for you, the love I have for us. The craft itself, and the result, is a thing of beauty.

In the Before Times (before I knew I was disabled, before I knew there was a community out there, before I knew I belonged) I had a cookie-cutter view of love. As a child I knew there was love in the way my mom snuggled me, laying my head in her lap with tender hands brushing my hair. I grew to learn that there was love in the extra jobs my dad took on to make sure we had what we needed. As a teen, I found love in small-town connections and seemingly everlasting friendships. I thought my life was full of love, even brimming with it. I built friendships and maintained family connections. I played to all the normative standards of reciprocity.

I thought I had woven this gorgeous tapestry together with friends and family members connected in a tight-knit weave. My tapestry's warp (the long, vertical threads stretched across the loom) was made up of the threads of my love, and its weft (the sideways, horizontal threads locking everything into place) was made up of the love that others reflected back to me. I thought I was weaving something stable and secure. I thought I was churning out yards of cloth from my threads.

But then I got sick. And I got sicker. And I started to cancel plans. Friends and family members witnessed my rapid deterioration, but no one outside my immediate family knew how bad it was. I didn't tell them because I knew they didn't want to know. I wasn't healthy enough to have fun. I was frustrated and anxious as I tried to make sense of a body that seemed to defy my every desire for normalcy.

A tapestry can't hold when warp and weft go at the same time. One thread snapping makes little difference in a woven piece, but when multiple threads splinter, the piece reverts to a shapeless tangle. My warp threads were straining under the pressures of internalized ableism. I had very little love for my failing body. I needed the weft to hold everything together until I could straighten out my warp. But those threads began to snap, one after another, as loved ones distanced themselves from me. I had banked on the idea that those threads were wrought of love. I thought they couldn't snap, but they did. I watched as my whole tapestry unraveled before me.

I didn't know what to do with the tangle of threads I was left with. I had scraps of love at my disposal, but everything seemed a mess. My warp was all wrong. I didn't know how to love myself as I watched my body decline. I grew up denying my body the love it needed, convinced by doctors and teachers that I was "fine" and had to just "toughen up." I had no love for my limitations. I wanted a body that could run on very little and churn out constant streams of productivity. I wanted to be independent, so I starved myself of rest. But a body can't survive without rest, self-love, and community support. Eventually my symptoms accelerated so rapidly that doctors were forced to interrogate what was wrong. At age nineteen I was finally diagnosed with hypermobile Ehlers-Danlos syndrome. EDS is a genetic condition that affects your collagen production. Because I have weak collagen, my joints, blood vessels, and skin are very fragile. While symptoms are diverse for EDSers, in my case, EDS looks like frequent dislocations and subluxations (partial dislocations), chronic pain, weak muscles, and poor blood flow. Like a thread spun too loosely, my joints and bones tend to split away from one another, even under minimal pressure.

My diagnosis compromised every vision I had of my future. Motherhood? Gone. Living abroad? Gone. Working a political career? Gone. Having a day without pain? Gone. All these threads that I had planned to place in my tapestry fell from my grasp. I felt like I had nothing left to weave. Instead of giving me the tools I needed to craft something new, doctors gave me a lengthy to-do list. I'd have to put off the tapestry until I could set up appointments with cardiology, neurology, orthopedics, gastroenterology, optometry, pain management, and physical therapy. I'd have to screen for the life-threatening comorbidities. No sense weaving something together, they claimed, if I were dying. There was an endless list of medications, supplements, dietary changes, physical therapy plans, and other "habits" to change before I could even think of weaving again.

In the months following my diagnosis I looked for threads of love in all the wrong places. I looked through countless medical journals and patient community posts hoping for a cure. I looked at my body through a medical lens, thinking, "What can I fix?" and "How much can I fix?" A few months after my diagnosis, I went to a meeting of the 2013 Ehlers-Danlos National Foundation Conference. I was excited to meet other disabled people who shared my "rare" condition. Doctors had told me time and time again that EDS was so rare (back then they estimated 1/20,000) that I'd likely never meet another patient outside my family unless I sought them out (if only I had known about Twitter). I thought I'd find disabled people who were adapting—people I could learn from. I didn't know how to weave a life together anymore, but I thought if I could just find one other person who was doing it, maybe I could simply mirror them.

I didn't find threads of love at that conference. Medical professionals with tenuous and exploitative patient connections dominated the conversation. I wanted so badly to find community, but this was not a space built from love or joy. People were held together by fear, desperation, and anger. I attended "community support" sessions for my age group and listened to peers share stories reeking of discrimination. People described how they were forced to homeschool or drop out of college. Others recounted how they couldn't find steady employment, and many had been fired over accommodations. I entered the room hoping I could find one thread to hold on to. I spiraled as I listened to others say that they had no friends anymore, that their romantic partners had left them, that no one was willing to stick around. If none of these people had found threads of love, how was I going to? People seemed resigned, but I was upset. Why weren't they angry? Didn't they want to talk about how unfair this was? I walked into the room hoping to borrow threads, or to learn to spin new ones. But the people in that room were clutching their own torn pieces, trying to repair holes in moth-bitten cloth. They had no threads to share.

The ironic thing is that I already knew how to extend disabled love, I just didn't have the right framing for it. My mother and brother were diagnosed alongside me that December. Our household was already held together by disabled love. Every time we dimmed the lights or spoke in low voices, my family showed love for those with migraines. When my brother tiptoed down the stairs in the afternoon to grab a snack, avoiding all the squeaky spots, he left trails of love behind him. He would gently shut cabinet doors and creep back upstairs as I dozed on the living room couch, a napping spot that seemed to have a special kind of magic for aching joints. When my mom honed herself into a weapon at every new medical appointment, all sharp edges and hardened eyes, she was teaching me a new form of love. I had plenty of instances of disabled love in my life, I just hadn't honed my self-love or awareness yet, so I didn't see them for what they were.

The threads I was weaving together back then felt inadequate. I was spinning threads of self-love that seemed far too thin to hold and far too dull to make anything beautiful. I was taking my medications, doing physical therapy, using mobility aids, and slowing down. I was beginning to gather reserves I could spin, but I was still jealous. Non-disabled friends were weaving their tapestries together—dating, making career plans, building lasting friendships, going on spontaneous vacations. I was endlessly jealous of the threads my friends seemed to have, spun together from spur-of-the-moment trips, all-nighters in the library, and drinking parties on the weekends. My nondisabled friends seemed to have piles and piles of threads—colorful, bright, distinct—made of spontaneity and freedom. I wanted threads like that, too.

I wanted more. I had no idea what I was doing or what I needed, but I knew that I wanted a community. I wanted a space to weave love back into my life. At first, I tried to bring together disabled people on my university campus. I grew heartsick week after week when I was the only student who appeared for disability awareness meetings. Sitting in the ALANA Cultural Center at Colgate University, waiting endlessly because "maybe they're just late" became a monthly occurrence. It felt like a sign that I wasn't supposed to love this part of myself, and a reminder that seemingly no one else my age did.

Luckily, instead of shutting down, I got angry. I scoured my university looking for disabled love. I found scraps in the library, reading works by disabled scholars Paul Longmore and Tobin Siebers. I found fragments in the memoirs I read and the theories I parsed through and the histories of disability rights I pored over. I found so many people fiercely demanding equality, justice, and inclusion. There were blogs, zines, and Instagram posts brimming with disabled love. I realized that even if I didn't have disabled community nearby, it was out there. I just needed to look for the threads that disabled people were already putting out into the world.

Love came in the form of Anneliese, the first (and only) disabled person who ever showed up to a disability awareness student meeting. Ahead of me by a few years, she was already a fierce advocate for disability rights. We shared lengthy emails bemoaning our struggles to secure meaningful accommodations. We drafted policy briefs to improve campus transportation, housing, and classroom and campus environments. We debated how to best attack discriminatory policies.

Anneliese taught me that some of the thinnest threads in the world, like silk, make some of the strongest materials. She spun beautiful threads, in tones I had never seen before. A quicksilver gray thread—a reminder that work can always be done lying down. An opaque fishing line—encouragement to try to build access even when that labor goes ignored by others. Together we spun. Threads to ground us, threads to acknowledge the harms done to disabled individuals who came before us, threads to voice current harms, threads to encourage others to keep fighting.

Those early attempts at activism sustained me and reminded me that I, too, belong in this world. In an environment where disabled people are rarely accepted, and even more rarely valued, having disabled love in my life at school was vital. Anneliese broke every rule I had mistakenly held myself to. She taught me to ask for what I needed, to be unashamed of defying nondisabled norms and respectability politics, and to fight for my inclusion. Our threads did little to change the tapestry of our institution, but I graduated knowing how to spin glittery, silken, undamageable threads.

Disabled love is spun from respect and mutuality, not reciprocity. Disabled love isn't about keeping score or competing to give the most. Disabled love doesn't demand consistency or perfection. Disabled love asks us to love ourselves first and foremost. It reminds us that we are not a healthy community if we push one another to give beyond our individual means. Disabled love tells us it's okay to cancel plans. Unlike nondisabled friends, my disabled friends never stop inviting me or rescheduling. They honor my boundaries just the same as I honor theirs, because disabled love is spun from honesty.

Disabled people spin threads out of nothingness. We hand the shuttle back and forth when we spend time together, build space for one another, and find value in one another's experiences. We map out new patterns, and make sure that every thread finds its own space to shine when we build and sustain access for one another. We dig through our reserves and share the threads we've spooled. When doctors take tools away from people, we show up with polished shuttles and shed sticks. When newly disabled people say that they have nothing to weave, we show them our finished works and remind them that there is more to this life than darkness. We reach out to those new to the community, those with shakily spun threads. Hand in hand, we twist our own materials to shore up weaker threads until each and every one of us can spin our own unbreakable strands. We spin skein after skein with care, curiosity, and understanding. Together, we weave rows of hope and laughter and joy to balance out those of frustration and despair. We borrow with care, and we share with generosity. We spin and weave and tamp down row after row of love when we build community together.

Disabled people know how to love like no others. We show our adoration for one another when we crack morbid jokes. We make one another laugh over very real, terrifying shit. We pay homage to one another by simply standing witness—to highs and lows, to cycles of grief and mourning and celebration. We find reverence in the stories shared with us, stories that teach us how to navigate, how to fight, how to resist. We say "I love you" in a million ways. When we murmur it at the end of phone calls, hoping that the simple sentiment resonates. When we scribble it all over medical notes as we help one another compile records, track changes, and figure out how to secure what we need despite a failing medical system. When we proclaim it, loudly, when we protest and make our stories public.

Disabled community teaches us how to weave love in a way that's hard to put into words. We weave to sustain ourselves, one another, and our shared histories. We send one another threads across time and space. We ship them off in envelopes with letters and postcards.

We trade them during Zoom calls where we do absolutely nothing together. We gift them over long phone calls peppered with silence because quietude is love, too. We unabashedly take them when we tell guests to leave already because it's nap time. And we leave them behind in heaps when we perform care work.

The threads whisper that we are worth everything. That it is worth rebuilding the world so that we have a place in its future. They remind us that our lives have value, even when the world disagrees. Row after row, the tapestry tells us that our lives are worth living, even when we start to have our doubts. It claims that undoubtedly, we are enough, no matter our needs. The full picture tells us that we are beloved. Perhaps our tapestries are made up of thinner threads, maybe they don't follow the patterns we expected or the color schemes we had hoped for. Nonetheless they are woven together from stronger stuff than we could have imagined. In the end, the final image is stunning.

Rosasharon Teaches Me to Breathe
On Animals, Disabilities, and Intimacies

Ada Hubrig

Breathe in. Breathe out.

She chose me.

While I was visiting my partner's family on their farm late one spring, a tortoiseshell kitten came barreling out of the tree line. Her half-gallop was a bit lopsided, favoring her right side to her left and causing her to run more akin to how I'd imagine a four-legged bird might move than a cat. I watched as she made a beeline toward us, digging her claws into my jeans and climbing atop my shoulder.

I fell in love with that cat immediately.

Because of the unusually intense flooding that year, we named her Rosasharon, after the character in John Steinbeck's *The Grapes of Wrath*. Even as a kitten, Rosasharon was sassy as hell—she fiercely claimed me as *her* person, and she would swat my partner's hand away from me or bite friends who sat too close.

While she was still a kitten, Doc Winter, the local veterinarian—a kindly octogenarian who lived up the street—took a liking to her. I would sit on my front porch reading, with Rosasharon curled in my lap in the evenings, and he'd sometimes stop on his routine jaunt to chat.

Leaning against my porch railing one evening, he held her in his arms. "You know, I hate to be the bearer of bad news, but I don't think she'll make it till spring."

"Well then, we best enjoy the time we have." I smiled back weakly, appreciating Doc's honesty but holding back tears.

Over the next months, Doc did what he could to help: he performed a surgery to remove her front claws—a procedure I'd normally consider a cruelty, but because she couldn't retract some of the claws she kept hurting her eyes and the claws that couldn't extend kept getting infected. After a particularly grim and serious infection, Doc suggested that declawing Rosasharon was the best course of action. He also drained the lump on the back of her head, which he believed to be an infected cyst of some kind.

He would tell me, on several occasions, that he was amazed that Rosasharon had lasted so long, that he was certain she wouldn't pull through that first winter with us. A few years later, when Doc—that kindly, cantankerous old man—passed away at the age of eighty-six, Rosasharon seemed to miss his visits.

Like me, Rosasharon had an atypical body in many ways, with her curved spine, a tail that was permanently arched and which she seemed to have no motor control over, a large lump on her head, her claw situation, an uncategorized gastric issue, and other ailments. Rosasharon and I both experienced chronic pain, and learned how to live in our pain together. In the eleven years we spent together, Rosasharon and I were both in a series of surgeries and recoveries. She would teach me, time and time again, how to breathe, how to live in a state of constant change and becoming.

Breathe deeply and slowly.

My pa, a Midwestern farmer with his mind always on the next task that needed doing, looked upon Rosasharon with disapproval. During a rare visit, he watched Rosasharon struggle to climb up on the couch next to me and scoffed when I bent down to help her. Disgusted, he asked, "Why don't you just put it down, put it out of its misery?"

I answered that she was a part of my family, but he wasn't very interested in my explanation. Before he passed, Pa often made the fact that I share my home with cats the subject of ridicule, and he had little patience for me or others whose labor or purpose wasn't immediately apparent to his particular brand of agricultural pragmatism. Pa had both a very different relationship to animals and understanding of disability than I—his views were not far removed from the cultural assumptions about disability held by those I was raised among in a working-class family in the rural Midwest.

For years, I had internalized so many of those ableist attitudes and beliefs. I bought into the idea that I had to be an exceptional disabled person, that I had to *prove* my life was worthy to the nondisabled people around me. I'd labor as diligently as I could, overexerting my body that I saw as flawed, broken, and undesirable. I'd try to prove to others—and myself—that I could overcome these perceived defects: I'd do what I could to help in the field or a summer camp or various construction jobsites or my family's butcher shop. I'd work summer jobs and grab any side gigs I could in college and graduate school. I would literally work myself sick.

While I've had disabilities all my life, I didn't understand myself as disabled until much later. I didn't come to claim disability until my late twenties, as I found community with other disabled people who helped me to find my way and feel less isolated and alone. I'm so grateful for these communities.

And for Rosasharon.

For much of my life, I had internalized a message that I was a burden, that if I couldn't work as hard as the nondisabled people around me, I was somehow not as worthy of love or peace or joy. I would hide my disabilities from others as much as I possibly could: intestinal bleeding and other gastrointestinal symptoms; a steady loss of mobility; being autistic in a world not made for autistic people.

But Rosasharon didn't hide any parts of herself from me, and I found it hard to keep secrets from her. While I always assumed myself a burden to those around me, it occurred to me I never once had thought of Rosasharon as a burden, but as a delight. Spending time with her, often simply reading and sipping a cup of tea as she'd curl up in my lap and we'd both drift to sleep on my recliner, was my ideal afternoon. I thought of Pa's question and his claim that she was in misery. Sure, Rosasharon was often in physical pain. So was (and am) I. But even in our pain, Rosasharon and I found so much joy in each other's company.

Rosasharon didn't have to labor through her pain or pretend to overcome her pains and illnesses. Just by being herself, she was enough. And she was teaching me maybe I was enough, too, that I didn't have to "overcome" my disability to be worthy of love or acceptance or joy, either. I could just sip tea, sit with my book, and breathe.

Breathe as calmly and with as much ease as you can.

Even as Rosasharon was teaching me to breathe, it felt like my body was tearing apart.

The medical name for my ailment is *fistulating Crohn's disease*, or at least that's frequently the most disruptive star in my personal constellation of overlapping chronic illnesses and disabilities. A few years after Rosasharon moved into my home, my disease progressed. My large intestine had corroded, and pathways of infection were forming through my body. I began a still-ongoing series of surgeries to keep me alive.

The medical term for what I was experiencing was "enterocutaneous fistulas," pathways that had formed between my intestines and the skin of my belly. By the time it was clear what was happening, sepsis had set in. An infection had formed through my abdominal wall, and much of the tissue on the right side of my abdomen had to be removed. The sepsis had been severe, impacting my ability to think clearly, and I remember that time in bits and blurs.

I do remember, vividly, hugging my partner for what I was worried would be the last time before an emergency medical team loaded me into a small fixed-wing craft in Nebraska and airlifted me to the Mayo Clinic Hospital in Minnesota, where I underwent a series of surgeries and procedures that all blended together in a flurry of pain.

What I remember more clearly is that for months after the surgeries when I was on bed rest, I couldn't sit up, much less walk, and breathing was painful. For a time, my body could not breathe without assistance and I was on oxygen.

During that time, Rosasharon was my constant companion: when I would sob from the pain or the loneliness, Rosasharon would curl up next to me. Her deep breaths would remind me, in turn, that I needed to breathe. She would extend her tiny, soft paw to my face, brushing my cheek.

I could tell Rosasharon things I was too afraid to tell anyone else—that I was worried I was a financial and labor burden on my family; that I didn't know how to cope with this new level of pain; that I was grieving a loss of mobility and coming to terms with a list of things I'd hoped to do one day that now seemed impossible.

Rosasharon, in pain and recovery herself, would curl next to me, purring and meowing back at me with her trademark sass. While some of the people—and especially nondisabled people—in my life seemed to have a hard time understanding that much of my loss of mobility would be permanent, Rosasharon accepted me immediately as myself and taught me to accept myself, too.

Breathe deeply, release, and let go.

In May of 2020, while many people were on lockdown because of the COVID-19 pandemic, my partner, my cats, and I packed up and moved to Texas for work. We didn't know anyone, we hadn't even seen the space we had rented to live in—one of the few we could afford—except for two poorly taken photos online. Without a single piece of furniture, we loaded ourselves into a van and drove the twelve hours from Seward, Nebraska, to Huntsville, Texas, in one go.

During the drive, I told my partner that Rosasharon was anxious and needed to sit in my lap, but that was mostly inaccurate. *I* was anxious and needed Rosasharon to sit in my lap.

That first year in Texas, when we knew so few people and, as part of our COVID precautions, only left home when work or other situations absolutely required it, was particularly isolating. But Rosasharon, ever the optimist, helped me make the most of each moment, often suggesting by pawing at my ankles that it was time for me to lift her up into my lap so we could snuggle, have our tea, and read. While the ongoing pandemic has been difficult for many reasons, Rosasharon and I did take some of the very best naps of our lives those lockdown afternoons.

While Rosasharon and I were usually pretty laid-back, calm souls, we definitely had our moods, too. Rosasharon would get grumpy and snarl on occasion—usually because she decided it was time for her supper and it was not actually time for her supper. When I would get overwhelmed from the demands of my job or from chronic pain, I would be a bit snippy, too. Rosasharon and I learned to completely accept each other as we were, a lesson that has helped me more fully love and accept myself and others in my life. For the first time, I was completely comfortable with my disability around another. I knew that I didn't have to act strong or be tough or pretend: Rosasharon and I could simply *be* with each other. After working so hard for years to conceal my chronic illnesses and autism from others, it was such an incredibly beautiful and meaningful experience to simply *be* with another, and to experience another in their fullness, too.

During our second year in Texas, as rain poured outside, I was cooking supper for my family when my partner called me into the living room. My partner told me that Rosasharon had stretched her body and then went limp on her right side. I sat with her on the floor, noting she was unable to move the limbs on the right side of her body or move the right side of her face. We'd later learn she had a stroke.

I picked Rosasharon up from the floor as gently as I could, and I held her in my arms as my partner called around to local veterinarians, trying to find one that was open. While my partner was on the phone, Rosasharon calmly lifted her fuzzy paw up to my cheek and looked up into my eyes, reminding me one last time to breathe as she took her own last breath.

It may sound like hyperbole, but I assure you it isn't: one of the most meaningful relationships of my life has been my connection with sweet, sassy Rosasharon. I didn't understand, until Rosasharon was part of my life, how necessary and important it is to be in community with others who experience disability, to share space with others who experience life in nonnormative ways.

From the moment she darted out of that tree line to holding her as she passed and even now, Rosasharon teaches me how to breathe, to give myself the patience and grace to be more myself, and each day is brighter because of it.

The Last Walk

Melissa Hung

Judith opens the door to her apartment, dressed in all black from her sweater to her Skechers. "We match," I say, and go in for a hug. We are similar in size, small and slender but solid. When we release she picks up the black belt bag. Made of smooth napa leather, the bag has gently rounded bottom corners, minimal brass hardware, and an adjustable strap. "Do you want this after I'm gone?" she asks. I make a noise, unable to find any words at first, then blurt, "I mean sure. Yes."

"It's our bag," she says.

If she had not told me she was dying, I would not have known. She looks the same, except that she's stopped coloring her hair—I'm used to seeing it oak-bark brown—and let the grays show through her waves. She doesn't look sick. But I know, as she does too well, that there are many ways to be ill, many ways for a body to be wrought and not appear so at all.

Judith tells me to write down my address on a piece of paper. I know she already has it but clearly there's a system here, so I write it down. She adds the piece of paper to a stack of other papers and secures them together with a binder clip.

Looking at her, I cannot believe it. How can a year go by without seeing your friend and now the thin line between living and dying is suddenly apparent?

"I'm not sure how long I'll be at this address," I say. "How long do you have?"

"Not long," she says.

Judith dons her bright blue, puffy down jacket. We leave her apartment, cross the shared courtyard to the front of the complex, and push through the wooden gate. It clicks behind us. It's a muted November day, chilly with gray skies. Her gait appears deceptively steady, but I know it's because of those sneakers, the only shoes she's found that give her the stability she needs. More than once, I had urged her to stock up on them in case they were discontinued. We walk west toward the nearby park, me on her right side, where she can better move her neck. She asks about my mom—I've recently returned from several weeks in Texas, where I cared for her—and I say things about radiation, chemo pills, gene mutations. How my mom wants me to sell her name-brand purses that she's barely carried because she doesn't think she'll be around to use them. Judith is close to my mom's age, in her early seventies, thirty years older than me. Her daughter is closer to my age. But we don't have a mother-daughter relationship. Judith treats me as a peer, a friend. I can feel the respect she has for me and I return it in kind.

We arrive at the park and turn toward its main feature, a dusty baseball diamond surrounded by an expanse of grass. Trees line the edges of the park. On the weekends, the sounds of shouting and baseball bats cracking fill the air as children play, but midday on a weekday, no one else is here. Judith points out a sign attached to the chain-link fence behind home plate, white letters on municipal green. It reads:

Please Remember
These are kids
This is a game
This is not professional sports
The coaches are volunteers
Thank you for your cooperation

She likes this sign, she tells me, because it says stop being a jerk without calling anyone a jerk. It appeals to people's better sides. I think about how this could describe Judith's own life's work. About how she taught creative writing to children in schools and to men serving life sentences at San Quentin State Prison. How she said the prayer of St. Francis every time she entered San Quentin, though she was Jewish. How she mentored the teaching artists who came through WritersCorps, the literary arts education program where we both worked. How she taught others the ways to get students to loosen their minds to creativity. How that first requires creating trust so that people feel safe enough to open up. How to listen, how to notice—listening and noticing being so much the work of writers and artists but also a core part of becoming a caring human being.

When I arrived at WritersCorps, which placed writers in schools, juvenile hall, libraries, and community organizations to teach creative writing to youth, Judith had been there for twelve years. We would work there together for nine. I was the administrator. I thought of my job as clearing obstacles for the teaching artists. I was the organizer, the money person, the spokesperson when one was needed. But Judith was always the heart. The ideas behind the program and how we ran it were all her. I was technically the boss, but she mentored me, too.

———————

What I noticed about Judith: She favored long-sleeve shirts. She lived modestly in a one-bedroom apartment with tall shelves full of books in the small dining area adjacent to the kitchen. She ate healthy, often opting for a salad. But she baked dense chocolate chip cakes for birthdays. She always remembered my birthday. She gave people second chances. She answered emails incredibly promptly. She was more organized than even me. She wore a silver ring depicting a theater mask on her left middle finger. She was particular; sometimes little things (or what I perceived as little things) set her off, but there was always a reason. Once, in my early days at WritersCorps, I brought bagels and cream cheese to a training, but Judith would not allow it. Choosing the bagels, cutting them, spreading cream cheese—it would all be too distracting, she said. She wrote poems with words like *carve*, *body*, *searchlight*, and *tree* in them. She preferred taking public transit and walking to driving. She checked up often on her mom, who lived a few hours away. She was not interested in owning a cell phone. But she used the smiling emoticon sometimes in emails. :) Her friends were of all ages.

What Judith noticed about me: Once, she wrote and mailed me a letter to tell me that she thought I was depressed. I hadn't even realized it.

We walk out of the park and find ourselves facing a construction site—new apartments, or condos more likely, going up where a trailer park used to be. So we walk the other way into a neighborhood of single-family homes, modest but pricey because this is the Bay Area. We come across a yellow house with a garden of cacti, succulents, and yuccas and stop to admire it, drought-tolerant but verdant, nonetheless. The plants reach up and out with their spindly arms and pointed leaves. One is nearly as tall as the house. To replace a lawn with cacti is a smart move. California has been in a drought for most of the years I've lived here. A cactus has adaptations in its roots, leaves, and stems to help it survive parched environments.

Sometimes you have no choice but to adapt. One day, I woke up with a medical mystery: a headache that would not leave. I did not know it then, but I had crossed over into the land of chronic pain, a place where Judith, who endured problems with her spine, neck, and back, had lived for much of her life. Migraines plagued her, too. She understood what it was like to go about your day with an undercurrent of pain beneath everything. How a good day was one in which you could ignore the pain for the most part. How you learn your limitations and try to avoid the situations that can set you up for a bad day. But how despite it all, you never knew what kind of day you might have, what might push you into a bad day.

We turn onto a busy street with cars zooming by, and head back toward her apartment. Judith recounts what happened to her since I last saw her—a year of emergencies in both our lives. The same month my mom was diagnosed with two cancers, Judith fell and broke her wrist on the sidewalk. The scratches on the front of the belt bag are evidence of the fall. The pain was so bad that she received four doses of fentanyl in ten minutes. But pain itself is only part of the experience of pain.

"Pain, as you know, is not just the physical sensation," Judith says as we continue down the sidewalk. "Pain is also the lack of stamina, the inability to concentrate. It's not being able to write."

In the land of chronic pain, you sit down in front of your computer or notebook and try to work, but you cannot think. You try to do tasks that aren't too taxing. But you are only going through the motions. At some point you realize that you don't feel well. You can't remember the last time you woke up feeling rested and refreshed. You wonder if it will ever happen again. It's not just the pain, it is the exhausting fact that you have been in pain for so long.

Judith tells me she is not afraid of dying. She has never been afraid of death. I do not understand what exactly is happening to her, the specific ways in which her body is collapsing. It's too complicated to explain, Judith says. And with what stamina she has left, she wants to use it for beauty, for loved ones. This time at the end of her life was actually rather enjoyable. Rid of all the medical appointments that were only marginally helpful, she spent her time seeing friends and family. In the mornings she received visitors. In the afternoons and evenings she lay down on the rug in her living room and listened to music, letting the memories come and go, washing over her like waves.

Back at her apartment, Judith makes some tea for me in her galley kitchen. I bring the mug over to her compact blue couch and we keep talking as she lies down on the rug. We talk as we have always talked, though we know this is the last time, catching up on our lives, sharing about writing projects. I tell her about a series of essays I've been working on and she asks if I had considered incorporating other art forms with it. I hadn't. Ever since we both left WritersCorps—she for retirement, me because the onset of my chronic migraine meant that I could no longer work full time—we'd get together about twice a year for meals and walks.

It was at one of our lunches that Judith realized that a twenty-dollar bill had fallen out of her pocket at some point that day. She used to carry a small backpack, but even that bit of weight had become untenable for her back. So she stuffed things into her pockets. That evening, I wrote an email to her suggesting the belt bag. It was a splurge, but she bought it.

We talk until Judith says she needs to nap. She gets up and we hug our final long hug at the door.

Who let go first? I don't think it was me.

A few weeks after our walk, I'm standing on a BART platform waiting for the train downtown when my phone chimes. I look down. A text lets me know that Judith has died. I can't stop the rush of tears. A man approaches to ask if I am okay. *No*, I manage to say between gulps of air, *my friend died.* He says he's sorry and recedes to wherever he had come from.

I don't remember now where I had been going. I was probably on my way to the indoor pool at the YMCA. Swimming is one of the only things that gives me a measure of relief from pain. While it doesn't erase the pain, it turns it down a notch for a bit. After a swim, my whole body feels looser, my head clearer.

Sometimes I imagine Judith gently drifting on her back in the water, her hair spread out wild around her, her body relaxed. No longer able to swim toward the end of her life, she floated in water-therapy sessions. The pain that wracked her body would ease for the hour or so when she was in the pool. The weightlessness of the water lifted the burden of her bones—a reprieve from gravity, from daily suffering.

A day or two after that, a bubble envelope arrived in the mail at my home. The return address was Judith's. Of course it was. Judith, forever punctual, organized, and prompt, even in death. I opened the package. There was the belt bag. Tucked inside the bag was a brief note of thanks from Judith. I adjusted the strap and clipped the bag around my waist. I have worn it nearly every day since.

My Journey to Motherhood
A Parenting Odyssey

Marie E. S. Flores

I was born with a rare neuromuscular disorder that impairs my balance, strength, mobility, and hearing. Although it has been one of my life's greatest challenges, it also made me a resilient person, inspired me to become a physician, and made me a strong and creative problem-solver.

Diverse disability and cultural experiences have been an integral part of my upbringing. I was born to a Colombian mother and an American father (who also has the same neuromuscular condition as I do), both of whom worked as biochemists at the National Institutes of Health (NIH). I grew up thoroughly immersed in both of their extended families, their research labs, and our multiracial Unitarian church in Washington, DC. I learned Spanish and Latino culinary traditions from my maternal grandmother. I also learned about various world cultures and cuisines from my paternal grandmother, who taught English as a second language and hosted Middle Eastern and African foreign exchange students in her home.

My childhood and adolescence included regular school and extracurricular activities all the other neighborhood kids did, but it also included repeated doubts cast upon my abilities. I worked hard to excel in school to counter people's stereotypical perception that because I use a wheelchair, I must have a cognitive delay as well. As a teenager, I yearned for the intimacy from boys that most of my friends had, but no one was ever interested in me that way. I would think to myself, "Everyone wants to be my friend, but no one wants to be my lover. . . ." I wondered if I would ever find someone to be happily married to and start a family with.

When I first met my husband, Luis, one of the things that made me sure I could trust him was that he also has a disability: he was born with microtia (one of his outer ears is not formed). After years of dating, Luis and I knew that we wanted to have children after we got married, but we wanted to wait a year, plus I had just started medical school, so my life was extremely busy.

Obviously, intimacy can be physical, sexual, and fun, whether pregnancy is a desired outcome or not. But several years went by and I wasn't getting pregnant. And as much as I yearned to become a mother, it got put on the back burner because of competing priorities: attending med school, applying to residency programs, moving to the East Coast to complete residency, getting my first job, and finally moving back to the West Coast.

To fill the void and "warm up," we got some houseplants and took care of those. Then we adopted a puppy; later we got another dog, and then a fairly large aquarium full of exotic fish. None of them died, so we felt ready to try again for the real thing.

By this time, we had settled down with a house and a stable income. But ten years had passed, and I was nearing my fourth decade of life. I tried taking fertility medication; no luck. So, admitting that we had a serious infertility problem, I found a reputable infertility clinic at UCLA Health in Los Angeles, over a three-hour drive from where we lived in the Central Valley of California.

The infertility specialist we met, Dr. Lindsay Kroener, was wonderful, and she took her time to get Luis's and my full medical and family histories. We then had to undergo multiple tests for all kinds of things, and genetic counseling before we could actually begin any kind of in vitro fertilization (IVF) procedure. Because I have a known genetic mutation that causes my disability, we were asked if we were going to test our embryos for this condition.

For us, it was a fraught question. For years, we'd embraced the 50 percent chance that our child would be born with my condition. What better parents could such a child have? Yet to the medical system, my condition is a preventable disease, and passing it on to another child is unethical, even cruel, so testing and embryo selection were foregone conclusions.

The nonphysician, proud person with a disability, and feminine parts of my soul were offended! They seemed to be devaluing my own life, and what did they know? Only the bad stuff, none of my joys and triumphs. At the same time, part of me also knew the suffering I'd endured, especially as a child. By age twenty-two, I'd dealt with multiple inconsiderate doctors and painful surgeries. Given the choice, why would I intentionally pass that pain on to my baby?

Ultimately, we agreed to preventative genetic testing on the embryos, not only for my condition but for others. The genetics team also attempted to test my husband for known genetic mutations that cause microtia since it runs in his family, but the tests all came back negative. This process took a really annoyingly long time; more blood work, more genetic counseling, saliva samples taken from me, Luis, and my parents, and seeing multiple additional specialists. Making a baby was not fun anymore. It was like a really tedious, unsecure job with tons of appointments and testing—and almost none of it covered by my health insurance. Every encounter was a reminder of all the things that could go wrong, and the probability of getting a normal embryo kept going down as I aged. However, this lengthy process also brought Luis and me closer together in anticipation of having our future son or daughter.

My medical knowledge helped me understand why these tests were needed and why the process was so time-consuming. I had patients who waited months or even a year to get a specialist referral or an expensive diagnostic test. But this did not dispel my impatience to make Luis a father. For years I had seen him bond with other children, and I knew what a good father he would be. I felt like our intimacy grew tremendously, envisioning the new parental roles for each other. But at the same time, I was going through yet another experience of my body—my very existence and personhood—being medicalized. It made me feel weak or "less than" other women who can get pregnant and expect a healthy baby almost effortlessly and at far lower cost.

When all the testing was completed after seven months, we could finally start the medications to do the retrieval of my eggs—and then the COVID-19 pandemic hit! The nurse called me right after the lockdown started to tell me that the retrieval had to be postponed. I was devastated. Although I had already waited years, the thought of having to wait a few more months was very stressful because I was an essential frontline medical worker at risk of getting this new deadly virus every day.

After a few months, I was allowed to proceed with the medications and we finally got to do the egg retrieval procedure. It went smoothly and resulted in five mature embryos. Unfortunately, four of them came back genetically abnormal with chromosomal trisomies or monosomies not compatible with life, and one did not have enough cells for this analysis. In addition, all five carried the point mutation that causes my neuromuscular disorder.

After the results came back, we got detailed genetic counseling about each one. The counselor even explained the probability of a false positive, or what usually happens to pregnancies with the specific results that we had if we were to proceed with implantation—a very high probability of failure or miscarriage. Knowing the medical side of it, there was no way that I would attempt to implant one of the four with abnormal chromosomes. However, I did consider an option of thawing the one that did not have enough DNA for analysis, re-biopsying it, and freezing it again to see if it was euploid (an embryo that has the correct number of chromosomes and is considered a normal embryo). But this process could decrease my chances of a successful transfer resulting in pregnancy. We still have not decided what to do with that embryo, and it is still on ice with the others.

We decided to try another retrieval with a slightly different medication protocol. This time we ended up with just two euploid embryos, and one of these did not carry my known pathogenic mutation. We proceeded to transfer this embryo into my body.

When we found out a couple of weeks later that I was pregnant, we were over the moon with excitement! Every day we talked about our hopes and dreams for our baby boy (known because of the genetic testing). We talked about names, we talked about how to decorate the nursery, and we talked about how we wanted to be parents. My husband would kiss my belly every night before we went to bed. When we went in for the first ultrasound and saw the heartbeat, I was overjoyed. We called him "Baby Dot" because that's what he looked like on the first ultrasound. This experience really brought my husband and me even closer together.

But our joy was cut short. When I went for my follow-up visit at about ten weeks gestation, my doctor did the ultrasound and let out a sigh—she could no longer detect a fetal heartbeat. Our baby had died inside of me. I had no symptoms of a miscarriage, no bleeding or cramps or physical pain. When she told me the news, I was completely distraught. The crushing emotional pain was unbearable, and I could not control the flood of tears that followed. I felt broken, my hopes and dreams for my future family shattered into a million pieces. It took ages to recover from this experience.

We decided to try an egg retrieval one last time and also started the process of applying to foster a child to adopt in case it didn't work. We did the same medication protocol and again ended up with only two mature embryos that made it to biopsy. I was so accustomed to bad luck that I was certain it was over. . . . However, I was shocked when I got the call from my doctor, all happy and excited, to tell us that one of them was euploid and unaffected with my condition. I screamed with happiness!

I still had many hurdles to overcome, but I had hope that we could still have a baby. Yet I was in the middle of changing jobs, selling our house in Hanford, and moving to the Los Angeles area. My infertility doctor was completely supportive of us waiting a few months to do the transfer until we got settled. I later underwent the procedure in September 2021, and everything went smoothly. However, after enduring so many disappointing setbacks, I did not want to tell anybody, fearing to jinx myself and lose this pregnancy as well.

We waited two weeks. I did my own home urine pregnancy test the night before the blood test so that I could be prepared for the disappointment if it didn't work. But I grinned when I saw there were two lines on the stick. The little sliver of hope became a shining beacon in my heart the next day when I got the call: "Congratulations, you're pregnant!" My hormone levels were indeed in pregnancy range and higher than at the same point in my previous pregnancy. Yet I was still afraid to celebrate wholeheartedly. My mind tried to rein me back to "expect the worst and hope for the best." Even though my hormone levels rose appropriately, I still felt terrified, every time we went in for an ultrasound, that the doctor was going to tell me bad news again. I even asked the nurses not to put me in the exam room where we found out our previous pregnancy had failed. They were very kind and understanding of my request.

When we saw our baby's heartbeat for the first time at around five weeks, I was so overjoyed. We called this one "Baby Peanut." Every week we went back for a follow-up and were reassured with normal ultrasounds.

But nothing can be easy in my life for long. At eight weeks gestation, I was at work, and when I went to the bathroom, I had bright

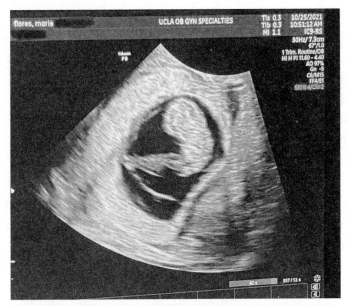

An image from an ultrasound of Marie Flores's fetus inside her uterus during the first trimester of her second pregnancy.

A photo of Marie Flores taken at the beach. Marie is smiling and sitting in her black-and-blue manual wheelchair, pregnant, and wearing a royal blue dress. Photo credit: Claudia Contreras

red vaginal bleeding. I burst into tears because I was certain that it was over, that I was doomed to lose another baby and not be able to become the mom that I wanted to be or to make Luis a dad. I called the clinic, and they saw me the same morning. To my surprise, Baby Peanut had a strong, normal heartbeat. He was totally fine, and the bleeding was coming from something called a subchorionic hemorrhage, which is like a bruise inside the uterus. I could not believe it, what a relief!

For the first two trimesters of my pregnancy, my husband and I did not want to talk to anybody about the baby. We hated the thought of discussing baby names or the nursery with anyone, as if that would somehow tempt fate, resulting in another miscarriage. As Christmas approached, we did not want any gifts from anybody, fearing that we could lose the baby at any time. After the holidays, I was hospitalized at nineteen weeks gestation with severe breathing problems and again worried that I was going to lose the baby. It was not until I reached viability, which is about twenty-three to twenty-four weeks gestation, that I felt like I could finally relax.

Then, all of a sudden, Luis and I started talking about how we were going to decorate the nursery and involve the family in planning the baby shower, and about baby names. We realized we had a ton of stuff to do to prepare for the baby to come home, and soon!

At the same time, I was having a lot of worsening issues with my own health; even just getting around in my wheelchair and breathing with this growing baby in my belly was a struggle. As hard as it was, I knew that everywhere I went, our baby was with me. Once I could feel him moving, I felt such a close connection to him—it is difficult to describe. I would talk to him all the time even when no one was around. I also talked to other women about pregnancy, symptoms, and challenges and changes in the body.

All my OB and specialist doctors at UCLA were wonderful in taking care of me, Baby Peanut, and even Luis. We made multiple

A photo of Marie and Luis Flores, a Latino couple, taken at the beach. Marie is pregnant and wearing a dark navy blue dress. Luis is wearing a white shirt, and the two of them are barefoot and sitting on a blanket in the sand, leaning against each other and smiling.
Photo credit: Claudia Contreras

plans for the delivery because of my advanced age and other medical issues. It was a very high-risk pregnancy, so I needed frequent monitoring. I unfortunately had several complications during a long labor and delivery at thirty-seven weeks, resulting in a C-section under general anesthesia. I actually wondered if I might die as the anesthesiologist put me to sleep. But once I was awake (phew!) and able to hold my sweet little baby boy in my arms, my heart filled with so much joy and so much love. It's like when you put up a pot of water to boil and forget about it, and it bubbles over. So then you turn it down, put the spaghetti in, turn the heat back up, and wait—then it bubbles over again and foams even more than the first time! That's how my heart felt. It was bubbling over with love for my miracle baby, this beautiful little human that we made.

So now I can *finally* say that I am a mother and I absolutely love it! It was surreal at first; people would call me a mommy, and I would

A photo of Marie and Luis Flores, a Latino couple, nestled close to each other outdoors in front of a palm tree. They are both wearing white shirts and smiling. Marie is holding her newborn infant son, Eliseo Markos Flores, who is asleep and wearing a blue jumper.

turn my head to look and see who they were talking to behind me. Being a mom is also the hardest thing I have ever done in my life, but it has been totally worth it. Yes, there have been challenges and exhaustion just like any new parents deal with, but we have found creative ways for me to be able to take care of Eliseo independently. For example, my good friend's husband is a carpenter, and he graciously built us a custom wheelchair-accessible crib so I could reach the baby from the side instead of from the top. I am also breastfeeding my baby, and that has created a tremendous bond between us. When I feed him, I snuggle with him, talk to him, sing to him, and love to read books to him.

Reflecting on this roller coaster of a journey has made me compose the following messages:

- To my Baby Dot, who I never got to meet: I will cherish the short time you grew inside of me but will be forever heartbroken for not knowing exactly why I lost you. I also still grieve the intimacy I was supposed to have with you that never came to fruition. Every year for *Día de los Muertos*, we put the box with your ultrasound pictures and baby booties on the altar. You will always be loved and never be forgotten.

- To my current son, Eliseo, aka "Baby Peanut," who is now over nine months old: I love you more than anything in this world and can't wait to see what you do in the future. You are a funny, curious, and strong little boy who knows exactly what he wants, just like his mama. I can't wait for you to be able to talk to me and Daddy. You are my precious miracle baby and have been the best thing that ever happened to me.

- To all the childless mothers out there: My wish for you is to achieve the role of parenthood you dream of. But I acknowledge the medical, financial, and structural challenges that can stand in the way of a safe pregnancy and delivery (or adoption). My hope is for society and the healthcare system to treat us as worthy of love and the natural human experience of having children if we so desire.

My bumpy pathway to motherhood has been an unpredictable physical and emotional marathon in more ways than one, yet I don't regret a single minute of it. I am grateful to all the people who helped me throughout this intense process without hesitation, especially my loving husband, Luis, as well as close family, especially my sister Anita, and my best friends, *Las Sucias*. I would also like to acknowledge the unconditional encouragement from my online support group "Physician Women Warriors" and the multitude of doctors, nurses, and other healthcare professionals who guided me to the finish line. There is no way I could have achieved this dream of becoming a mom without their love and support.

To the You that Used to Be Home
An Anatomy of a Disabled Heartbreak

Mia Mingus

Heartbreak comes in many forms, just as love does. The heartbreaks of broken friendship, comradeship, community, and family between fellow queer disabled women of color have been the ones that stung the most. This is a telling of parts of my truth. This is what I have excavated from the ashes of the messiness of being human and the ways we break each other's hearts. This is what I leave evidence of, even if only for myself.

Disabled Heartbreak

If this were before, I would, like I always did, start with "What did I do wrong?" I would cling to "Someday . . ." and "We can work it out," no matter how hard or how deep the pain from all you did and all you didn't do.

I would tell you about how I rushed to the hills of forgiveness with open arms and waited there for you for hours, days, years . . . a decade before hanging my head, arms wrapped around myself, and slowly, defeated, turning to leave. A loneliness inside of loneliness.

I would tell you about how you broke my heart, irrevocably. And how what happened broke my spirit, too. How it hurt for so long and how the pain was so deep that, today, over a decade past, I can still remember just how it felt.

And even still. Unbelievably. I have kept your room inside of my heart clean and ready. I still open the curtains each morning and close them each night. I change the sheets and sweep and dust. I leave fresh flowers in the warmth and lay an extra blanket at the foot of the bed in the cold. And I still feel the sharp ache of my own hope and commitment in the stinging reality: I am still your home, even though you are not mine.

A Lifetime of Longing

I don't know disability through anything other than my own life. I only know how I longed for you long before I met you. How you were something like a mirage at first. How you thought the same of me, because we had been endlessly traveling through the desert we had been banished to by a world that had lost its way.

I only know how I had never seen a mirror, so I made do with muddy puddles and the ever-moving current of the river. I became what was needed to survive: part chameleon, part magician; part housewife, part scavenger. And so did you.

Maybe reflections are not supposed to become real. Maybe they are always better as mirages. Maybe then they will never have the chance to reflect the sun's rays as a weapon. A beating heart at the mercy of a magnifying glass. Maybe then they will never learn how to burn.

Why do we burn each other alive? Why do we take our best swings in an embrace?

Sometimes I still wish I could ask you, "Why?" Why did you leave our home to burn? Why did you not help to put the fire out? Why did you watch me wipe the soot from my sweaty brow again and again, my clothes riddled with ashes and burns as I raced to grab another bucket of water to throw at the flames? Sometimes I can still hear the pop and snap, smell the stench of the smoke, feel my heart beating inside my chest. Sometimes I can still see you sitting there, frozen in your shame and stubbornness, lost in your pride and fearful safety.

I walked through the ruins after it was all over. I sifted through the rubble and found all that remained. A heart I made for you. A day spent in the redwoods. A week in the lemony sunshine. Baked goods. A thousand calls and a million more laughs. A fold-out table, a small bundle of thyme, and two cafés.

And again I waited. Holding the blackened treasures in my arms, to share with you, give to you. To grieve together at all that had been lost. To rebuild together.

Sometimes hope can be the cruelest teacher.

The Cowardice of Shame

I remember watching you run and hide behind a clump of bushes once as I passed by, years later. I was still holding on to hope then, too, even after everything terrible had happened. I didn't know that there was still more of my heart that could be broken—a lesson I would learn from you again and again and again for years to come. I was foolish and still believed that you believed in the words you would spout about love and friendship and how much I meant to you.

I wish you could have shown up for me, for us, for yourself. I wish you could have been able to turn and face us, even if just to say goodbye, even if just to help close the wounds, both mine and yours.

Every time I think of you, I think of the cowardice of shame and the cruelty of silence. Every time I think about you, I remember how mean you were . . . and how much I loved you.

Knowing someone's unhealed trauma can be a kind of poison. A fire burning in a sealed room.

Sometimes I wonder what you looked like when you received my two letters in that first year. If you took them for granted. If you tucked them away, like you did your heart. Maybe you wished I would reach out one last time, bridging the cavern you put between us. Crossing the rapids and traversing the stone and thorns; trying to see through the darkness. Shivering from the storm, breathing with exhaustion from the journey. A tired fist knocking on a heavy door.

Why did you always leave that work for me? It was treacherous and terrifying. Why did you not face fear and leap, too? This question breaks my heart.

Watching someone starve from want of connection and care is nothing to forgive. A full plate of food seen and smelled from inside a cage. Perhaps you were starving yourself, too, but you also know what it means to be disabled. You also know that disabled loneliness is a kind of loneliness that can only be understood by fellow disabled people. You also know how cruel it is to lock disabled people out of disabled community. We experienced that together from another queer disabled woman of color and vowed never to do the same to each other. Why did you break that vow?

Homecomings

If this was before, I would hug you and cry and tell you how much I missed you and how grateful I was that we could be in each other's lives again. I would cook you your favorite meals and play your favorite music. I would sit with you and hold your hand, your favorite thing.

And we would talk long into the night the way we used to. I would tell you how much I love you and how lonely my heart was without you.

I would softly whisper ever so gently, ever so tenderly, that as a disabled adoptee, the enormity of "home" weighs heavy on me every day, but with you it felt a little lighter. That "home" is everything and nothing at all, both there and not. That "home" is a quiet grief that stretches from before I can remember and follows me wherever I go. I would tell you how happy I was that you were home—that I was home. Again.

Maybe as queer disabled women of color, we make our homes inside of each other because there is nowhere else to build. Because our best efforts always seem to infringe upon someone else's space. So, we build inside of our love and friendships, create walls and windows to hold us, tables to gather around and soft fires to remind us that there is still warmth left in this world for us. That was what it felt like with you. That was a kind of home that I had never felt before, and I can still remember that pastel joy like the feeling of sunlight on our faces.

To the You that Used to Be Home,

I keep your room inside of my heart clean and ready. I am still your home, even though you are not mine.

Care During COVID
Photo Essay on Interdependence

Kennedy Healy and Marley Molkentin

This photo essay was originally published on the Disability Visibility Project blog on February 8, 2022. Though images here are printed in black-and-white, image descriptions have been written to reflect the full-color images from the original blog post. View the original post at disabilityvisibilityproject.com/2022/02/08.

The photos accompanying this essay were taken in the winter and spring of 2021 in Chicago, Illinois. Our conversation was recorded and edited for length and clarity in January 2022. The lack of representation of formalized in-home care during and before the pandemic led us to create this project. We share it in the context of a global pandemic that continues to cause great suffering to many underrepresented groups. This is the story of two people with relative privilege, told in solidarity with all those discarded by the state and public.

KENNEDY: My name is Kennedy. I'm a twenty-seven-year-old Fat, Queer, Crip. I receive state-funded home-care services that allow me to utilize personal assistants, or PAs, who help me with bathing, dressing,

A landscape photo of two people in bed in the morning. Marley, a young white woman with long red hair, kneels on the bed next to Kennedy, a fat, white disabled person with short brown hair. The window shade behind the bed is open, framing Marley as she lifts Kennedy's leg, bending it at the knee, as though to stretch it. Both Kennedy and Marley are wearing cloth face masks.

hygiene, household chores, and more. Though my life is structured around care, it is a reality that is invisible to many people around me.

MARLEY: I'm Marley, I'm twenty-three, and I graduated college with a photojournalism degree and no job in the middle of the pandemic. I found Kennedy's PA job posting in a queer Facebook group. I was the first PA she hired under COVID, essentially trusting me with her life due to her high-risk status. Though I knew nothing about care work, I spent the next year working for her, learning from her, and ultimately creating with her.

KENNEDY: One night as we were doing our routine, we decided to shoot a photo project together. I had never seen care documented in an

A landscape, side-profile photo of Marley moving Kennedy through a room using a ceiling Hoyer lift. Facing each other in masks, Marley and Kennedy are framed by a hallway and a bedroom door as Marley reaches up to operate the lift in which Kennedy is suspended. Warm light pours in from the bathroom door behind Kennedy, though the rest of the surroundings are dim. Kennedy holds the remote operating the lift. Her naked butt and legs hang down from the sling.

authentic way that wasn't super medicalized, staged, or stale. And I had never had a care worker who was a photographer. Marley introduced me to the concept of self-portraiture, which we chose as our medium because of the constraints around COVID safety. We felt it was important to share our story. This was months into our relationship. But I want to start from the beginning. Marley, I'm curious when you first came across my application online, what drew you to apply?

MARLEY: I already knew a little bit about care work because I have a friend who uses home-care services. I don't have a healthcare background, but I liked the idea of working hands-on with one individual, in a home setting. While there was a certain risk with COVID, it was also safer than many other jobs. I really liked how up-front and transparent you were. I felt like our values really aligned: politically, identity-wise, both being queer, and valuing COVID safety. The pandemic launched our relationship even more intensely because we both felt a great responsibility toward each other's health and well-being.

KENNEDY: I'm glad that you did apply. Before COVID, there was a moment when we were living under Trump, and Bruce Rauner as the Illinois governor. Until more recently, I wasn't aware of any politicized disabled people working at the Illinois Department of Human Services (IDHS), which maintains the Home Services Program the PAs are funded through. The services, compared to when I first moved to Chicago in 2012, all started to dwindle. So even before the pandemic, hiring and maintaining PAs was a huge struggle given all the different barriers the system puts in place. And that's for someone who the state deems worthy of any services at all (i.e., a US citizen who is disabled "enough").

I've always spent a ridiculous amount of time coordinating my care, and COVID compounded that. In the summer of 2020, I lost some PAs due to moving neighborhoods and needed to hire new folks. I think early in the pandemic we were like, "Oh, we'll just wait it out." Then we started to see how long this was going to be and that we still had to do things like move and switch jobs. It was all incredibly daunting and felt really impossible. You were the only stranger I hired that summer. I was asking that your other job be remote, or that you not use public transit, which is how most people in Chicago get around, especially low-wage workers. It just felt like a crapshoot. And now we have this project.

MARLEY: It was such an amalgamation of things that came together in the worst time, but with the perfect timing for this project to happen. What were some of the other struggles that you experienced?

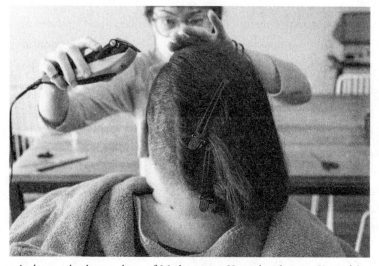

A close-up landscape photo of Marley giving Kennedy a haircut. Kennedy's head is seen from behind, with chin-length hair on the right side of her head sectioned off with clips. Marley faces the camera in a mask, peering over Kennedy's head, re-shaving the left side of Kennedy's hair with clippers. There is an orange towel around Kennedy's shoulders, and tools for cutting hair are blurred on the wood table behind them.

KENNEDY: There are a lot of barriers to hiring and maintaining care workers. The state limits the hours we have to work with. The shifts are short, sometimes you need care early in the morning, often I go late at night. The pandemic made decisions and protocols even more difficult. With the help of some friends, I eventually drafted a document about what was expected of people at work and outside of work pertaining specifically to COVID, which again makes the job harder to fill. But this was so necessary for my survival. You always worry about abuse or theft when hiring a stranger to work in your home. Now I feared that people would lie to me about their COVID precautions, too.

There were few resources for obtaining proper PPE. The state sent one set of gloves and one mask for each PA, which was just offensive. It got really tight between three PAs that first pandemic winter. I felt like we were playing burnout musical chairs. When time-off requests come in or when someone has a sore throat, how do I handle that? Making all those little decisions and maintaining my own mental health was incredibly difficult. What did you find some of your barriers to be as a care worker?

MARLEY: First off, my pay was minimum wage for a job that is so deeply valuable to our world and our well-being. Another big barrier that was hard on me was transportation to work. I don't have a car, so before COVID I took public transit everywhere. But then I started riding my bike for COVID safety. In the summer, it was nice. But in the winter it snowed so much I couldn't always ride my bike, so I had to just walk thirty minutes in the middle of the night.

One other barrier was the COVID anxiety. I got into this frame of mind that was necessary for survival, but it was really anxiety-inducing. I felt like if I rub my eye accidentally while I'm in the grocery store, did I essentially just give my boss COVID? Am I going to get Kennedy sick? What if she dies? And then it turned into: if I do this small thing, I might kill Kennedy.

KENNEDY: Everyone around me was having anxiety about my survival or were not that worried about it, which also felt like shit. I personally had to kind of balance things. While I know this is a catastrophe, and we do need to take precautions, how do we not spend every moment catastrophizing? Which leads to my next question: What sort of coping mechanisms or joy did we find?

MARLEY: We did have a lot in common and it was easy to be ourselves and crack jokes. Some of the humor was dark at times, in relation to the COVID stuff, but then I think we both had these funny, weird Midwestern childhoods that we joked about while we played '90s R & B in the shower. There were a lot of fun moments for sure.

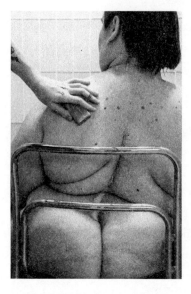

A portrait photo of Kennedy in the shower as Marley washes Kennedy's back. Kennedy is facing toward the pink-tiled walls of the shower with the back of their head, back, and butt filling the frame. Kennedy's head is turned slightly toward the camera. Kennedy has a long scar down the center of her back and multiple back-fat rolls and freckles. A metal chairback frames Kennedy's body. Marley's hand reaches in from the left with a purple bar of soap.

KENNEDY: Yeah, over these COVID winters, I've had to create things to maintain my mental health. I've had over twenty regular PAs since 2012, because that is how bad the turnover is. My relationships with the PAs who've worked since COVID hit are much different. Everyone has had a COVID experience—it's a global pandemic. But being high risk and receiving in-home care is such a specific pandemic experience to live through. We were sort of each other's pod, and it's been great the ways we've collaborated. Creating the project itself, to me, was a coping mechanism. Would you agree?

MARLEY: Completely—I don't know how seriously we took the idea at first, but then it seemed like more and more of a very real possibility that these photos could actually be vessels for people to understand us and give a fuck about care work and disabled lives during the pandemic. I think so many things were out of our control; this was something I could control. I can't control COVID. I can't control if my roommate might expose me to COVID or if somebody coughs on me at the grocery store, but I can show up with my camera and we can photograph the same stuff that we do every morning and every night and show people what we see and show people the value of what we live.

KENNEDY: Yes, and COVID made the project way more raw than something we would have shot pre-pandemic. The stakes were different, and that changed what we wanted to put out there. The intimacy of the photos was a way to take back power that gets stripped from disabled people through things like bad media representation, abusive care, or a myriad of other kinds of violence disabled people face.

MARLEY: Care work has always been undervalued, misunderstood, and misrepresented under capitalism. Media portrayals of disabled life have been harmful overall. Then COVID happened, and there was more coverage about health/care workers and disabled people. But there was a lack of understanding, empathy, and media portraying the lives of these communities that we all should have been prioritizing.

A portrait photo of Kennedy sitting naked on a chair in her pink-tiled shower, holding a hot-pink loofah across her chest. Kennedy gives a sharp look to the camera. Their catheter dangles from below their stomach. Kennedy's feet are dark and her skin is wet. Marley stands to Kennedy's right, lifting one of Kennedy's arms and directing the shower stream onto Kennedy's armpit with a detachable showerhead. Marley is wearing a mask.

KENNEDY: I know that before working with me you had some disability frameworks, but how did doing this project as your master's thesis while working in care work shift your perspective even more around ableism?

MARLEY: It was unavoidable. Learning about your life, learning about your perspectives; you had so much knowledge to pass on to me. You trained me on how to be a care worker and a big part of that is understanding ableism and power dynamics. You gave me books to read and creators to follow. It became a huge part of my life. Now I just give so much of a fuck about ableism. Every time I would bring this information to my classes, people were shocked. "Are you serious? Disabled people don't have marriage equality? Disabled people are kept in forced poverty if they receive services? You don't get any paid sick time?!"

KENNEDY: In a pandemic . . .

MARLEY: Every time I would tell my classmates this, my close friends this, my partner this, they were all shocked. It shifted the perspectives of all the people in my life.

KENNEDY: You really dove in in a way that nondisabled PAs usually don't. That speaks to your personality, commitment, and passion. It's one hundred percent, Marley, all the time! And yes, people really don't understand care in a political way, even if they care for children, elders, or friends' mental health. Needing help is something we're taught to hide, and the pandemic put a huge magnifying glass to our needs. We can really see how our government wants to either fund violence or fund care and where their priorities lie. It's helped me to start to think about care as an antithesis to violence and as what we need to end violence of all sorts. In-home care is just one facet of that.

Frameworks like disability justice and abolition don't believe state programs can be reformed into something that works. Discussions about care collectives and mutual aid are all really helpful in terms of people building the kind of world they want while these other systems collapse. I dream about some sort of structure where a lot more people around me are able to provide me care. Not just three to six PAs; like fifteen to thirty community members who are with me long-term. And they all live in a world where they have the time, energy, and resources to do that. I think the photos you took, and the way that they captured these really intimate and slow and gentle moments that I have with care workers, really speak to the value of people spending time taking care of each other.

A portrait photo of Kennedy's face filling the frame as Marley's hands surround it with a blue towel. Kennedy's eyes are closed, mid-smile, their face dotted with water droplets. A tattoo is visible on Marley's left arm.

This Is My Solemn Vow

Maria Town

To have and to hold,
for better, for worse,
for richer, for poorer,
in sickness and in health,
to love and to cherish,
Until death do us part. This is my solemn vow.

Our first conversation happened at a board meeting, and now I was considering proposing. I met Cheryl when I moved to a new city. I reached out to a local chapter of an organization I'd been involved with in a different city, hoping to meet people, and ultimately, I met the love of my life. Cheryl was the chapter copresident, and after a few monthly board meetings, we became friends. More than a year later, a friendly dinner after a long day at work turned into something altogether different, when I got home at two a.m. and messaged a friend, "I don't know what just happened. Dinner became the park, the park became playing Uno and listening to Patsy Cline. That transitioned to driving around and talking and getting Frosties. I think I just went on a date?" Eventually, Cheryl cleared up any uncertainty and formally asked me out. Fast forward, and we moved across the country together. It was a huge step for me. I had never lived with anyone I'd dated before, and just a few months after we moved in together, the pandemic hit. While some people realized that they absolutely could not spend every day together, I found myself increasingly in love. Eight months into the pandemic, I decided to propose. Spoiler: She said yes!

As we started to plan our wedding, my wife and I went back and forth over what we wanted to say in our vows. Writing our own vows and sharing them in front of friends and family felt too intimate. The traditional vows felt incomplete. If we used the traditional vows—"to have and to hold, for better, for worse" etc.—I wanted to add "until death *or the state* do us part."

Most people probably don't think about the end of their marriage before it's even begun, but from the moment we got engaged, I was all too aware that if either of our access and support needs changed, and we needed personal-attendant services or home and community-based services, we would have to get divorced. As a person with developmental and physical disabilities, it's easy to assume that if anyone's care needs changed, they would be mine. However, my wife could just as easily acquire a disability that drastically altered her ability to care for herself.

The primary way Americans pay for home and community-based services is through Medicaid, a federal program that provides healthcare to low-income people and families. Paying for these services through private insurance or out of pocket is almost impossible, unless you are independently wealthy. Because Medicaid eligibility is determined by your income and the amount of assets you have, even if a specific individual is not working and has no assets, if they are married and their spouse is working and has assets, this income can cause them to become ineligible for Medicaid and the many life-sustaining programs it provides. We aren't talking about a huge number of assets either. While eligibility for Medicaid differs greatly across states, the one thing all Medicaid programs have in common is that their income limits are painfully low. This creates a marriage penalty within Medicaid where marriage is discouraged and divorce sometimes required in order for disabled people to access the care and support we need to survive. Medicaid is not the only means-tested program where marriage penalties exist. Similar issues exist in Supplemental Security Income (SSI), the Supplemental Nutrition Assistance Program, Temporary Assistance for Needy Families, and more. All of these programs are disproportionately used by disabled people to survive.

What results from this is an impossible, inhumane choice for disabled people: choose between legally committing to the person you love or the resources and supports you need to survive. The moments when a spouse may be most needed, like a hospital stay or a traumatic event—the "for worse," "for poorer," and "in sickness" moments—become the moments when marriage is the greatest threat to your well-being. Yes, until death or the state do us part, my love.

Of course, many disabled couples are in committed relationships and do not want or feel the need to get married to have their relationship validated. Nonetheless, this should still be an option available to everyone, and it is a marriage equality issue few Americans know about. As a queer disabled person, it is difficult to see how some in my community have the right to marry while others in my community, LGBTQIA or straight, cannot. The state does not acknowledge that marriage penalties violate our human rights because these

Medicaid policies simply reflect the ableism rampant in our society. When I called my mother to tell her I was engaged, I asked her what she thought. This was a mistake. Instead of saying she was happy for me or excited for me or jumping full speed into wedding planning, she responded quite simply, "Maria, you need to take better care of your health." I paused and somehow got up the courage to say, "Mom, did you say that because you actually mean if I become more disabled and need more care, Cheryl will leave me?"

"Yes," she said simply.

Even in the eyes of my mother, my marriage was over before it started.

Although I was hurt and mad at her response, I wasn't surprised. The idea that someone who needs more assistance and care is not an attractive or worthy romantic partner is not new. It is a widely held belief that is deeply entrenched in American society. Talk to any disabled person about dating, and one of the first things they'll mention is concerns around disclosing their disability for fear of being told that their disability is a "deal-breaker," of being perceived as a tragic, burdensome figure rather than as a person full of life and sexual agency with an appetite for romance and companionship. Countless examples exist of people asking internet advice columnists if it is okay to break up with their partner who's been diagnosed with a medical condition. As with most things on the internet, this is yet another example of "Don't read the comments."

The stigmas and beliefs that disabled people are not worthy of love, romance, or companionship can have truly dire consequences. Pamela and Stephen Krupse were married for forty-two years, and actively involved in their community. Pamela developed Alzheimer's disease, Stephen became her caregiver, and ultimately he shot and killed her. Stories about Pamela's murder painted a sympathetic picture of Stephen, framing his shooting as an act of desperation, or even compassion. A major newspaper even called it an act of love rather than "a malicious intentional act of hurting another human being." Pamela Krupse's murder and the subsequent media coverage is tragically not unique among stories of homicides by family caregivers. More accurately, it mirrors the typical set of circumstances in which these events occur. When I think about Pamela or any of the disabled people murdered by spouses or partners every year, I think about vows—vows to love and cherish in sickness and in health. I think of vows by law enforcement to serve and protect. Vows by journalists to cover stories accurately. Vows of support by family and society at large. Vows all irrevocably broken. And though each of these stories breaks my heart all over again, I vow to myself to bear witness, mourn their deaths, and work to end these cycles of socially sanctioned violence.

Love may be a many-splendored thing, but love, like everything in society, can be corrupted by ableism. The reality of navigating love as a disabled person comes with a painful awareness that love often comes with conditions, that you can be loved so long as you are not an inconvenience. No article I'd seen put this so clearly than one I came across in the summer of 2020. In the *New York Times* column called "The Ethicist," a woman asked if it was unethical to break up with a man because he had Crohn's disease. Regarding her question, the writer stated that she doesn't really know how to support her beau and further said, "I want to shield myself from the pain, but I also feel like a terrible person for even thinking about it." The columnist Kwame Anthony Appiah replied:

> When a potential partner is already seriously ill, committing to this person may be committing to a life as a caregiver. (The

specific condition you mention has a wide range of severity; it can be mild and well controlled or genuinely debilitating.) You don't owe it to anyone to accept that burden. . . .

"You don't owe it to anyone to accept that burden." The words rang in my head. The quiet part had been said out loud and published for all the world to see. I felt an urgent need to counter this narrative. I went to Twitter and posted a reply to Appiah, a columnist with a massive public platform at a major newspaper. I told him that people with disabilities and chronic conditions can manage our own lives, and that this advice from The Ethicist is incredibly hurtful and dangerous. Disabled love is beautiful, I said. The tweet resonated, many people responded, and my friend Sarah Blahovec suggested that "Disabled love is beautiful" should be a hashtag. I agreed and subsequently tweeted a selfie with the accompanying text:

A white woman with long, thick brown hair wears lipstick and smiles. She stands in front of a photo wall.

My life is full of love and worthiness.

Those who love me care for me and I for them.

When someone trusts you enough to communicate intimate details of their body or minds, embrace those details for the gift they are. I am not a burden. #DisabledLoveIsBeautiful

Soon, my Twitter feed was full of commentary and images of disabled people asserting their worthiness and celebrating their love. Queer and trans folks, multiracial couples, young, old, wheelchair users, spoonies. The flood of tweets reflected the diversity of the disability experience and articulated the many different ways disabled people experience love and access intimacy. Some highlighted their romantic partners, sharing stories of how they met their spouse coupled with stunning engagement and wedding photos. Others shared photos of their friends and the deep love they felt for them. Disabled people discussed the love they feel for their disabled pets! Disabled and nondisabled parents alike shared posts about their disabled children, emphasizing the profound joy that is loving their disabled child. Many people highlighted the self-love that came when they embraced their disability and their care needs. Couples where both partners were multiply disabled shared stories of how they support and care for one another, without being made to feel like a burden. Some shared stories of how their partner seeing them as they were helped them to truly see, accept, and love themselves, even in moments when it is difficult to do so. Lots of people mentioned the love they feel and the care they receive when they are in community with others, particularly other disabled people. And, in working to counter the narrative that disabled people are burdens and unworthy of love, the hashtag

#DisabledLoveIsBeautiful created a brilliant and bold community moment bonded by shared intimacy and vulnerability.

As articles and stories continued to be written framing disabled people as burdens in relationships, members of the disability community used the hashtag #DisabledLoveIsBeautiful to counter this narrative. While I am consistently frustrated by how often this narrative comes up, I do love that now, in addition to rage tweets, my feed is full of #DisabledLoveIsBeautiful tweets and reminders that we, as disabled people, have the power to define ourselves and to determine how we want to be in relationship with others. The ways in which our bodies and minds often demand that we quickly get over any infatuation with the myth of independence and force us to engage in interdependence allow us to see love as it truly is—as a practice that requires mutuality. Even the practice of self-love is emboldened through affirming experiences within a beloved community.

Eventually, Appiah posted an addendum to his original column. The #DisabledLoveIsBeautiful hashtag worked, and the author has been compelled to provide a more nuanced response to the original question. He wrote:

> To assert that the letter writer shouldn't feel obliged to pursue a relationship she doesn't feel up to, then, is to address only half the story. The man she was briefly seeing deserves someone who sees him as a whole human being with much to give—he deserves someone who wants to share his life out of love, not some sense of scruple.

He expressed regret that he did not say more in his initial response and acknowledged how we all can become disabled and, in a roundabout way, how we are all harmed by ableism. I am proud that

#DisabledLoveIsBeautiful generated some more nuanced stories and provided disabled people with a tool for visibility and narrative change. However, I know that this hashtag will not fully end the stigmas against disabled people as unworthy of love. Even if social perceptions of disabled people drastically changed, this stigma would continue to persist because multiple structural factors remain in place.

In the very first post where I wrote "Disabled love is beautiful," one of the first responses read (edited), "We've been told all our love isn't beautiful which leads to so much internalized ableism." Policies that penalize disabled people for marrying or encourage us to divorce reinforce the notion that disabled people are not worthy of love. Policies that segregate disabled people from their communities, friends, and families further deny our communities the joy of our presence and love. Inaccessible infrastructure and insufficient public health policies force disabled people to isolate, and reinforce the notion that we didn't belong in the first place. Out of sight, out of mind. Why should we be loved? Why should we love ourselves?

Historically, marriage was never about love. It was an economic agreement to uphold heteronormative patriarchy. United States policy also prioritizes biological families, while restricting who can marry and who can bear and raise children.

Disabled people experience love and give and receive care in a variety of ways, but most of those relationships are incredibly difficult to make official in the eyes of the state. It doesn't matter how intimately involved and vital a partner is in your life, if you want them to be covered by your health insurance, formally involved in your medical decision making, or to be taken care of after you die, all are practically impossible unless you are married or related. What would a policy scheme look like that acknowledged all the manifestations of crip kinship?

The stigma surrounding disabled people that casts us as burdens and marks us as undesirable and undeserving of love and intimacy will not be diminished, much less extinguished, until we recognize care work as vital and necessary. This recognition must accompany changes in systems, resources, and policies that make it easier to access, pay for, and sustain care work. Thinking back to the vows that so many couples take on their wedding day, such changes surrounding care work make the "for better" times better, the "for worse" times manageable, and "in sickness and in health" possible. Imagine how my mother might have responded to the news of my engagement if she'd known that no matter how my needs changed, no matter what happened in my life or my wife's, that we could receive support and services we needed to thrive and would not be penalized for doing so. Would she have been able to respond with joy rather than fear that her disabled daughter would

A ring light holds an iPhone, which looks onto Cheryl and Maria as they read their vows. Cheryl and Maria both wear long white wedding dresses. A black service dog wearing a harness lays on Cheryl's dress. They are surrounded by orchids and greenery.

one day be left alone and heartbroken? Would she have been able to recognize that disabled love is beautiful rather than have her perspective clouded by ableism? To be honest, I don't know. But I can hope.

Our engagement was relatively short. I told my now wife, "I do not want a long engagement. There are benefits to marriage that we fought to have and I do not want to have to wait for them!" Not only was it short, our engagement was nothing like I pictured it would be, and neither was our wedding. All of our engagement- and wedding-related activities took place during the COVID-19 pandemic, and, although it was not what I expected, our wedding was intimate and it was beautiful. Our wedding was held virtually with only three other people attending in-person. As is so often the case for disabled people, we were very late getting started. We wound up not being able to get into our Zoom room because so many people joined the meeting! Captioners and sign-language interpreters who had worked with me for disability-community events provided the access support for our wedding. Our friend's service dog decided to take a nap on the train of Cheryl's dress, becoming an honorary member of the wedding party. Initially, Cheryl and I arranged for a wedding officiant, but they got COVID a few days before our ceremony. We ultimately officiated our own wedding and declared ourselves married. It was a moment full of the self-direction, agency, joy, partnership, and love that disabled people are so often denied.

While we did reference certain aspects of traditional vows, we did not include "until death *or the state* do us part." Instead, we created intentions of our commitments to each other. I committed to Cheryl that:

Recognizing that the external conditions in life will not always be smooth and we may lose confidence in ourselves and our partnership, we pledge to see all these circumstances as an opportunity to open our hearts; to accept ourselves and each other; and to generate compassion for others and further commit to changing the systems and conditions that created these hardships.

Finally, as we committed ourselves to each other, we recognized that two people in love do not live in isolation. We continue to learn the lessons of friendship and of the tremendous act of giving one's love to another in the company of our community. We recognized that our love is a source of strength with which we may nourish not only each other but also the world around us. Our community of Zoom wedding attendees typed, vocalized, or signed responses as they pledged to remain steadfast in their support, surround us with love, and reach out in times of joy and trouble. Disabled love—whether self-love, romantic love, or community love—is beautiful.

The Exhaustion of Pretense and the Illusions of Care

Khadijah Queen

In my desperation to get some real sleep for the first time since January 2020, I said yes when, in October of that year, my acupuncturist asked if I wanted her to get rid of my "false steam." She asked if I was sure, and I said yes, again. Care is a kind of intimacy. A layer of knowing that involves exchange and trust and consent. For me, a person on the asexual spectrum, intimacy has nothing to do with sex or romance. Instead, it involves tending, protection, nurturing—and that can come from friends, family, strangers, and, especially because I am disabled, care workers. I remember the light pressure of the acupuncturist's hands anchoring my ankles to the clinic table before she left me to process that energy shift in the dim, curtained space.

It worked; I slept. I did less work. I said no a little bit more often. I asked for a break, took a week off from teaching to process grief, even made a few small collages and drawings again in the open space and composed a commissioned poem out of morning haiku and journal scraps. But my duties remained, care work I couldn't outsource—my family and I are all disabled. My son and my niece (ages twenty and eighteen at the time) and my elderly mother all lived with me, in a home I'd just purchased on my assistant professor salary. Their needs: urgent, daily, all-encompassing, and left up to me. And at the same time, seeing me struggle to keep up with work amid the management of medical appointments and meals, they kept some of their needs hidden from me—which meant emergencies could and did erupt. Ambulances, ER visits, frantic calls to the nurse line. I tried to hide my stress at home; I didn't want them to feel like they were a burden. But the more I tried to hide the mental and physical toll, the more evident the damage actually became.

In a crisis, I'm amazing. I calm, soothe, assess, strategize, harmonize, coolly implement solutions. Daily tasks? Not my forte. My mind prefers delving deeply into something singular—like silviculture, family-owned French wineries, poetry. The constant interruptions of caregiving and self-care unmoored me, and I couldn't maintain a set routine. I got distracted, sidetracked, sucked into time-holes of random curiosity about sub-Saharan birds and the sacking of Carthage in 146 BCE and binge-watching *Drive to Survive* while the dishes piled up and mail went unopened.

Performing non-novelty tasks (cooking, cleaning, errands) runs counter to how my brain works. Friends reminded me not to forget about my own needs, but as a working solo parent caring for extended family, how could I avoid sacrifice? The world is not built for disabled people, so we take on the pressure of creating a real life outside of the illusion of systemic support. We often can't access that support, whether due to the infinite fiery hoops of bureaucratic paperwork, or, if by some lucky stroke we do gain access, we might experience its random and persistent violence and gaslighting. Navigating that

bureaucratic maze taxes already low energy reserves and further insti-
tutionalizes the isolation and exclusion of an already marginalized
population. We cobble together our own supports.

But that extra effort takes a toll. Stress manifested in my gut. I
went to the ER in November 2020 to find out I had IBS, rapidly
growing fibroids, and some random thing going on with my liver that
they said they'd "monitor." Meanwhile, the deadly wildfires raging in
California traveled a thousand miles to turn the Colorado sky a hazy
orange, and for days we had to close all our windows against the ash.

Then, my mother—who has dementia—had an episode that I
couldn't emergency-control into the clear, a dramatically unsafe hal-
lucination that sent me scrambling to find the proper facility for her.
She insisted that she could live on her own, but she put dishwater in
the greens and a mountain of salt in the soup she'd been making per-
fectly for decades. She put on her clothes inside out and refused to take
showers or allow me to help her with hygiene. She became obsessed
with rewriting the numbers in her phone book, and was probably taking her medication incorrectly—but she insisted she could do it herself, and the more I tried helping, the more she cursed me out. She
stopped leaving her room, preferring that I or my son bring her a tray
of food, which she'd half-eat. My vibrant, funny, larger-than-life diva
of a mother was disappearing into the illness, into her most negative
characteristics, and I had to find a way to help her live through it with
more dignity and better medical attention. During a pandemic.

With help from a regional program for seniors in crisis—one
that couldn't help in a preventative sense, but that's another story—I
quickly found a suitable care facility not far away. I moved her in,
paying professional movers because she insisted on packing her tiny
room with furniture from Montgomery Ward catalogs. Yes, they
still exist. I grieved, processing the loss of our very close relationship

in favor of something more adversarial, fraught, heartrending. Our intimacy—gone. She didn't want to know us, her children, anymore—new delusions haunted old memories, and her obsession with danger fractured us.

Still, disabled people know persistence. It took countless specialists and infinite patience to find the right diagnoses for my son. It took until the summer he turned nineteen for us to know he is autistic as well as gifted, that he suffers with migraines and sensory processing disorder, not "laziness" or "too many sweets" or "not enough sleep" or "too much gaming" or, in a common indictment of me as a single mother, "too much instability." I tried so hard to prove school officials, doctors, and evaluators wrong; I strove to be the stabilizing force in his life, his buffer against pernicious stereotypes of young Black men that threaten his well-being, his access to resources, his very life. And I am lucky to have his permission to disclose this; I ask, I am transparent, I am honest to a terrible fault.

Terrible, because that honesty has turned into oversharing on more than one occasion. I'm sure there were instances when I said too much, with too much emotion, especially at the wrong time to speak. I found that tended to get worse at certain times of the month—a joke culturally, but a truly overwhelming hormonal disruption for me. My doctors had for years blamed my extreme monthly mood swings on plain old PMS, then fibroids, then perimenopause. Since I seemed "fine," looked "fine," could still function even though their usual birth control remedy didn't work for me, no one investigated further. I'd heard the accusation "You're too sensitive" so many times in my life that I had long embraced it. What better way to use sensitivity than to become a writer—a poet? That defiance took energy to maintain, however, and its source is not infinite.

Almost a year to the day after my mother's mental break in October 2020, I had my own. In a chaotic and stress-filled moment, I planned my own demise in a way that felt scarily implementable. The energy level I had maintained for most of my life just disappeared—that false steam—but in the wake of ongoing grief about my mother, the pandemic, my son's illnesses, my family's illnesses exacerbated along with my own, I lost the ability to sleep. I couldn't keep up with working, cooking, cleaning, caregiving, and general self-maintenance. Instead of two or three times a week, I ordered takeout almost every day. I struggled to keep my own and my family's medical appointments and complete my writing projects and show up for online events and answer email and grade papers and design new syllabi and attend meetings and do uncompensated diversity work while Black during a global pandemic-recession-uprising-environmental collapse. I looked fine on the outside, but I felt isolated even with colleagues offering to help.

The Dissolution left me with what iconic poet and playwright Ntozake Shange might call "some simple bitch/widda bad attitude," one who had little desire to hustle or struggle or push herself to do more than the bare minimum. I disappointed people. I said no a lot more, said no to things in advance, in a long email auto-responder. I ignored major projects, missed out on a big opportunity. I cried a lot, I raged, I fell deeper into a disinfecting spiral as the pandemic wore on and on and on. Even with all the steps I'd taken to ease my load, my mind started collapsing. I felt burned out, hazed, ashen-hearted. I couldn't fight the bombardment of intrusive thoughts, so they took over, and I didn't even recognize myself anymore.

I had felt the disaster of the virus coming in December 2019, did as much preparing as I could to protect my high-risk self and family. But after two and a half years of maintaining a personal system of protection from SARS-CoV-2, and the abrupt loss of an exciting travel schedule and social life with no certainty as to when or whether it would return, chronic stress veered into deep depression territory. I called a hotline. I spoke to a woman who sounded Black, like me, who understood on that unspoken level the monumentality of what I was experiencing. The intimacy of that conversation helped to re-anchor me to who I was; I felt recognized, and realized a glimmer *did* remain. She got me a referral that saved my life.

Now that I have an official ADHD diagnosis, I understand that I underwent the dissolution of a social mask that had been in place for my entire adult life—a mask that I thought I'd perfected as I became more well known in my field. As an unknown, I gravitated toward intimate conversations from the start. Poetry is like that. Stranger-poets connect immediately, on the already-deep level of the poem, sharing intimacies with someone you might never encounter again except in a poem. As I published more, whatever eccentricities or social awkwardness I displayed got perceived as part of my identity as a poet—she's too sensitive, too intense, too strange, too *much*. Yes, I heard those whispers amid the praise. The strength of my defiance overruled any sense of exclusion before the pandemic. During? I've had to learn an intimacy with myself that I hadn't taken time for, that de facto isolation and exclusion has impelled. I am relearning who I am with new information, including facts about how hormonal fluctuations greatly exacerbate ADHD symptoms. Post-Dissolution me doesn't pretend, sets boundaries, says no, hasn't anything to prove—and so refuses proofs. I like her. I might even finally love her.

The world asks us to be quieter, to do less, *be* less. Be less colorful, more neutral, more predictable, more obedient, less spontaneous; to eschew "excessive" expression in favor of modesty, genuflect to the uniformity of it all unless we're in service of profit—the capitalist spectacle of entertainment. In conventional social settings, cultural norms demand that we don a bland façade, to sit still when our bodies demand movement, to resist the "disruptive" urge to fidget and doodle and blurt movie lines and sing and move, to stop doing multiple things at once and "just" *focus.*

Hiding or suppressing natural impulses is called masking. And we—who are not neurotypical—manage because we've been conditioned to do so, to connect but also to protect ourselves. The exhausting, debilitating, anxiety-inducing, and depressing effort of masking affects how we think about ourselves and other people in profoundly negative ways. I didn't understand that until I could no longer maintain the illusion of *fineness.* The public self I presented could have eaten the real me alive, disappeared me, dissolved my whole self instead of just that surface construction. Every time I feel like I have to put it back on these days, to talk to a person in charge of something I need or a family member needs access to, I smell a sizzle—sharp, acidic, and my newly built mind-self rejects that harm. I'm practicing more refusal, unlearning forty-seven years of compliance. Those of us whose disabilities aren't physically apparent often live in the schism pretense creates—we're fine until we're not, pretend until we can't, our minds and bodies suffering through the unnecessary demands to which ableist culture clings.

Whether disabled or not, creative people—contrary to persistent myths about the starving artist—require care, a nontoxic workplace, and a support network that shores them up as they are. That's no different from any other human being, but sometimes, superhuman expectations get placed on folks who create for a living. They are set as unreasonably as the expectations of perfection and silent endurance placed on people who care for families and strangers. Folks may see the super-competent or high-performance face we show the world and think we've got everything in our lives settled and under control.

And while that performance (perhaps, at least in my case, powered by hyperfocus) is real, we do adopt public personae for professional purposes, in order to do what we love and share what we know in style and in sometimes glamorous circumstances despite our discomfort. American culture is fascinated by what's behind the public veneer, too, but only enough to reinforce the importance of maintaining it—or to be titillated by the violent spectacle of its destruction. That isn't true intimacy. For me, true intimacy means striving for complete knowing; I'm interested in acceptance and non-transactional relationships, not consumption or competition.

That eschewing of surface ties might seem at odds with the fact that Los Angeles helped raise me. My city as surrogate parent reinforced what my biological parents told me: to look perfect, to watch what gets desired and rewarded in order to emulate it, to speak perfect English, to act as if perfection were natural and effortless, to walk in sunny California spaces as if upon a pageant stage. I used to live in the mirror. Not out of vanity, but to practice masking errors on the surface of my physical presentation in public—an intimacy of enforcement—and I made social errors all the time, talking out of turn or saying something too bluntly or not paying attention when expected to. I used to "space out" so much as a kid, I got teased. A popular refrain: "If you weren't Black, you'd be blonde." Kid me leaned into the misogynist presumption. I let people think I was an airhead, blamed my astrological sun sign—Gemini—and mostly got let off the hook of remembering boring things I didn't care about, like math formulas or anything with too many procedural steps.

My memory is long, however, and visual. I learned to read by the age of three and vividly recall my father teaching me at breakfast with the newspaper. Ads, comics, sports. I remember the smell of coffee and newsprint and Dad's orange juice, and he'd let me drink some from his giant glass if I got the words right. I remember my feet on his lap, standing as he held the paper with one hand and me around the belly with the other.

Hyperlexia, or early facility with reading and speaking, is a common symptom of ADHD. So is eidetic memory. So is social awkwardness, disorganization, fidgeting, interrupting, sensitivity to rejection. No one who loved me had language for any of those things, but I turned to language as escape. I still love that instant connection. I read every book in the house, all inappropriate for my age—all the Robert Ludlums, all the Stephen Kings, all the Danielle Steels, all the Walter Mosleys, all (yes, all) of Mom's *Encyclopaedia Britannica* volumes from A to Z. Ah, the 1980s. I read all the C. S. Lewis and L. M. Montgomery and *Choose Your Own Adventure* books my fifth-grade teacher Mrs. Schenck let me borrow when she saw how fast I sped through them. Eventually, I devoured all of my dad's encyclopedic volumes on Black history and Western civilization. Then I read all the Lois Duncan novels in my middle school library, all the Sweet Valley Highs, all the V. C. Andrews. In high school I discovered Toni Morrison, Maya Angelou, Alice Walker, Ntozake Shange, Marita Golden, J. California Cooper. I read them all and then read the writers they thanked in acknowledgments. I read Zora Neale Hurston, Toni Cade Bambara, James Baldwin, and Gloria Naylor. As an adult, I found the work of Lucille Clifton in a bookstore and read every word; I dove into the melancholy multiplicity of Fernando Pessoa, the elusive intensity of Lyn Hejinian, and continued alphabetically in bookstores and libraries.

My hyperfocus on reading—and, eventually, writing—got me all the way into graduate school despite many, many financial and circumstantial obstacles. People sometimes call the hyperfocus that is such a feature of ADHD a superpower, but no—we are human. We just use our brains differently. Or, said another way, our brains require stimuli and structures that neurotypical spaces tend to pathologize. However, the way neurodivergent brains work can be an asset, too, especially when known intimately, when nurtured and cared for and respected. I don't mind sounding like I'm on a soapbox. Having ADHD means that my sense of fairness cannot be suppressed. Is it linked to the dysregulation of executive function and the lack of dopamine production in my brain? I don't know the answer to that; but I do know that I can't help despising bullies, barreling toward solutions, and rejecting injustice.

In poetry, in prose, in books, I could find worlds where imagination didn't feel like pretense. Instead, that pretense was stripped away—the writer crafting an intimacy in its place, allowing human truths to starkly exist through voices and characters freed of the false veneer they wore in front of each other, unable to hide from any lies they might tell themselves.

In the summer of 2022, the acupuncturist asked if I needed stress relief this time. I had just returned from two weeks in the south of France, writing and attending a literary conference, which rejuvenated and relaxed me. I was buzzing with ideas, bursting with projects—zero stress in sight. I said, "No, but I could use more energy."

I have my steam back, and the language to describe it.

The Most Valuable Thing I Can Teach My Kid Is How to Be Lazy

Elliot Kukla

"Abba, I have an idea," says my three-year-old. "Put on your pajamas and your big mask, turn off the light, and get into bed."

"That sounds great," I say, honestly. I strap on my sleep apnea mask, change into soft, worn cotton PJs, and crawl under the fluffy white duvet with my child. Within seconds, they are lulled to sleep by the familiar gentle wheezing of my breathing machine. They know the sight and the sound of my sleeping body well; I have lupus, an autoimmune disease that causes chronic fatigue. On a good day, I can get by on ten hours or so of sleep. When my condition flares, sometimes for weeks on end, I need to sleep for much of the day and night. Before my child was born, I was afraid that my fatigue would make it impossible for me to be a good parent. And it's true that I am often juggling parenting needs and exhaustion. What I didn't anticipate is that prioritizing rest, sleep, and dreaming is also something tangible I can offer my child.

They see me napping every day, and they want in. We build elaborate nests and gaze out the window together, luxuriously leaning on huge mounds of pillows. Most three-year-olds I know fight bedtime, but we snuggle under the blankets on cold winter evenings, sighing in synchronized delight.

America in 2022 is an exhausting place to live. Pretty much everyone I know is tired. We're tired of answering work emails after dinner. We're tired of caring for senior family members in a crumbling elder care system, of worrying about a mass shooting at our children's schools. We're tired by unprocessed grief and untended-to illness and depression. We're tired of wildfires becoming a fact of life in the West, of floods and hurricanes hitting the South and East. We're really tired of this unending pandemic. Most of all, we are exhausted by trying to keep going as if everything were fine.

Increasing numbers of people are refusing to push through this mounting weariness. There are currently 10 million job openings in the United States, up from 6.4 million before the pandemic.

This trend is being led by young people; millions are planning to leave their jobs in the coming year. Some middle-aged people decry the laziness of today's youth, but as a chronically sick Gen X parent, and as a rabbi who has spent much of my career tending to dying people as their lives naturally slow, I am cheering young people on in this Great Resignation.

I have seen the limits of the grind. I want my child to learn how to be lazy.

The English word *lazy* is derived from the German *laisch*, meaning weak or feeble, and the Old Norse *lesu*, meaning false or evil. Devon Price, a sociologist who studies laziness, remarks that these two origins capture the doublespeak built into the concept.

When we call people lazy (including ourselves), we are often pointing out that they're too tired and weak to be productive, while often simultaneously accusing them of faking feebleness to get out of work for malevolent purposes. As Dr. Price puts it, "The idea that lazy people are evil fakers who deserve to suffer has been embedded in the word since the very start."

Shunning laziness is integral to the American dream. The Puritans who colonized New England believed that laziness led to damnation. They used this theology to justify their enslavement of Black people, whose souls they claimed to have "saved" by turning them into productive laborers.

This view has endured in American culture. Hundreds of years later, working to the point of self-harm to build the boss's wealth is still lauded as a "good work ethic" in America, and the word *lazy* is still connected to racism and injustice. It's poor, unhoused, young, Black, brown, mentally ill, fat, and chronically sick people who are most often accused of sloth. We rarely hear about lazy billionaires, no matter how much of their fortune is inherited.

For decades, I feared being labeled "lazy" because of my chronic fatigue. I pushed myself past my physical limits, all the way to severe illness, to prove my worth. Disabled activism taught me that stigmatizing rest is not just bad for my body; it's bad for the world. The pandemic demonstrates, in a visceral way, how staying home and doing less can be a form of activism. The pandemic has also illustrated how respite is not widely available to most essential workers in this country, with tragic consequences for everybody. The lack of sick leave, family medical leave, and the opportunity to work from home in essential, low-wage jobs has thrown kerosene on the viral fires of the pandemic.

Even as we look with hope toward a post-pandemic future, we will still be living on a fragile, warming planet with increasing climate disruptions. It's urgent that we find ways to work less, travel less, and burn less fuel while connecting and caring for one another more. In other words, it's critical that we un-shame laziness if we want our species to have a future. The world is on fire; rest will help to quench those flames.

Right now, as the Omicron variant spreads wildly, the Centers for Disease Control and Prevention has factored keeping people at work into their decisions on guidance, at times making it more dangerous for immunocompromised people like me to get healthcare or leave the house. As a high-risk person, I am painfully aware of how profits and productivity matter more to those in charge than my survival does. As Sunaura Taylor, a disabled activist, points out, our grinding economic system inevitably leads to treating disabled people as disposable, while trapping able-bodied people in dangerous, exploitative jobs. "The right not to work," says Taylor, "is an ideal worthy of the impaired and able-bodied alike."

Laziness is more than the absence or avoidance of work; it's also the enjoyment of lazing in the sun, or in another's arms. I learned through my work in hospice that moments spent enjoying the company of an old friend, savoring the smell of coffee, or catching a warm breeze can make even the end of life more pleasurable. As the future becomes more tenuous, I want to teach my child to enjoy the planet right now. I want to teach them how to laze in the grass and watch the clouds without any artificially imposed sense of urgency. Many of the ways I have learned to live well in a chronically ill body—by taking the present moment slowly and gently, letting go of looking for certainty about the future, napping, dreaming, nurturing relationships, and loving fiercely—are relevant for everyone living on this chronically ill planet.

To be sure, it is my privilege that allows me to teach my child to be lazy. Many people in this country and elsewhere spend all their time working, some holding multiple jobs. Many still struggle to afford housing and food. For too many, laziness is not an option.

But rest should not be a luxury; our time belongs to us and is not inherently a commodity. Reclaiming our time is an act of sovereignty over our lives, deserved by everyone. "Rest," says the nap bishop, the Black activist Tricia Hersey, "is a radical vision for a liberated future."

Today, my child and I are playing a game of hill. We are lying under a giant pile of every blanket in the house, pretending to be a hill studded with soft grasses. Their warm breath is on my neck, skinny limbs splayed across my soft belly.

"Shh, Abba," they say. "Hills don't move or talk . . . they just lie still and grow things."

I am teaching my child to be lazy, and so far, it's going really well.

What Getting My First Milwaukee Back Brace Was Like

Ingrid Tischer

Because my memories go back to the age of three and no further, it seems as if I came into existence as I was (just barely) walking with my mother, and occasionally my father, through the long hallways of Rochester's Strong Memorial Hospital sometime in early 1969.

In the confusion about what was wrong with me—cerebral palsy atypical was their best guess and a misdiagnosis until I was eleven—it must have been a strange relief to the neurologists and orthopedists to come upon scoliosis, a particular problem, discrete and treatable.

Scoliosis, the name for curvature of the spine, gave them the opportunity to bring a small sense of order to an unwieldy whole. Dr. Agneta Borgstedt, the pediatric neurologist who knew me best, and my parents finally decided it was necessary to treat the worsening condition with a contraption called a Milwaukee back brace. They knew, though I didn't until later, that I would possibly wear it until my twenties.

Clinic visits from that time always included me bending forward from the waist as doctors, residents, and medical students ran their index fingers down the length of my bare back. Their diagnostic procedure spoke in simple declarative sentences: "Her spine has two major curves that will need to be braced."

Orthopedists are carpenters and gardeners. They revere the symmetrical and stake the drooping stalk. The fingers on my back never found the vertical line of a straight spine. Their fingers waved this way and that, slowly, sometimes as a medical student hesitated and an instructor said, *Yes, follow the line, it's right in front of you.*

I was always x-rayed front and back, and side to side, standing and lying. The X-ray table, covered in cold linoleum, had tape marking where exactly to lie on it and then where to stand. The camera was heavy-looking but so well-mounted and mobile it might have been a dragon gracefully swooping in to take a closer look at me. I stared it in the eye as the light flashed.

Standing still and holding my breath for three seconds was easy. Wearing the lead apron was no bother. When I saw the film later in the day, the hazy crocodilian sway of my vertebrae explained what was wrong with me better than anything.

Dr. Borgstedt said that scoliosis as severe as mine would lead to deformity and pain. Untreated, in time I wouldn't be able to breathe because my spine would curve so far inward it would invade the space my lungs needed.

Most scoliosis patients are girls in an adolescent growth spurt; the muscles that anchor the spine on either side are unequally matched for a time and one side pulls the spinal column into a curve. Muscle-strengthening exercises were the first level of treatment, then bracing, and, as a last resort, fusing the spinal vertebrae together, preventing any curvature—and ordinary bending.

My appointments took us from the upper floors of the hospital down to the maintenance level, where orthopedic diagnoses met orthopedic devices.

The first brace shop that I remember was dusty and loud with the sound of saws. The floors were cement and dark, marred linoleum. The lights were like those in garages. Scraps of leather punched with holes for buckles in this pre-Velcro age lay scattered on workbenches. The room was filled with the presence of metal, for braces, for tools, for the grab bars a patient grabs to stand still and straight during the plaster casting.

Making a brace that extends from the neck to the hips took numerous appointments, multiple fittings, and a variety of materials including metal, leather, plastic, and a lightweight fiberglass-based foam.

The months-long process of crafting the brace began with two body stockings and orthopedists marking strategic pressure points on the outer stocking with thick black pens. They bickered: "She needs a lateral—" "No. A cervical collar will attend—" and poked regions of my back where, apparently, the curves were most severe.

My mother stood watching, arms crossed, a pucker of concern on her face that made me determined not to be bothered by anything.

She was flanked by several men in white coats and work shoes who were perhaps interested in the sight of an unusually young scoliosis patient. The wrapping of wet plaster gauze felt warm and comforting at first. The caster had a kind face the same square shape of my father's. It was no hardship to stand very still, holding the metal grab bars overhead as he did his work.

By the time the plaster became uncomfortably hot, I liked him well enough to impress him by staying utterly calm while he sawed the cast in half with a round surgical saw, making it vibrate. Unlike my older brother, I didn't have many opportunities to show physical courage; I wasn't going to miss it.

He cut through the inner layer with a pair of blunt-nosed scissors, cracked the shell in half and slipped it off me, taking the marked-up body stocking that was stuck to it.

I stood alone for a minute with my hands still gripping the bar above me, blinking in the bright light. My mother swooped forward to cover the chill of my near nakedness before the men. It was a mix of chill and relief to be so exposed after the stiff wrapping of plaster.

*   *   *

We were in my mother's bedroom, she and I, one afternoon after her lie-down and before supper took over. She said I needed to try wearing the brace now that the fittings were done. It was home with us, in her closet, on the floor next to her shoe rack.

I wasn't worried. I had been through so many fittings while men with thick, rough fingers pushed a pressure pad here and there and told my mother bluntly it had to be tight—"Tighter, sorry, it's gotta really squeeze her"—that I had a quiet, waiting calm for whatever was next. The thing wasn't comfortable, that was for sure, but it didn't hurt. All those fittings had been about making it not hurt.

The Milwaukee back brace in her closet looked like the offspring of football hip pads and a frame for body armor. In later years my braces would make me skeptical of assumptions that all corsets were painful. The braces did constrict my movement, yes, but if one hurt, it meant I'd outgrown it and it was time to begin crafting a new one. As an adult I would privately roll my eyes when friends told me I was too vanilla to understand bondage. Perhaps not. But living in back braces for ten years of my childhood informed my understanding of physical restraints in a way that they perhaps could not understand either.

———————

Every brace was different of course, as each person's spine was different. It worked on the support-and-contain principle. Flat, vinyl-covered pads were attached to a metal frame extending from the neck to the waist. The pads pushed the back muscles at strategic spots to counter whatever weakness was allowing the spine to curve. Those pads had to push hard to make a difference.

My brace had several pads positioned near the shoulder blades and the lower rib cage. A metal collar would surround my neck, stopping me from looking down easily unless my whole self from the waist up dipped forward. One long bar in the front and two in the back that spoke of erector sets traveled from my shoulders down my torso to where they were affixed to the molded plastic girdle cinched in at my waist.

This girdle, a hard plastic mini-corset that came down to cover my groin and behind, stopped just short of where my thigh began. The lower edge had been painstakingly trimmed and smoothed—too long and it cut into my legs when I sat.

There wasn't a lot of actual coverage above the girdle, but it still kept me from moving freely. A metal screw held the collar together at my neck; a leather belt buckled the girdle together. It would have been impossible to put it on myself even if I had been old enough since all the fastenings were in the back.

The orthopedic craftsmen had shown my mother how to put it on me. This was her first attempt at doing it at home.

Kneeling and concentrating, she held the back bars and opened the brace like a particularly stiff book as I stood with my back to her. I slipped my arms through the empty space between the pads but stopped because the girdle pieces were still too close for me to slip between. She creaked the thing wider, and I was in.

"How's it feel?" she asked, taking a puff on her cigarette. It was a warm, humid day, and it didn't feel good, but it didn't hurt.

"Okay," I said.

"Well, let's see if we can fasten it right," she muttered. The neck screw took a minute but spun easily once she had the pieces in place. "One down," she said.

I stood still, balancing myself by keeping one hand on her bed. I was wearing the new, long undershirt they said I would need to wear to keep my skin from being rubbed raw at the waist, and to absorb sweat. The plastic of the girdle may have had hard foam padding on the inside and was dotted with air holes, but my skin had to be protected.

My hair was already snagged in the collar. Tears prickled my eyes as innumerable small hairs pulled out. "My hair," I said, trying not to move my head but wanting to twist around to see her.

"Hold still, hold still," she said. "What? Where does it—"

"My hair!"

Her fingers delicately pulled most of it off the back of my neck and to the side, and she said thoughtfully, "We've got to cover . . . okay, let's finish getting this on first."

We both sighed.

She buckled the girdle tightly enough so that I was aware of wearing this enveloping thing, but my body inside slipped and slid against it. She noticed. "That's not tight enough," she said regretfully.

She tightened it so much and so quickly, I gasped. "No!" I blurted.

"Okay." She sounded a little frightened, and loosened it. There— it felt more like it had at the hospital. Snug, and it moved with me.

"How's that feel, honey?" I tried to walk a little in it, but that was too hard; I needed to see my feet.

The room had its usual late-afternoon light, plus the lamp's. The sky was darkening for rain, and the warm yellow glow was too much. It was suffocating.

"Off! Take it off!" I had worn it; that was enough. It was too tight and I couldn't get away from it.

My mother and I were facing each other. How did she know what to do? She was sitting on the white woven bedspread with the window behind her head. My parents had a nice low double bed even I could climb up on. I stood supported by her knees.

"We have to leave it on for a little while," she said evenly. I must have looked panicked, but I didn't know what to say because I was half-grasping that *Of course, this was what it had all been leading to.*

"Just a little while longer today," she said.

I said, "No."

"Honey."

"No!"

I tried to wiggle around in the thing as if to shake it off. Which just left me breathless and more disturbed.

"Just a few more minutes today," she said, taking my hands in hers. I didn't say anything.

"I know this is so hard," she said.

I nodded. I couldn't speak.

"I know it's hard."

I breathed. "It's okay."

She didn't say anything for a minute. Shook her head. "No. It's not." She tried to bring me closer, but I didn't want to move and I couldn't bend anyway. "Honey, please. Cry if you want to."

"I'm okay." The room was horrible, horrible in its drowning yellowness.

She nodded, looking at me. "All right." She paused and stood up, propped me against the bed, opened the closet door where the brace had been. "I want you to do one more thing today and then we're done."

She was looking down at me and walked back over to take my hand. "I want you to look in the mirror, see the brace on you."

No. No. No.

"Come on," she said quietly.

Next to my mother: a tiny, bent girl with my face, scared and sad, and skinny arms, skinny legs, sideways-looking flattish feet. All buried up to the neck in a humpbacked, wide-hipped robotic disguise, out of which my head, arms, legs, and the rest seemed to extrude, ill-matched pieces, graceless in their own right but now inhuman as well.

I was ugly. Ugly as I saw the Genesee River bridge in winter on a tense ride home from my grandparents' farmhouse. An outline of black iron spotted with dirty snow against a gray sky. Surrounded by smokestacks and tree branches. I remember all of this.

I moved my arm; inwardly I felt it, a smooth glide of a sweeping gesture, but I saw the same motion in the mirror and it was a jagged upward lurch. An ugly movement.

Now I was sobbing and the face was so sad, I couldn't bear to see the girl I looked to be, who wasn't at all the girl I was. The pinching closeness of the brace, the weight, the pain on my mother's face that came from me were bad, more than bad enough. The worst, however, was the betrayal of my own face. It was miserable-looking and wretched.

I did not know what to do with my face. It had shocked me and given me away to everyone else at the same time. I could handle being me but not that face, because that person was not me.

My mother was unfastening the belt and loosening the screw. When she slipped it off me, I nearly collapsed from the relief. I could feel her heart beating against my back, and my arms could press against my stomach again; the world briefly concentrated in the space of my body from neck to thigh. My mother hugged me and hugged me, the brace lying on its side next to my pants and shirt. I felt everything for a while that evening, as if nothing had ever touched my skin before.

Igniting Our Power by Reclaiming Intimacy

Ashley Volion and Akemi Nishida

Intimacy is such an intriguing word, but what is intimacy, actually—and how about disability intimacy? As members of disability communities, how do we experience intimacy differently from those who are not part of these communities? These are questions that brought us, disability-community friends and scholars, together to chat, and our conversations became this chapter. As two disabled women of color who are each coming from queer, migrant, and other communities, we became friends partially because of our common scholarly and personal interests around intimacy, care, and, above all, community building. We understand the importance of these topics, not only through an academic lens, but from navigating the world with a disability in our everyday lives. It is through the lens of our everyday lives that we understand the importance of discussions around intimacy that often goes underrepresented. We began this conversation to further the discussion around intimacy in the disability community.

One thing we realized immediately is that intimacy is tricky to define because of its complexity and ever-evolving nature. But this is what makes intimacy so interesting, intimidating, frustrating, and fun to talk about. Growing up, we had a vague and narrow idea of what intimacy is. Our conversation says, "F that!" Intimacy is anything but narrow. Within our conversation, we invoke our power through our articulation of intimacy by describing how these moments positively validate the very nature of our existence. However, we could not fully explain what intimacy is without discussing what we refuse to call intimacy. This conversation will not leave you with one concrete definition, but hopefully, you will want to dive deeper into how we can define intimacy as people with disabilities.

AKEMI: How can we rethink intimacy by centering disabled people's experience or crip and disability wisdom? Shall we start by talking about what crip wisdom is to us—a phrase we first encounter in the book *Skin, Tooth, and Bone* by Sins Invalid?

ASHLEY: Crip wisdom for me is everyday conversations. It entails a sense of creativity. We turn different things into what we need them for. We may take something that we would use for cooking and use it for a totally different aspect of our lives. For instance, I remember my friend and I were having a conversation when I first started to do my own laundry. I couldn't figure out how to put the laundry detergent in because those containers are really awkwardly shaped and weird to handle, especially with my limitations in my hands. She mentioned to me laundry pods that you could just throw in. Even though it sounds simple, it actually gave me the ability to do something big that I couldn't do before. Just that small suggestion led me to do things differently.

Having those conversations that nurture connection and comfort with another person is a form of wisdom for me. In these conversations and these moments of crip wisdom, I feel comfortable being who I am, and having my whole sense of self realized, which I don't get often.

AKEMI: Crip wisdom to me is unique wisdom that emerges from everyday experiences of disabled, sick, Mad, fatigued, pained, Deaf, blind, and/or neurodivergent people. I wanna start by naming diversity within disability communities or categories, because when people hear the word *crip*, some people automatically think it signals only physical disability. As Ashley beautifully summarized, crip wisdom is creative tips and everyday experiences of disabled people.

Crip wisdom is our resistance or our crip middle finger to this ableist society. If you just hear the phrase *crip wisdom*, it may sound like an oxymoron in the larger ableist society. How we put these words together is our resistance to say that what we learn from our everyday life is valuable. This disability genius-ness is totally our fuck-you to those who see our lives as trivial and valueless in a very eugenic way. The phrase itself and how we use it is resistance.

I see crip wisdom as a way to transform society and envision our everyday lives in a very disability-centric—inclusive and accessible—way. It shows us how we can live in a different way from this US, individualist, independent BS. I wanna emphasize crip wisdom as a vision and dream and also our transformation of this ableist society.

ASHLEY: We can redefine intimacy by centering crip wisdom because society thinks of everything as just black or white. They don't see the color in between. Redefining intimacy in this way can show us that intimacy doesn't have to be one thing or have one definition.

Intimacy is more than romantic and sexual intimacy. Intimacy can be just looking at someone because you know what they're going through. Just this intimate connection of understanding and comfort.

In the United States, we're taught that nakedness is a very intimate and private thing. Yet, I have to show people my body every day to receive the assistance I need. I have to be vulnerable in ways that other people wouldn't even dream of. Intimacy means something *deeper.* Being naked in the presence of others doesn't necessarily mean intimacy, because it's forced on to me based on care.

Intimacy comes in the spaces where my friend might look at me and know I'm going through something hard that day. She'll know that I'm not in the space to have a conversation. She'll just bring over my favorite treat, give me a hug, and leave. Intimacy for disabled people can be more of an emotional connection but on a *deeper level.* It is this moment of intimacy when you're seen fully. That can be rare.

AKEMI: I like how you're thinking of intimacy in a very personal way and distinguishing intimacy by describing it in different depths. Intimacy feels deeper and not just superficial "my naked body being touched by your hand," stuff like that.

Since I was born with a disability, I always hid part of my disability as much as I could by putting my disabled hand in my pocket. I realize my disabled hand is rarely touched, 'cause I didn't allow anybody to touch it. When they did, they gave me disgusted faces that, in turn, gave me lots of visceral feelings.

I have friends who have similar disabilities to mine, and we hold each other's disabled hands. That touch is very deep in the way you described. It's more than sexual and romantic—or it may be a mix of all of that. Because when my hand holds their hand, first, there is a visceral reaction. My hand rarely feels the warmth from other hands. But when our disabled hands touch each others', it is a physical way to feel recognized for our whole selves and our humanness. Feeling affirmation of our very being or our existence with every part of myself. I don't have to present myself as a human by hiding my disability. It feels like this person validates, acknowledges, and values my existence with every part of myself.

A dictionary describes intimacy as a *warmth* or *a long association*. When we think about intimacy from a disabled person's perspective, it's more than that. It's a very deep *affirmation* that it's okay for us to live. It's okay for us to be who we are and take up our space in this society. We are loved and valued and worthy of intimacy with each other.

ASHLEY: Intimacy within disability communities helps us grow as individuals and make new pictures of what we believe in our everyday lives.

Intimacy is a means to survival. It's like a safety net. It's knowing someone's there for you when you may not be able to be there for yourself sometimes.

AKEMI: Disability intimacy affirms our fundamental existence, which changes the way we think of ourselves: "We are worthy of love! We deserve intimacy!" It is not solely a disability-community thing. We are thinking about it through a more intersectional way as disabled women of color. When I think about intimacy through such an intersectional lens, it deepens its meaning 'cause it shifts our understanding of who we are and our relationship to society. People coming from marginalized communities are showing and expanding what intimacy is and does.

AKEMI: **Can you think of particular ways disabled people are deprived of intimacy?**

ASHLEY: I think ableism brings assumptions of how we cannot experience intimacy because nondisabled people never had intimacy on the same level as disability intimacy. Sometimes, ableist thoughts can limit us because other people may think of intimacy in a certain way: sex and sexuality.

AKEMI: By ableism, we are not simply talking about ableism in isolation or in silo, but we recognize how racism shapes ableism, ableism enables sexism, and vice versa. When I thought about this question, first I was thinking about how physical barriers are one of the most obvious ways we are often isolated from one another or from general society. The more I think about what you said—I started thinking that in this ableist society, disabled people began developing different ways to be intimate or opened up what intimacy is by developing intimacy beyond just "two people in person in physical space together."

I think about how ableism poses psychological and emotional barriers for us that keep us from experiencing intimacy because of internalized ableism. We might desire and daydream about intimacy, but at the same time, feel we don't deserve it in real life. Or we might be afraid to seek intimacy due to the fear of being rejected. Without denying such reality, I wanna amplify what you said about how disabled and other people from marginalized communities simultaneously push against very narrow notions of intimacy and reframe and rethink our experience to think about where intimacy comes up in our everyday lives, even though the hegemonic society might not agree with our notions of intimacy.

AKEMI: What experiences do we refuse to call intimacy?

ASHLEY: I refuse to call anything that is in my day-to-day care routine with financial compensation a moment of intimacy. Intimacy comes in those moments when I might go on vacation with a friend who has a different disability than I have, and we work together to meet both of our individual needs. During our vacations together, I don't pay her to do any of the care work she does, but it is a mental health break for us. I will call that intimacy because it comes from a deeper level, from a reciprocal relationship. When it comes to everyday paid care, I am working on refusing to call such care intimacy. I receive so much paid care that, honestly, it's hard for me to separate what is intimacy and what is not sometimes, even though I've been receiving it for the last twenty years.

It is hard to separate what is intimate care and what's not, because my attendant has been with me over five years. My care worker is one of the closest people I have in my life, especially during the pandemic because we made a pod together when everyone couldn't go out into the world. I want to acknowledge that intimacy develops because you spend so much time with that person. Oftentimes, from the client's perspective, it's hard to separate what the paid work is and what the intimacy is, because you spend so much time together day in and day out. She cared for me the most and even saw my emotional break-downs.

Sometimes it does get complicated in terms of intimacy, especially when it comes to a really good care worker who takes their job with pride and does outstanding work: sometimes you can internalize that as being more than what it is. That is a very hard thing to navigate and something that I'm still learning how to navigate myself.

AKEMI: What I refuse to call intimacy is anything forced on us. The term *forced intimacy* (the term put forward by disability justice activist, Mia Mingus, to describe how disabled people are often forced to be in intimacy with their personal assistants) is helpful to understand able-ism embedded in daily care activities. But at the same time, like you said, I feel the word is an oxymoron, because I don't wanna call anything forced on us intimacy. Intimacy is a very personal thing. It's up to each person to define what is intimacy or not. I like how you draw the clear line of, "When my naked body's involved, it is not necessarily intimacy." That's a really clear line you're drawing, that anything forced on us, whether it involves a naked body or not, we refuse to call it intimacy. I think it's powerful for us and for disability communities to refuse something to be called intimacy and to reclaim intimacy in our own terms. I like how you're seeing yourself and other disabled people as a judge to decide and tell the world what's intimacy and what it is not. I wanna reclaim intimacy based on pleasure and the deeper feelings that you talked about.

AKEMI: What are the unique kinds of intimacy we are able to develop because we're disabled?

ASHLEY: Intimacy and the way we create and develop intimacy is an important aspect of our disability identity. It teaches us different ways to look at what intimacy is and what it is not. Early on in my development as a disabled person, I would have described intimacy in the strict guidelines that I'd seen on TV, purely physical.

I think the uniqueness provides us ways to look at intimacy, and not just a physical aspect. It allows us to look at it in different ways of emotion or access. That's why my scholarly work has primarily focused on *access intimacy* (a term put forward by Mia Mingus to describe intimate feelings disabled people experience, when their access needs are met organically) because we don't have words, sometimes, for the different types of intimacy that we experience. I think this gets us to expand our thinking and our knowledge base. As we develop our self-identity, our thinking about intimacy grows, too, and we're able to be more intimate with people. I keep thinking about how you said previously that within a lot of these intimate moments between disabled people, we get to feel like our whole selves are being valued. I spent so many years being like, "I can't be intimate in this way," and being really depressed about it and being like, "I won't get that fairy tale that I see on TV."

To be honest, that feeling has not 100 percent gone away, and I wanna acknowledge that, because when we talk about disability identity and pride, we give off the idea that we're these totally enlightened human beings, and we don't have internalized ableism anymore. It gets lessened, but I think we'll always have a little bit of internalized ableism instilled in us from society.

AKEMI: I love how you talk about how intimacy prompts us to grow or is a necessary element for our growth. You clearly described how ableism makes ideas of intimacy very narrow, but we say, "F that," and we rebuild, expand, or fundamentally create what intimacy is for us. Intimacy isn't just the romantic naked bodies touching each other; it's about affirming our value and existence, allowing ourselves to love and to be loved and to take up this space together and to make us feel not alone.

If we reclaim intimacy in such ways, not only human friendship but also foods, arts, and relationships with animals and nature sound like very intimate parts of our lives.

Oftentimes, humans are horrible, and we feel safer, more loved and comfortable with animals, nature, or even with food. We've experienced intimacy in so many ways. For example, when I was young, I saw this disabled woman of color dancing at a feminists of color conference. I didn't understand the choreography or meaning behind the movements, but the movement was so powerful that I started crying. I had never cried because of art or dance, but somehow the dance caught me in a very deep, intimate way. It was an intimate experience I had with art.

Once we experience intimacy—being validated and valued—we refuse to settle for less, and we even refuse to call some mainstream notion of intimacy we internalized previously as intimacy. Reclaiming and expanding how we understand intimacy will bring even more self-affirmation. Disability intimacy brings a positive spiral!

We understand disability intimacy as our way to broaden how we view or define intimacy. We envision a world that acknowledges, validates, and embraces our unique forms of intimacy, crip wisdom, and essentially our existence—allowing disabled people to form deeper connections with others. In the world we envision, there are no longer obstacles to experiencing intimacy and our intimate experiences are not surveilled and punished. To envision and advocate for disability intimacy, then, we must embrace a world where people will no longer experience eugenics or life in incarceration. Through intimacy and crip wisdom, we envision a world where disabled lives are not only accepted but uplifted and centralized for the beauty that we all bring to the world. We want a world where we can experience different forms of intimacy freely!

Primary Attachment

Yomi Sachiko Wrong

The baby arrives on a warm afternoon in August, so achingly new and little more than six pounds.

I note her luscious smell, her serene face framed by a thicket of black hair, the way she is bundled in a soft pink blanket. I think of her mother doing this tender act of care before the state took the babe away. I imagine it was wrenching.

Because how do you relinquish a child you've just given birth to? She had no choice. They parted with a promise of weekly visits and a plan for reunification.

I find her mother's first name on the emergency placement paperwork and speak it to the child every single day. So she will know and not forget. I do various other things to support their connection, much more than is expected or required, but as days stretched into weeks, then months, I inevitably became Jellybean's primary attachment.

I stay attuned to the shifting dynamics and my positioning within this mother-child relationship, now a triad. I try very intentionally not to overstep in my role as the baby's caretaker and guardian. I check myself when the arrangement becomes difficult, complicated, messy. When the plan for reunification begins to unravel, partially judging myself for judging the baby's family.

I don't know the child's kin, the full truth of their circumstances, or how they feel about her being raised by a stranger. Resource parents, as we are now called, are largely kept in the dark about family histories and the complex backstories leading up to a child's removal.

We are expected to step swiftly into a gap, love deeply, and at the same time, remain detached from the outcome. It's ludicrous.

The US child welfare industry is a broken, violent machine rooted in ableism, white supremacy, and systemic oppression. We are all ensnared—parents, children, caretakers, attorneys, and social workers with big hearts and best intentions. As a Disability Justice dreamer, I believe that if we practiced collective care and wrapped support around struggling families, perhaps more children and parents could heal together, without ever separating. As I advocate and organize for a better world, a just future in which state power cedes to community control, I must navigate conditions as they are. I do my best in this situation with Jellybean not to use what small leverage I have to replicate harm.

I have a heart for children. I've witnessed nieces and nephews enter our family and have felt a burning emotional tug to help nurture and protect them. They are my babies, too. But my role in their lives has always been as a supportive aunty. Now, I am a mother.

The day-to-day care of Jellybean's body—the feeding, the cleaning, the comforting—intensifies our attachment to each other. I am her protector, her silly playmate, her morning sing-along song, her evening massage, her two a.m. reassurance. We spend time each day skin-to-skin, our bodies co-regulating, learning to trust. I become her sun and her moon. She, my North Star.

When I was asked to care for Jellybean, it was presented as an emergency. The desperation of the social worker felt palpable.

"Could you please help out?" she pleaded with me over the phone. She said that the babe would likely go to a shelter otherwise.

"Could I? Could I really?" I asked myself.

Such a major decision. Though I'd been licensed to care for foster children for a while, this was my first long-term placement. My emotions were a mix of fear, excitement, and . . . what? Self-doubt. Feelings of inadequacy. Internalized ableism, that old bitch, came to taunt me again.

Could I manage as a disabled single parent?

I called my sister. She encouraged me that we could take this on as a family. Then she raced to Target for baby supplies, and I had just four hours to get everything ready, not fully knowing what all Jellybean would need from me. And then she was here. A social worker pulled up to the curb and handed the bright-eyed girl over to me. My god.

At age fifty, I had long released any urge to bear my own children. I was diagnosed with infertility in my late thirties and had to grieve what would never be. After much internal healing, I reconciled that I would never see the play of my features on a newborn face or pass on many other genetic traits I highly value.

Still. I wanted a family, so I looked into adoption. But the part where you have to promote yourself to prospective biological parents? Create a profile? With pictures? No. This felt unaligned with my values.

So, I attended foster parent orientations, thinking that supporting children and families might be better. But I grimaced through so much classist, racist, ableist talk about "damaged" kids in crisis; it felt like they were actually trying to scare prospective caregivers away. A deeper truth is, I was nagged by fear that no one would find me—a Black, disabled woman—desirable to rear a child. Across the country, disabled parents lose custody of their children, get reported to Child Protective Services on specious grounds and/or denied the right to form families based on ableist assumptions of who is fit to parent.

These concerns kept me just shy of moving forward. And then the world turned on its head and I learned to release what didn't serve me.

In late 2019, my life imploded. And I was still plucking the shrapnel out of my heart when a series of catastrophic events unfolded.

The COVID-19 pandemic struck in early 2020.

I became seriously ill in January.

My beloved friend and chosen little sister, Stacey, died in May.

That December, my poppa contracted COVID and died a few months later.

As the pandemic wore on, the losses piled up and grief closed in around me. I was grasping for anything to keep myself rooted on this side of the realm.

I stacked my blessings against my heartaches.

I had a new home, a wonderful family, *the* best dog.

I had beloved community and many deep friendships. My badly bruised heart stretched, as an early flower arches for the sun, toward a life and future unknowable, one I wished to be filled with aliveness, joy, authenticity, and pleasure. Slowly, slowly, I inched closer to that warm light, centered myself right there.

I planted a wildflower garden and grew food. Went back to college. Hiked new trails with my pup.

I again researched foster care programs and signed up for the virtual classes. My plan was to offer respite care to kids needing a safe place to land for just a little bit. I would see how these short-term experiences went before considering a longer-term commitment to an older child.

I understood enough about early trauma and family separation to know my default would be to always push for and support reunification. I believed I could bring a disability justice politic to this heartwork, a politic that affirms not only collective care but the inherent worth of all bodyminds. I wanted to help children recover and rebuild from the damages life inflicts, never imagining I would be called to nurture a newborn, one who has yet to show deep imprints from the stresses and the hurts that systems of oppression inflict on us all. I prayed faithfully, sought wise counsel from others, considered ways to build and raise up a sovereign, tender, resilient little human.

"We have one heart, you and I."

My mother's words echo back to me. In our beginning, after I was born, we bonded under the watchful eye of the neonatal staff. I was a mess of broken bones—both arms, both legs, a fractured skull. My lung collapsed. It was a traumatic birth. Hospital staff laid me in an incubator lined with lamb's wool, the softest bedding they had, and waited for me to die.

But every day for a month, my lovely, brave mother took two city buses to come see me. Sometimes my big sisters, who were two and a half and four, would be with her. She said they quietly watched through the glass window as she gingerly gathered me up in the lamb's wool and sat in a rocking chair. She sang, hummed, and soothed. Coaxed me to eat, to live. "I held you to my chest so our hearts could touch."

We forged a new embodied experience.

When she could finally take me home, she was free to learn my body and how best to care for me. She said she had to overcome her own fears and feelings of inadequacy in order to show up fully as my mother.

For my whole life, it is her touch that evokes safety and assurance. I am most at home under her glow, which emanates from the body care that she gave to me, that was specific to my needs, the gentleness of it intensified by my fragility. She taught me to trust this primal intimacy. I do my best to follow her steps now, for my Jellybean.

We know that infants must form an early attachment to a sensitive and responsive caregiver. This social and emotional bond is imperative, as it lays a foundation for all future relationships in that it signals to babies that it is safe to express needs and negative emotions. And I see this play out with my baby girl, this raw need for attention, care, and touch that her very survival depends upon, and how urgently she puts forward this demand to me, her primary attachment figure.

When Jellybean is in distress, she must be able to count on me to respond in a patient, comforting manner. I study and learn her cues; what it looks and sounds like when she needs to be held or expel gas, or is feeling overtired. I composed a deep vibrational sound just for her, and when she is fussy, I put little fingers or toes to my lips and murmur this until she settles.

But our early days were chaotic. I was so anxious about hurting or dropping her. I tried my best to anticipate her desires, but we were strangers and our bodies were not yet in sync. I faltered a lot.

This fumbling is totally expected of new parents, of course, but I had the added pressure of the ableist gaze, and that nearly broke me. Because some of us have internalized the ableist gaze so that it is always on us, judging and disciplining us, even when no one is looking.

Fostering unfortunately requires much interaction with social workers. I do not much care for social workers. They represent my own early trauma.

Once, an agent arrived at my front door to assess the baby's health and well-being. Upon seeing that I am disabled, however, the focus quickly shifted from an inquiry into an uncomfortable surveillance laced with the agent's assumptions and biases that I had to interpret and defend against.

"So, you live here alone?" she asked more than once, taking in my modest two-bedroom cottage.

To allay what I saw were her growing concerns, I offered that I had a strong, vast support network and flexible work schedule. There would be no problem caring for the infant, I assured her with all the confidence I could gather, but I felt heat rising. I politely reminded the worker that I had already been thoroughly vetted and approved to take this on. I was managing her and my dignity in the way I had learned to do over my whole lifetime as a Black disabled person.

During this first visit she fixed me with an uncomfortable stare. My sister paced in the background, ready to pounce. But understanding this was my battle, she stood down.

When Jellybean fussed and I lifted her, the agent gawked with stupid amazement.

I am a little person (LP), and Jellybean is an average-size baby, so she just about covers the length of my torso. I have large hands and slender fingers perfect for piano playing. My frame is petite. I am at once delicate and sturdy. I had to quickly learn to handle Jellybean by way of the particularities of my own body. Which is another way of saying I learned to crip motherhood.

Our relative size difference means nothing to me, but it's a concern for some people, and this worker was obviously uncomfortable seeing how I manage with the baby.

I am of course accustomed to this kind of social management that's necessary for disabled people to do all the time. But I recognize that the stakes of this specific encounter are high, because this agent holds power and is here to judge me as fit or unfit to be the primary caretaker of this wee one.

I have ample upper-body strength to lift and hold a newborn. However, my elbows do not fully extend so my range of motion is limited. When I pick Jellybean up, I do so slowly, deliberately, in a series of steps involving careful wheelchair positioning, seat elevation, and body mechanics.

My hands touch and move and connect to the baby, yes. But I also use my chair and lap and adapted baby gear to do the care work. Now picture a lovely choreography of hands and arms and lap and chair and assistive technology as I carry out the tasks of feeding, changing, comforting, and cleaning this precious one.

Jellybean hasn't yet learned to attend to her own body and so depends upon me to do that in a consistent and gentle way. It's hard physical work, and disabled parents always need to be resourceful in developing patterns of interaction between our own and our babies' bodies.

Whenever I go to lift her, Jellybean instinctively arches forward to offer an assist. She's expertly attuned to my functioning. It's remarkable to see this in a newborn, because it demonstrates an understanding that her survival depends on that arching and on my response. Our synergy is, to me, quite gorgeous.

But the agent is weirded out. The way I move and do things is not the normal way by her standards. During that same first visit, instead of asking how their agency might support me to care for this child, she asks how I care for myself.

"Do you cook?"

"Yes."

"And feed yourself?"

"Yes."

So now she's made me into the baby. Her interrogation invades what should be the most intimate of human acts.

This is why I prefer to parent Jellybean in private. Tucked away in our little house, baby, dog, and I get on just fine. Our life together illuminates fresh pathways to intimacy.

I remember on a walk one day through a redwood forest, some months prior to Jellybean's arrival, a dear friend asked, "What sparks desire for you?"

And I had nothing.

I had become numb to arousal, romantic or otherwise. Grief does this. But now, nurturing this baby? New levels of ecstasy and bliss.

I am intoxicated by the scent of my girl's hair, her slobbery kisses, the sound of her lips smacking in her sleep—a tasty dream, I think, of a warm bottle of formula or a spoonful of pureed sweet potato. She is my Jellybean because when I first held her, I had a sensory explosion reminiscent of sticking my hand into an Easter basket, rooting through the plastic green "straw" filler, and pulling up a handful of jelly beans. She is every color and flavor at once. A delicious hit of dopamine.

This new physical and emotional intimacy is for me a source of wonder. And yet, the sensuality of mothering is something my body recalls from so many moments of intimacy with my own mother.

And I know from other disabled mamas that this private/public management of our parenting is the way. When we talk, disabled parents share private truths about the rewards and challenges of child-rearing in the larger sociocultural milieu. We help, hold, and encourage one another.

Christina, another LP mama, sends me a sling like the one she used to carry her baby girl, Olivia.

Rosemarie, who has very short arms, shares how she maneuvered each of her floppy newborns.

My friend Sunaura explains how she laid in bed for weeks after giving birth to her daughter as a way of bonding. To move the child, Sunaura gathered the baby's garments in her mouth and pulled her to where she needed. Like a mama cat. I love this imagery!

I find these examples of the very specific interactions that disabled parents have with their newborns so very affirming.

I am enough for this baby. My care is adequate. I am enough.

"Don't worry, she won't remember any of this."

Well-meaning people say this about Jellybean, hoping to reassure me as I fret about her emotional development. They insist that the early rupture that led her to me won't be burned somewhere in her psyche. I know differently.

The literature on early trauma is clear: injurious things we experience as young'uns, even as infants, can and do make a home in the bodymind.

But what is also true: we can mitigate trauma with early intervention, love, and care. With less ego and judgment as we act in the best interest of children and their families.

I was fortunate to have a primary figure to attach to, and if emotion imprints memory, then I pray Jellybean will know deep in her cellular structure the different ways she was held in her first year of life. Not just by me and the village we formed around her, but in various ways by her first mommy, who loves her so.

And beyond this year? Only God knows.

Before going to sleep each night, no matter how exhausted she was, my grandmother Viola did two things: she washed her feet and she prayed on her knees at the side of the bed.

I can still hear her giving thanks for her day, for small mercies, for good health. She prayed for her children and grandchildren. She said other things that I can no longer recall, but witnessing this ritual of my grandmother speaking to her Creator each night was safety and comfort to my little-kid heart.

So I pray with Jellybean nightly. We give thanks and praise for the people who love and help us, for our little home and our goofy doggo. We pray for her parents, for their care and protection. After she's asleep, I ask God for the strength to accept whatever lies ahead for us all.

My life as a mother is a cauldron of emotions—joy, sadness, anxiety—all swirling, all the time. I want to know this child forever. What her voice might sound like at age three, thirteen, twenty-one, but I don't know that I will ever hear her speak. And that makes me very sad.

Healthy attachment involves letting go, bit by bit, knowing that impermanence is inevitable. Everyone, eventually, leaves. Sometimes, leaving is best. This is my practice. Loving, letting go. Loving, letting go. Loving. I'm getting there.

I have surgical scars on all of my limbs, and Jellybean likes to touch and trace the ones on my arms with her chubby fingers. I will never know what her infant eyes and heart perceive when she looks at me, but may some part of her always remember these scars and these arms that embraced her. Amen.

Elegy for a Mask Mandate

Ellen Samuels

For a year, maybe two, I knew
that you loved me. I saw it
in your eyes, the windows

to the soul, the only part
of your face I needed to
see to believe. For a season,

maybe two, you went
with me everywhere, holding
hope like a parasol over

our heads. I thought we'd
created a new world, where
the sick and the well

could be citizens of
the same country. I held
your disinfected hand at

the theater, in the grocery
store, places I hadn't
gone for years. I knew there

would always be the
resisters, the ones who since
childhood called me *queer*,

cripple, *lazy*, *hysterical*. But
you muffled them with your
handsewn cotton, your

filter inserts, your N95s. We
learned to speak a new
vocabulary, to understand

what it means to protect
each other so we all survive. In
my home now, in my lonely

bed, I'm still speaking those
words to the silent house: *My mask
protects you. Your mask protects me.*

PART II

Pleasure and Desire

Skin Hunger and the Taboo of Wanting to Be Touched

s.e. smith

The physical therapist has a warm, friendly voice and a manicure that glitters as she lowers the table to make it easier for me to transfer myself, paper crinkling beneath me. I am in a strange parody of a massage treatment room; instead of generic Orientalist art on the walls and Native American Flute Serenade Disc Four, there's a cutaway diagram of a slightly alarmed-looking person with a void where their genitals might be, hanging crookedly by the door, and the whir of a white-noise machine in the hall.

She asks if I am ready to begin and rests her hand lightly on my shoulder; a thoughtless gesture, one she will make with dozens of patients that week as she probes and adjusts their bodies in search of the things that are wrong inside them. But I feel her hand like a brand, every nerve tingling as she trails it across my back, feeling out the topography of vertebrae and muscles, a cascade of fire that spills across me before she's even begun. I shiver.

"Is this okay?" she says, in a soft voice, and "Yes," I say, but then I wonder if I can recall the last time someone who wasn't a medical provider touched me. Did I hug a friend when I ran into him at the movie theater, or just imagine it? I search my tingling nerves for the memory and *yes*, there it is, the baby. The last human being I touched was the baby, who catapulted himself across the living room to chew on my knee.

But when did I last see the baby? I wonder, as she works some kind of dark witchcraft on my back, twisting it in a direction I didn't know it could be twisted, making something *shift* so I gasp, but it is because for once I am not in pain.

Some call it skin hunger—the intense desire for physical and not necessarily sexual intimacy shared across people and cultures. Even in hug-friendly California, I am often reminded that the United States is a touch-averse culture, that gestures like holding hands or cuddling together on a couch are laden with sexual connotations even when none exist. The body of work on the need for touch is limited, focusing primarily on new parents and infants, but suggests that contact has mental health benefits as well as social ones.

The most famous research on skin hunger is also the most grim, a series of monkey studies conducted by researcher Harry Harlow in the middle of the twentieth century. Harlow's macaques were subjected to extreme isolation, in some cases entirely deprived of contact and clinging to "mothers" made from wire and cloth. He dispassionately observed that this deprivation produced "devastating and debilitating" results among the study subjects.

There is a popular sense that disabled people are un-date/touch/knowable, that we neither want to establish romantic and sexual relationships nor are we capable. To put it mildly, dating in this landscape is challenging.

A few years ago, I went out to a bar with a partner, forcing much shuffling of chairs and sentiments to accommodate his wheelchair. I was excited for my friends to meet him, pleased to introduce a person I'd talked about for weeks.

As soon as he left for the bathroom, one of my (now former) friends brayed: "Does his dick work?"

It wasn't simply the question that made me push my chair back, get up, and walk away, texting him to meet me outside when he was done. It was the casual sense of ownership over his body, the probing interest in our relationship, the surprise that someone "like him" could even find someone to date, let alone fuck. It wasn't the first or last time someone made a comment like that around me, desexualizing the entire disability community with their hand perched smugly on a drink, eyebrows raised in surprise when I didn't humor them as they speculated about how little people have sex, whether a facial difference ruins the mood, if Deaf people vocalize in bed.

This isn't just the case with physical impairments, but also with mental health conditions; we may not necessarily be framed as physically incapable, but we are deemed dangerous, frightening. "Bitches are crazy, am I right?" people say when women don't do what they want them to. The crazy ex-girlfriend is such a compelling trope that she has an entire television show and an evocative mental image in the form of the bunny boiling scene in *Fatal Attraction*. Crazy people are inherently unstable, too unsafe to date, but we're also liars, cheats, held prisoner by our medication.

For a while, I experimented with OkCupid, like most of my generation; time after time, I'd leaf through a profile, get excited that someone shared my interests, wrote an articulate and engaging description of themselves. But when I filtered our match questions, nearly inevitably, the ones about mental health would surface first. They'd never date someone with a mental health condition, or someone who takes medication to manage mental health.

Sometimes they'd see that I'd looked at their profile, message me. "You seem pretty cool," they'd say, with the confidence of privileged people who don't have to sift through match questions to determine whether prospective partners engage in discriminatory comments about them. I'd never reply. What's the point? To be told "I don't mean you"? To perform pleasure at being told I'm not like the other crazies?

Eventually, I left OkCupid, but the minefield surrounding disclosure is still a constant in my life. "Disclosure" itself suggests I have something to be ashamed of, and as someone who is openly crazy, it's hard to imagine a situation in which I start dating someone and they *don't* know. But there is a difference between knowing and *knowing*. Being upfront from the start helps weed out hateful people, but comes with risks, too. The risks that someone will dehumanize me, will view me as an easy target for violence.

Talking about wanting touch, feeling starved for it, is taboo. And we also live in an era when men routinely exert ownership over women's bodies, insist that they "deserve" relationships, where lack of intimacy is used to justify physical and sexual violence. Thus, there is a certain tension between these things; we acknowledge that disability is stigmatized, that disabled people who want intimacy deserve intimacy, but they are not entitled to intimacy.

These conversations become fraught; how can I say that I fear I'll never date again without feeding the monster? No one owes me their touch; I am starving for it just the same.

Sometimes people seem to hear "you are required to date disabled people even though it makes you uncomfortable" or "you are required to stay with an abusive disabled person (whether or not their abusiveness stems from their disability)" when we talk about these things, which hurts; it's both not what we are saying, and a perpetuation of harm. No one should feel pressured to date someone who is not right for them, to stay in a relationship that is unsafe or unfulfilling; no one should put another human being in either position. Yet, the belief that disability on its own makes someone an unfit partner is deeply disturbing, carrying with it a sense of cold indifference.

Within the disability community, some people feel it's defeatist to have these conversations, that speaking a thing makes it true. This push to remain silent places icy fingers at my lips when I would speak, buries the skin hunger that burns from the inside, crackling with every move, overlooks the discrimination that fuels it. It becomes an amplified isolation, to be rejected for our disabilities and rejected again by the disability community for saying so.

I think of this when I meet a friend for tea and we go to the beach afterward. We've left our shoes above the waterline, letting the sand scrunch between our toes as the sun sets, bleeding away at the edge of the horizon and turning the water gunmetal gray tipped in gold. It is the first time we have seen each other since her wedding, and there is a moment of awkwardness that eventually dispels as we settle into old rhythms, old ways of knowing, finishing each other's sentences, and predicting each other's questions. I am reminded that intimacy goes beyond touch, that it is something innate in the way we relate to each other. I try not to let my jealousy show, thinking that she will go home to a loving wife and I will return to stony silence, broken only by the wind whispering in the trees. *Failure, failure, failure.*

She pats me on the shoulder, tells me it can't be as bad as I'm claiming, someone will appreciate me for who I am. Someday. She tells me I'm beautiful, smart, funny, worthy of love, but alone in the darkness of my house, in the empty expanse of my bed, her comments will feel like stings, reminders of personal failure; for surely if I was all of those things, I wouldn't see someone's face politely close when they learn about the whole of me, wouldn't be immediately classified as undateable, unfuckable, unwantable, when I'm introduced to new people, wouldn't see someone's eyes stray to my cane for a transparent mental calculus—I will not be sporty enough for them, cannot keep up, will never be enough. I will go to sleep with the ghost of her hand on my shoulder, skin hunger gnawing just below the surface.

"I'm sure you'll find someone," she says, and I think, *will I?*

Know Me Where It Hurts
Sex, Kink, and Cerebral Palsy

Carrie Wade

I have cerebral palsy. That means something different for all of us:
some of us walk with braces; some walk without anything; some use
wheelchairs; some have hands, feet, and faces that do their own thing;
some stand on their toes; some communicate verbally; some don't.

Personally, I don't exactly pass as able-bodied. Most people know
something is "off" as soon as I stand up (as one college professor not-
so-gracefully put it, "I looked at you and went '*hmmm*'"). But sitting
down, almost no one can tell, so I inhabit a middle space that confuses
people all across the ability spectrum. People with CP have literally
asked where mine is, as if it can be located. It's true that I lack many
of CP's obvious markers, and aside from stairs without handrails and
clawfoot bathtubs (seriously, why?), I don't have to battle many physical barriers. But literally walking the line between able-bodied and not
has given me an up-close look at how people think about disabilities,
and I will say this: if you're not able-bodied, it's really hard to get
people to take you seriously.

They will tell you how brave and inspirational you are, for sure (which, of course, is more about them than you). They'll tell you God loves you extra. Bonus points if they are also crying. But they're uncomfortable, on some level, with you making your own choices—especially if those choices might have painful outcomes. Everyone around you will manicure your life so that you don't have to experience difficulty. Things will happen around you rather than to you. Risk-taking isn't presented as an option. There are a couple different assumptions at work here: first, that you've already *been through so much* that you deserve the gold star of a decision-free life, and second, that you are a child in need of constant protection. That becomes a self-fulfilling prophecy: when everyone takes care of you, it's damn near impossible to grow up.

When I talk about these issues with straight people, I always say "the other difficult thing to do when you have a disability is get somebody to fuck you." They laugh, I laugh, and we can all move on without really pausing to examine why that is. But I'll admit that's not the whole truth. Yes, sex with a disability is a tough sell, but not (just) for the reasons people assume. In my experience, the hardest part isn't convincing someone else you're desirable—it's convincing yourself that your body is worth pleasing.

Anyone who's come out, if only to themselves, knows a similar feeling: acknowledging that your desires are valid even though they're not the ones you were "supposed" to have. When I came out in high school, I knocked cerebral palsy to the furthest psychological back-burner possible. Now I had a new "thing" to focus on—and one that people around me, even if they didn't understand it, had at least heard of before. I was the only physically disabled person at our school who wasn't also in special ed, but there had been other out gay people there before I came along, and there would be more afterward. I was no longer by myself. It didn't feel as lonely. And unlike with disability, there was a prescribed narrative for how to deal with it, which I obviously embraced to a tee: I announced my gayness during a Gay-Straight Alliance meeting and was promptly elected club president for the following school year. It doesn't get much more Coming Out 101 than that.

I compartmentalized my disability and my sexuality like it was my job, until after college. Then I realized I wanted to actually have sex instead of just picking it apart in sociology class. So, like any self-respecting queer, I turned to the internet—and met Alex.

In her first message, she admitted she was in the bathtub, drinking wine to keep her courage up. In retrospect, bathtub computering is probably a bit of a red flag, but what impressed me at the time was her complete honesty about being nervous. It made me feel safe, like I could be, too, and that's exactly what I needed. I wasn't sure what else would happen, but looking across the table on our first date, I knew: *You are the first person I'll sleep with.*

First-time stories are always fun/mortifying, but that's not the one I want to tell you, because that's not the one that woke me up to the fact that my disability and sexuality have to breathe the same air. That happened about a month later, when Alex rolled over in bed and asked:

"So . . . how do you feel about bondage-y things?"

Remember for a moment that I had just gotten used to having sex at all. So my initial reaction was along the lines of UM WHAT I HAVE NO IDEA CAN I PHONE A FRIEND. But beneath that, I asked myself something else: How often are people this open about what they want? I wanted to please her but was also interested to see what this would mean for me and for my body. It's not often people invite me to take physical risks. So I agreed to try it.

And then . . . nothing.

I braced myself for the start of our little experiment, but things unfolded pretty much the same way as before. The delight of never knowing quickly gave way to frustration. I suspected why but didn't want to believe it. Sure enough, when I finally asked, I got the answer I had feared: "I'm afraid I'm going to hurt you."

What that said to me was, "This woman still thinks I'm a child."

Up to that point, I thought I'd done everything "right": cultivated a functional relationship, finally let someone see me with my clothes off, said yes to sex, talked about my body, listened about hers, been willing to try new things, behaved like an adult. But it turns out it hadn't worked. All of a sudden, the "nice" formula that had made my disability palatable—acknowledge, but don't dissect; laugh it off when things get tough—failed. I had literally done the most grown-up thing I could think of with this person, and she still saw me as vulnerable. Not in the way that brings people closer, mind you, but in the way that makes them afraid to touch you. Makes them think you're breakable.

Instead of screaming in her face, which is what I really wanted to do, I turned her question back on her and asked: "Who's better at pain than I am?"

As a way to get a grasp on the whole CP situation, people like to ask me, "Does it hurt?" In pain/not in pain is a good/bad binary that they can digest. It allows them to categorize my body in a way that makes sense, and tells them whether they should feel bad for me or not. I always say no because I don't want to give anyone (more) reason to look down on my body. But let's be real—there are screws in my spine. Of course it hurts. There's at least an unpleasant twinge happening somewhere all the time. So what people should really be asking is whether the pain is Old or New.

Old Pain I'm used to: the tightness in my hips when I don't stretch in the morning, the pressure where my legs meet my back when I walk too far. It's not that I don't feel it; it's just been there for so long that I know not to get nervous about it anymore. New Pain is where it gets scary because it stops having a name. I can't immediately catalog it or diagnose it as benign. At best, disability allows you to create a tenuous peace with your body, and any time it decides to violate that mutual agreement can be terrifying. You take the time to learn it—what it likes and dislikes, where it functions best—and stick to that routine, until New Pain reminds you that you're never quite going to have this figured out.

The upside, though, is that I can handle pain like a pro. It's easier for my body to feel pain than to feel good. Now, maybe I could have both.

The next time we had sex, Alex said, "Close your eyes—I want to try something."

I did, but it didn't matter much, because she tied a blindfold around my eyes first thing. Then I felt my hands go up behind my head, and heard a *click, click.* I didn't expect handcuffs on the first try, but there they were. And then I felt the first pinch—right on my nipple. And then another on the other side.

"Is this okay?"

"Keep going."

I never asked her to stop, which is a shame, because our safe word was *dinosaur* and I *still* think that's amazing. But alas, there was no *dinosaur,* and when she took the blindfold off, I saw that my chest was covered in clothespins. (When you're in your twenties, nipple clamps are expensive, so you work with what you have.) I'd never seen my body look like that. She must have been pretty impressed, because the first thing she said was, "I've never been able to do that before. Nobody has been able to take that many."

It's not often (i.e., almost never) that I get told I'm good at a physical activity. But now my body, which had spent so many years letting me down and making decisions without my consent, had gone and done something absolutely right—and done it *better*. It had done something other people's bodies, "healthy" bodies, hadn't been able to.

So often we're told that the "right" partner will "look past" our disability or "love us anyway," like they're on some sort of humanitarian mission. In that moment, I realized what complete and utter bullshit that idea is. The problem is not our bodies—it's the misguided assumptions people project onto them. That we shouldn't want them. That we don't know how to use them. That they need to be cured. *That's* what I want the people in my life—friends, family, partners—to look past. I don't want them to look past me. My disability is essential to my body. It's a tough belief to stick to, and one that requires constant reinforcement, but it's the truth.

A disability often compounds body shame, because so much talk is focused on what your body will never be able to do. You barely ever see any bodies that look like yours, especially outside a doctor's office. And when you do, they're never beautiful; they're apologized for. But that night, I realized that my pain tolerance and the things my body did well were assets rather than things to be run from or ashamed of. To know that what had been perceived (especially by me) as defective about my body was actually what made me desirable, powerful, and sexy for the first time ever—that moment was beautiful.

Staring at Curvature

Travis Chi Wing Lau

I distinctly remember the sensation of pivoting my body around to expose my back to the camera. Trepidation, those first shutter clicks that simultaneously felt so slow yet so fast. The sudden realization that the uneven contours of my back were quite literally in someone else's hands. That the truth of my spine's meandering (or dare I say it, queerness) had been "shot" and "captured," the violence so intrinsic to the everyday language of modern photography. But the work here was as much about relinquishing as it was about reclamation: the letting go of narratives imposed upon my own curved form, narratives that do not so easily strip away like articles of clothing.

How these histories of pain curve so tightly around me.

It was when I was still living in Los Angeles, still figuring out what it meant to be a newly out gay man in one of the most unforgiving gay meccas in the country. In my vanity as a then nineteen-year-old, I had enthusiastically agreed to be one of the models for a friend's fashion and design thesis project. Seven of us were chosen to show the range of his handiwork, which aspired to a garish ornateness that barely fit any of our bodies. Manhandling us before the show, he came off hasty and impatient; the many bundles of nerves entwined tightly around years of work expected to lead to a viable career in an already oversaturated industry. The stakes were high, so we followed orders: *just be very fucking still.* Obedient little mannequins like the ones he threw about in his studio as part of his "process."

Backstage before we were to step onto the short runway, I realized I was the only man of color in the lineup. In retrospect, what saddens me is that this realization felt obvious—as if such tokenism were expected and thus forgivable because I was doing a friend a favor. *This isn't about me.* But I certainly did not look like the others: they and their blasé quips about being nearly naked as if it were natural. After more than a year out and about in West Hollywood, I had come to know intimately that particular brand of condescending self-assuredness— conventionally attractive, white gay men reveling in the rush of having their bodies consumed by the gaze of others. And, reluctant as I am to admit it now, I envied it, wanted it precisely because it felt so inaccessible to me.

After the runway presentation, we were shuffled backstage for final photographs directed by the designer. Several pieces of the garments that I had been wearing—a sheer, tight jerkin and a patchwork overcoat draped over my shoulders and back—had begun peeling off my body by the time I exited the stage. As I made my way over to the makeshift backdrop to stand for photos, my friend rushed over to fix the "disaster" walking toward him. *Is this how you looked onstage?* he questioned me angrily. Amid all my anxiety walking for the show, I had not noticed the pieces almost fleeing from my form. I could only watch in silence and shame as he aggressively adjusted the pieces on my body only for him to give up entirely when the fabric would not submit (or rather, my body would not submit). *How am I supposed to work with your back like this? Your shoulders are completely uneven and your ribs just stick out like that. I mean of course the clothes aren't going to sit right on you.* Marking the points of ill fit with a felt-tip marker, he sighed, shook his head, and pushed me in front of the lights, where the photographer began to shoot. The other models averted their eyes as the flashbulb went off in bursts. I think the photographer mistook my blankness of expression as an attempt to model, when in fact all I wanted to do was to disappear altogether, my exposed body marked full of errors.

Click, click, click, click.

I met Den Sweeney via Instagram when I unexpectedly came across one of his striking images of Philadelphia, a city I was then still getting to know. I had always wanted to learn photography, a craft that somehow made a series of dials, buttons, lenses, and screens into images with a force that exceeded the frame. After an evening of teaching me the ropes with a DSLR camera I'd never learned how to use after having had it for years, Den asked me offhandedly over dinner if I had ever been in front of the camera.

I was at first caught off guard by the directness of his questioning, how it evoked the last traumatic time I submitted to being photographed. But, as I have come to understand him both as a friend and a fellow creative, that directness was a manifestation of Den's sincere approach to photography as a powerful medium of storytelling, particularly those stories that don't get told enough or at all. I finally shared with him the incident in Los Angeles that had left me still very raw, and he asked me if I would be willing to be photographed the "right way." Rather than explain what constituted this "right way," he modeled it, over the course of the several hours that comprised our first shoot together, this time with my back to his Nikon D810 camera.

Den's studio at the time was the living room of his family house in Northeast Philadelphia. Because he lived alone, he could make his space truly his own, infused as it already was with memories from his own childhood. Displayed on his walls were the many people and places he had photographed over the years, from performing violinists to the Canadian Arctic, from hockey players to Boathouse Row. Den had a story for each of them, each told lovingly as both remembrance of and pride about a life's work. His home contained not a trophy cabinet of prints but instead a tender archive of collaborations spanning decades.

During that first session, Den walked me through the meticulous process of composing and lighting a subject, which in this case was myself. In contrast to the haphazard and rushed experience of the thesis show, Den insisted we work at the pace of our bodyminds, especially knowing that experiments in pose and motion could cause me pain. His direction was gentle—invitations to adjust, to reacquaint myself with the form of my own body for results we would evaluate together each step of the way. Naked as I was for the first time before someone else who was not a partner or a caregiver, I felt an access to intimacy that until then had been inconceivable because of the safety I felt in my vulnerability.[1] I knew I was in safe hands rather than in front of fetishizing eyes—hands that wanted to, as Den likes to describe

---

[1]   Mia Mingus defines "access intimacy" in multiple ways across her writings, but particularly relevant for this experience is how she describes this phenomenon as that "elusive, hard to describe feeling when someone else 'gets' your access needs." See Mia Mingus, "Access Intimacy: The Missing Link": https://leavingevidence .wordpress.com/2011/05/05/access-intimacy-the-missing-link/ and "Access Intimacy, Interdependence and Disability Justice": https://leavingevidence.wordpress .com/2017/04/12/access-intimacy-interdependence-and-disability-justice/

his photographic method, "make" or cocreate an image together with me that tells the lived experience and history of my disabled body on my own terms. Photography for Den has always been care work, the photograph being evidence of the care given.

Yet, at that time, I was still developing a disability consciousness and a vocabulary for talking about my body in pain. Over multiple sessions, Den helped me invent a visual grammar for my kyphoscoliosis-related disabilities in a way that dignified my sensations and chronicities as themselves worthy subjects of artistic expression. We tried to actualize what Tobin Siebers describes as disability aesthetics, which "refuses to recognize the representation of the healthy body—and its definition of harmony, integrity, and beauty—as the sole determination of the aesthetic. Rather, disability aesthetics embraces beauty that seems by traditional standards to be broken, and yet it is not less beautiful, but more so, as a result."[2] For Siebers, disability aesthetics, by daring to imagine the vast spectrum of human variation, reveals the unspoken ideologies of healthiness and ableism that underpinned what was worthy of being painted or photographed. We began to ask questions about the history of photographic portraits: *What did it mean to have a queer, disabled body of color in pain as an aesthetic subject in the face of a tradition of portraiture that only objectified such subjects, if it represented them at all?* This question underpinned our multiyear collaborative project, *Curvature* (2015–2018), which put some of my earliest poems about my scoliosis-related disabilities in conversation with Den's portraits of me.

In one of our earliest pieces, "Triptych," we experimented with a lunar metaphor in a composite image of multiple portraits of my back from different angles:

This piece began as a series of experiments with contrast lighting

---

2   Tobin Siebers, *Disability Aesthetics* (University of Michigan Press, 2010), 3.

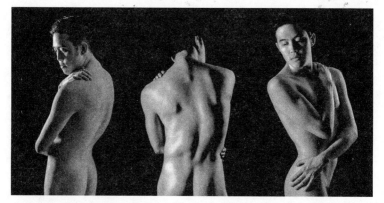

A grayscale composite photograph against a black background of three different nude photographs of myself, a Chinese American gay man. *From left to right:* Facing to my left with my shoulder toward the camera and my right hand on my left shoulder; with my entire back facing the camera; turned to the right with most of my torso exposed to the camera, right arm on my left shoulder, and left arm on my right hip.
Den Sweeney, "Triptych" (2016)

that accentuated the natural shadows on my back and created what looked to us like the topography of the moon's surface. "Triptych" became central to the project because it helped us find the distinct aesthetic of *Curvature* as a portrait series, which drew significantly from gay photographic influences like Robert Mapplethorpe and Herb Ritts, both of whom celebrated the erotics of the nude male form, often in the stark contrasts of black and white. The quiet strength of these pieces helped me rediscover the capacities of my body—to flexibly hold unusual poses or remain still for long periods—rather than fixate on its incapacities. Curved but capable of so much that I myself had worked to deny.

I loved the crip time of our process: taking our time over the span of a day to photograph hundreds, sometimes thousands of raw images that we would whittle down over weeks and months into our favorites, which would be edited into stylistic uniformity with the rest of our project.[3] We worked without expectations. We allowed ourselves opportunities to play, to let my body and its vicissitudes determine what poses to try, even if they were better in imagination than execution. Sometimes, what we first thought were "failures" were in fact *the* shots that would become the defining images of the day. For example, a photo that features me kneeling and holding the legs of a wooden stool that Den often used in his studio, which we ended up titling "Entanglement."

I was fascinated by its simplicity but also its sturdiness, which felt apt as another concept metaphor for our project. To arrive at the right image, we experimented with multiple variations for my pose that involved different interactions between my body and the stool, some more painful or awkward than others. Here, the impasse of the chair's fixed solidity was not an obstacle but a challenge to improvise my body's range of motion around, beside, and through. While the photograph shows the straining lines of my back, arms, and toes, the position was ironically one of the easiest to hold, one almost pleasurable to maintain because I could support myself against the stool. This pleasure was only revealed to me by our experimenting with ways of interacting with the stool that did not involve conventionally sitting upright upon it, a position that would have exacerbated my pain without support. I let my body navigate me around an object I thought I knew but in fact did not. My back's form and sensation invited us both to imagine new relationships between my bodymind and the space

---

3 "Crip time" describes a shift away from linear time toward an embodied, lived sense of time that reflects the rhythms and needs of specific bodyminds navigating time and space. See Alison Kafer's *Feminist Queer Crip* (Indiana University Press, 2013), Ellen Samuels's "Six Ways of Looking at Crip Time" (*Disability Studies Quarterly*, 37.3: http://dx.doi.org/10.18061/dsq.v37i3.5824), and Margaret Price's *Mad at School: Rhetorics of Mental Disability and Academic Life* (University of Michigan Press, 2011) for different articulations of crip time.

of the studio and the objects that populate it. The stool had not only become an intimate rest for my body but also a cocreator in the photographic process.

But despite more than three years of working together, I still experienced moments of discomfort, many less physical than emotional. While I came to embrace the liberating vulnerability of being photographed in the nude, I found myself doubting at times what felt

A grayscale nude photograph of me kneeling with my toes pointed to the side of a wooden stool with two legs and a crossbar. My right arm is clasping the opposite leg of the chair, while my left arm is draped perpendicularly over the crossbar. My face is cast in shadow as I look downward with the lines of my back directly exposed to the light.
Den Sweeney, "Entanglement" (2016)

like a vanity project featuring me as a repeated subject. *Was this just self-indulgence justified as art?* Den would never allow me to entertain this line of self-deprecating thinking, even as it lurked in the margins of every photograph we made together. I have since realized how deep this doubt runs and how much a part of my crip experience it animates. This unease in my gut is a trained reaction, a product of being socialized repeatedly into a world that has treated me like the designer in Los Angeles did so many years ago, who has only profited from his

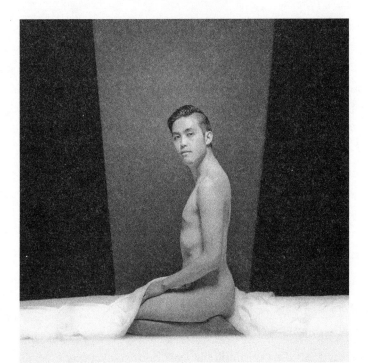

A grayscale nude photograph of me sitting upon my shins with my hands placed on my upper thighs. A white sheet is draped over my hands and knees, but the entire left side of my body is exposed, and I am looking directly back at the camera.
Den Sweeney, "Untitled" (2016)

objectification and denigration of other people in pursuit of his craft. *Curvature* has felt like a "risky practice" of self-exhibition that is also a rebuttal, one that joins a tradition and community of "disabled artists and artist models [who] choose to parade their abnormalities and display their spectacular bodies to shake notions of normality to the core."[4] It is ultimately a refusal to accept the casual and shameless ableism of a world of aesthetics so gatekept that bodyminds like mine ache in the space we attempt to take up, if we can access it at all.

After three years away from the camera's eye, I recently sat for a portrait by Columbus, Ohio–based photographer darren lee (dee) miller. Doing this portrait felt like a tender reunion with dee, whom I had met in 2020 when I first moved to Columbus. They had shared early pieces from their portrait series in process, *How Do You Want to Be Seen?*, which began at the start of the pandemic, and later invited me to create an image for the series. Much like Den, dee embraces a collaborative approach to photography that displaces them as a figure of authority and instead empowers the subject to author their own depiction and its accompanying caption. Having experienced the creative potential of such a deeply dialogic practice of shared vulnerability, I knew I could trust dee with my curvature.

After talking through the project's fundamental question and my vision of how my portrait might answer it, we met on a muggy July morning at an old Victorian home belonging to one of dee's colleagues. We were drawn immediately to the bathroom as a space, which had already been used in another of dee's portraits that had lingered in my memory ever since I first saw it. The bathroom's liminal quality between the quotidian and the private felt particularly appropriate: it

---

4   Ann Millett-Gallant, *The Disabled Body in Contemporary Art* (Palgrave Macmillan, 2010), 15.

A composite photograph of me seated on a white clawfoot tub in the middle of a bathroom with wood floors and walls painted with vertical stripes of light blue, mustard yellow, and brown. In the background, there is a toilet, a white sink, a small rug, and a mirror, which shows a reflection of me that is another portrait in which I am seated in the same position but turning to look back at the camera over my left shoulder.

darren lee (dee) miller, "Travis in Pearls" (2022)

is simultaneously the site of the erotic, the shameful, and the human. dee had remembered their colleague's clawfoot bathtub, which exemplified these layers of meaning built into a space so ubiquitous in modern culture, but also provided an unusual surface for my posing with my back turned to the camera. I had to develop an intimacy with the bathtub that bore my nakedness and with the strangeness of a private space that was part of another person's home. Holding my pose on the edge of the bathtub proved challenging for my spine over the course of the session, which had only curved more since the last time I was photographed. But like Den before them, dee's meticulous care for my bodymind's needs—supporting my pose, limiting the time spent per pose, helping me into positions with their own hands—allowed me to achieve what I most wanted to portray: my spinal curvature itself insisting on being seen on its terms. *What might it mean to have disability meet the viewer's gaze rather than what the gaze expects to see?* dee provided the means by which I could ask this question boldly yet safely. The beauty of a crip trust.

The embedded, culturally reproduced expectations attached to my bodymind were precisely at the heart of this portrait. As a scholar of the eighteenth century, I have become intimately familiar with the long tradition of Orientalist portraiture that exoticized and fetishized Asian bodies as part of the imperialist project of British empire—both as sexualized objects and as exploitable labor. dee's entirely coincidental plan that day to have me wear a necklace of pearls unexpectedly indexed this longer history of the pearl's commodification as jewelry and its connections to the Orientalist aesthetic. While my Chineseness has always been legible upon my body, dee's portrait reconfigures its relationship to my disability and queerness through this uncanny aesthetic so unique to dee. As Richard Leppert writes of the perverse racial dynamics still alive in Western portraiture, "the white man has identity, the [racialized] has anonymity; by in large they do not merit names, but they are 'useful' as cultural objects precisely for their colour-difference . . ."[5] I instead wanted this portrait to insist on my presence as a subject of multiplicity rather than a limited object. Nakedly queer, crip, Asian, painfully imbricated.

And in this way, I stare back. First my spine, then my face uncannily meeting the audience's gaze in the bathroom mirror. "Refusing to

---

5   Richard Leppert, "Art, Aesthetics, and Male Genitalia" in *On the Nude: Looking Anew at the Naked Body in Art,* eds. Nicholas Chare and Ersy Contogouris (Routledge, 2022), 197.

wilt under another's stare is a way to insist on one's dignity and worth," Rosemarie Garland-Thomson argues of the power of staring back.[6] I remain indebted to two photographers who have taught me how to look and why to look, in this case at myself as represented by their eyes. Myself, who for years refused to be exposed to the cruelty of the flash before I realized it could be compassionate. I stare and finally witness myself staring back.

---

6   Rosemarie Garland-Thomson, *Staring: How We Look* (Oxford University Press, 2009), 86.

republics of desire
disabled lineages of longing

Leah Lakshmi Piepzna-Samarasinha

For my mother, and myself.

My ancestors are disabled people who lived looking out of institution windows wanting so much more for themselves. . . . My ancestors are queers who lived in the American South. It's because of them I understand the importance of . . . living life big, even if it is dangerous. All of my ancestors know longing. Longing is often our connecting place.

—Stacey Park Milbern

1. night kitchen

It's a Thursday night and the lights are low. It's just me and the cat, dancing lightly around my kitchen, cooking kimchi fried rice as a mix of late-nineties industrial hits plays in the background, $5 warm white twinkle lights from Target strung above my windows and my forty-seven-year-old disabled femme joy, cooking for myself, solitary on a weekday night.

I am a middle-aged, crip autistic nonbinary brown femme, living through a third COVID winter of immunocompromised isolation. And I am happy. In my solo uncle femme apartment, not in love with any one partner, but learning to be intimate with myself. I have a lot of love in my life, a lot of pleasure, a lot of freedom, autonomy, and peace. My life is real, not something to fear.

It might sound strange, to be celebrating being a disabled person living alone in pandemic year three. Last weekend, I hung out on a disabled Zoom for hours, listening to other sick and disabled folks sobbing three minutes at a time about how they hadn't been touched for years, how totally abandoned we felt by the abled and non-high risk—those people who live in a completely different world and left us behind in ours.

I'm not separate from this. Of course there are times when the crip isolation hits deep and I feel like clawing the walls, grinding my teeth at supposedly radical friends posting mask-free selfies in bars I haven't been to since February 2020, feeling like if I watch any more TV—no matter how "premium" it is—I'll shoot myself. (At the height of the lockdown part of the pandemic I had HBO, Apple TV, Paramount [for all the New Queer Trek shows], Hulu, *and* Showtime; I was like *fuck it, we're all dying, I will disassociate and watch things with an incredible production budget.*)

Like so many disabled people, I honed my crip solitude skills long before the pandemic first broke in North America. When the pandemic came and I had to shield to survive, I was already an expert at solitude. I knew how to live online and in books, in masked walks and phone calls, knew how to make group online movie nights and dance parties feel amazing, not a weak approximation of the real thing.

But I hadn't lived alone since 2006. I hadn't wanted it, I thought, and I definitely hadn't been able to afford it. When Seattle became ground zero for COVID in North America in March 2020, I was living with friends I loved and my partner of five years in a magic house with a hot tub nestled in an improbable urban forest in South Seattle, a house found through Craigslist after a burnt green seven-day candle and some of the most fervent prayers of my life. I loved that house and the people I lived with passionately. It was my dream-come-true house of the forties I had survived into.

Within a month of lockdown, my roommates had to move out because me and my partner were high-risk, and our roommates (partners who shared air) were, too, but one had too many exposures at their emergency room job for us to live together safely. A year later, my partner and I broke up; they moved out and away. And I started living alone, for the first time in fifteen years.

I sank into it in an explosion of wonder and joy. *Finally.* Finally I had access to my secret heart, the thing I'd lusted after for years: the ability to wake up alone, walk around my house in my underwear alone, jerk off and write and walk around muttering to myself without having to negotiate or explain it to anyone. Make whatever thing—fancy, or sausage and greens in a pan—I wanted for dinner, invite people to hang out on the porch, or hole up for days writing till 4 a.m.

I was crushing on that feral autistic wolf femme solitude like a perfect date. I had not known how to say that I wanted, needed this. Hadn't known that it was okay that this was a need, this autonomous autistic lust for solitude.

I hadn't known it was okay to have autistic needs, because for all my life, even before I knew that I was and that's what they were, I had been punished for having autistic needs. We didn't have words for what we were, my All of a Kind autistic family. But I can remember so clearly, when the concept of *learning disabilities* first became a thing at the rust belt private school I attended (first as one of a handful of scholarship students, then my mother got a job teaching there so I could go for free) my mother saying that those white boys who were struggling with school, they weren't stupid, they were *learning disabled*, and there was a thing called classroom aids and support for them. My saying to her, so tentatively, *I think maybe I have something like that, too.* The fear written on her face, and how she said, quietly and with devastating clarity, "Those boys can afford to have something wrong with them. You can't." I had to be smart and weird and quiet and not make trouble. Needing help and being cognitively different wouldn't be viewed with wonder and curiosity if I did it. It'd just be the one excuse the school would need to kick me out. Mixed-class brown scholarship kids aren't allowed to be disabled, too.

Twenty years after that car-ride-home conversation, I figured out I was autistic—part of what my friend Naima calls the "great 2010s middle-aged BIPOC queer autistic revolution." And even after some time passed—I wasn't curled up shaking anymore the way I had when the test results first came back, in one long *oh shit* terror that if anyone knew I was that horrible thing I would lose all my friends and gigs—I was still used to sneaking off to do my Autistic Weird Things where no one could see. Kind of like sneaking off to smoke a cigarette used to be. Except this time, I was waiting for everyone to leave the house for work or school or vacation so I could revel in eating the same meal every day, hyperfocus on writing or in a research hole for eight hours straight, rereading the same Marge Piercy novels I'd loved when I was twelve. And mostly, sink into a silence and focus that felt like sucking on pure oxygen. I'd internalized that living alone was a selfish luxury, a fear of intimacy that surely came from trauma I needed to overcome.

But when people were around constantly, I felt my brain going dark from not enough breath.

And also there's the minor factor of: What disabled femme over forty *wants* to live alone? Don't you know how lucky you are not to be Alone? Aren't you desperate to be "cashed in," a capital-*P* Partner stamping you approved as loveable, valid, desired? If you're so lucky as to have a partner bringing you cups of tea and spooning you, and you love them, and you're disabled, and you know that the ways this ableist world says your bodymind is one big fault sign means you're lucky to have them or anyone at all, you must be really nuts if you want to throw that away for some amorphous things called solitude and autonomy. What kind of freak chooses walking around in their underwear like some weird uncle muttering to themself over Life Partnership?

I live alone now, but I don't feel isolated or lonely. In the morning I stretch, say love words to my cat, check the Discords I hang out on, my Signal feeds, WhatsApp messages, and regular texts. (One brown immigrant femme friend said to me once, *We need three kinds of text: Signal for the security culture friends, WhatsApp for all your overseas homies, and regular text for everyone else.*) I catch up on a series of voice memos left by a friend living isolated in New Mexico for the past twenty years because the air is clean and doesn't flare their MCS, turn on my friend's early show on KEXP, and text them when I like one of the songs. I grind my coffee, pour the water and stir till it blooms, sip my daily cup as I jot notes in my big 8-½×11 black spiral-bound artist notebook's big pages with no lines to hold back my sprawling autistic handwriting that even I can barely read. Sometimes I trade voice memos with loved ones and comrades all day and all night. My DMs swell with flirt and different kinds of love, people I am breathing with.

I feel sexy, a hot haggard uncle femme in my late forties in a black

A-shirt and my little booty shorts. My grandpa black slippers slapping the floor; my rumpled, unapologetic silver, magenta, and tamarind curls and close fade. My big eyes, tired grin, my knowing myself.

Being crip, you don't always have many possibility models. I'm always beating the drum of this statement, but like, you really don't—especially for us middle-aged and getting older ones. Too many of us die or are disappeared, and even when we don't, we have to hunt to find the stories. You might know a younger crip who was a ball of fire partying it up in the club at twenty-six, but because of the Born to Die Young curse hanging over our heads, you don't get many pictures of crips in their thirties, forties, fifties, heaven forbid beyond. The two options we're given for disabled adulthood are often either a fiercely stamped-approved normality—*See! I bought a house! I have a job! I have a Life Partner!* Or a back room of parents' house/homeless shelter/nursing home. There's not a lot of images of the in-between, or the beyond.

Yet there are many of us living odd, good, sexy, settling-into-ourselves, disabled, middle-aged and older lives. We get to where many people, abled and disabled, reach at midlife—that bone-deep knowing and unapologetic *I don't give a fuck* acceptance of self—but crip and neuroweird style. We do it even deeper and weirder, as we sink deep into knowing what crip neurodiverse weirds we need to thrive. The pandemic and the many disasters that came to my life in 2020–2021 were no joke, but the solitude and god-is-change they gave opened the door to being intimate with my feral, autistic solitary self in the way I'd always needed and rarely been able to get.

Here I am, becoming the young illder I didn't know existed. And needed. Becoming intimate with myself.

Healing my disabled lineage of longing, desire, and neurotype, too.

2. my mother's window

I am second-generation disabled. The disabled autistic child of a disabled neurodivergent, probably autistic mother. A woman who spent her life longing.

Like all children, I move in her legacy. I make decisions in this life about how I will repeat what she did, or break the chain and invent something different.

My mother looked out a lot of windows.

My mom was a polio survivor, a working-class Irish and Ukrainian/Galicia/Roma girl, a survivor of physical and sexual abuse from her parents and the men of the local Catholic church, stories she whispered in fragments to me when she pulled me over to her at the turn at the top of the stairs in our house. She could walk, with pain, and she was likely taught, as many polio survivors of her era were, that she could regrow her nerves if she just worked hard enough—look at FDR, he did it. Told that if she could walk and pass as able-bodied, she should thank her lucky stars and never dream of mentioning she was anything else. She didn't use the D-word to describe herself. That would've killed the narrow slice of freedom and possibility she had access to.

But she was disabled. And neurodivergent—never calling herself any label, teaching me to lie to doctors on the *Have you felt depressed lately?* question of the annual wellness exam starting at age five. But clearly a person living with panic, depression, disassociation, and different facets of her personality that didn't remember one another.

Clearly also autistic. Clearly also trusting no one. Except, sometimes, me.

My mother always thought she was ugly.

I remember her looking at her face in the mirror and sighing. Her face falling as I held up a dress from the Worcester, Massachusetts, Filene's Basement sale rack and telling me it was "too young" for her, when she must've been no older than forty-four. The cedar chest where her pretty, fun treasures, the Belgian lace and deerskin miniskirt she bought and rocked the year she lived in London in 1969, lay folded away, unworn. Relics of a brief moment when she didn't hate her body.

The stories my mother told me about her childhood were all about being smart, "different," and ugly. Being asked to dance once in high school only to have the boy who asked her and all his friends laugh and laugh at the idea that she could ever have thought it was real, that anyone would ever ask a girl as ugly as her to dance. She was the only girl in her high school class not married and pregnant at sixteen or immediately after graduation, something that was never ascribed by her to being disabled, but about being too smart, "odd," ugly. But those are all code words for disability.

To be smart and neurodivergent and a survivor of more abuse than she could name, and post-polio, was to be ugly in my mother's world. To be ugly was to live in shame, your body the butt of every joke. But, maybe, also to know and be able to access an escape from violence and early marriage, to get college instead. Sometimes ugly, crippled, too-smart, working-class girls are allowed college. The trade-off is being desired.

In her world, in this world, there are dumb, pretty girls and smart, ugly/"interesting"-looking girls. And we were number two.

All the stories my mother shared of joy, of desire and sensuality, of loving the fuck out of her life, were about being alone. She was that impossible thing: a working-class, unmarried girlwoman in her twenties and thirties in the '50s and '60s, renting her own apartment, working as a public schoolteacher, not living with her family. Smoking Gauloises out of her single-girl apartment's window late at night, satisfied and alone. Occasionally going on dates, but buying takeout from the diner and lying that it was homemade because she hated to cook. Saving up her schoolteacher money to go on solo vacations to Ireland and Paris in 1964. No one had taught her this. She'd looked it up in the library of her dreams, her working-class disabled femme ingenuity. She picked the lock of her life with it.

All the stories my mother shared about dating, sex, and love were about unfulfilled desire. Having a silent crush for years on a young man—beautiful, leftist, smart—who, like her, was volunteering for Kennedy's presidential campaign, then slowly coming to realize he was gay and uninterested. Then marrying my father, her dark and beautiful and definitely not from central Mass hope, who turned into her crushing disappointment, her necessary compromise. He was smart and weird, too, but raging and bratty, bad with money, spending hers, unemployed and drunk on the couch, shouting at her and her child and making them cry. And gay, or bisexual, and not touching her; they had separate beds from the time I can remember. Yet if she left him, it would be proof: Her disabled body. Too ugly.

So many stories of pining. Never ones of getting satiated. Filled up. Fed.

I inherited the story of her disabled, neurodivergent femme longing. The feeling of holding yearning in your body, in your solitude, for something you never get, because, after all, look at you.

And sometimes it's better that way, because you're safe. No one will see your crippled weirdness. No one will rape or abuse you. You get to control your desire: your fantasies, the orgasms and dreams you have at night when everyone has finally left you alone, they are yours and yours alone. And you love being alone. You are free there. Your brain flies there in your hermitude.

Pining is looked down on. Something we run from as disabled queers. We want to prove the stereotypes wrong: that we are fuckable and desirable and lovable, and we can get what the abled and normal do—sex, dates, partnership. We dress up cute, shoot selfies, are insistent about how gorgeous we are and how hot our sex is.

But in a world where disabled people are some of the most vulnerable to both rape and rejection, perhaps sometimes we use pining and fantasy, relationships that stay in longing and away from ever being actualized, as a way to create a freedom space of dream that is safe. Perhaps as neurodivergent queers, we sometimes have sex and access pleasure in ways that stay in fantasy, text messages or shared jerk-off fantasies—sex, love, and desire that don't fit the neurodivergent idea of Real Sex, Real Relationships. For us that's a brilliant hack, making up some hot shit that doesn't hurt with all our wild brains. Riches.

Sometimes staring out the window, longing for so much more, is still a place of freedom. Because the longing for so much more means not accepting the little they've given you. Means using your brain to hack out an imaginary safe space where you can be touched and loved and still have all your weirdness and delicious solitude. It's perhaps the most safety you will ever know.

Desire, free from rape and cut just right for your neurotype, that you don't have to find words to explain. Existing in a world that's years before having words for either your neurotype or your desire.

3. wanting the world

I grew up filled with my mother's dreams of escape for me. She hope, hope, hoped I would get away and do things she'd never seen—marry a nice, safe man (whatever that was), get a job with health insurance (she was very in favor of my brief period where I wanted to go to Harvard and become a plant geneticist), live in a place where weird, smart femmes were safe. All of which meant inhibiting the world.

But she always pulled me back from that cusp. Most of the nerdy attempts I made at independence, whether it was taking a ten-minute walk off the dead-end street where we lived to the mailbox half a block over, taking the bus to the library, or going to an Amnesty International teen conference in Boston (I know), were met with her bewildered incomprehension, panic, and also rage. When me and the two friends who'd gone to the conference were thirty minutes late because we'd stopped to get a slice of pizza (and still were home by 7 o'clock) we were met at the door by her crying hysterically—she'd called the police and the fire department—and my father bellowing with rage. How could I do this to her? How could I want to leave her? I was her autistic peace, her best friend. Seen as a little adult, parentified and sexualized and adultified in ways I should never have been. How could I want to abandon her to be touched by the world?

I grew up and got away anyway. My parents couldn't stop me from going to college, it would've looked too weird. They got nervous when I graduated and went on a trip to Toronto to meet my best friend from an early Riot Grrrl listserv, where autistic me spent hours hanging out typing messages, met a lover I fucked and fell in love with on the floor of the Toronto Anti-Racist Action house. And fell in love with the city, too, the way its alleys and tiny parks and fruit-and-veg shops and queer brown art opened their arms to me, easy. My parents must've known I wasn't going to move back in with them then, to be the maiden aunt, the celibate, nunlike child who would never break free from them. They were right. I moved to Toronto with two backpacks as soon as I could, finished all my classes as independent studies, and faxed my thesis in from the community radio station where I was running three shows. I knew I needed to put a national border between me and them to get free, to survive what I knew would come next.

Not only did I break free; I asked if they would go to family therapy to talk about the abuse. They told me I was sick and needed help and to come home and they would get me some. I didn't. My heart broke, but I also wasn't surprised. I changed my number so the twenty calls a day of screaming and begging and crying and veiled threats of forced treatment and conservatorship, things that would never allow me to leave, would stop.

In my little shitty perfect basement apartment, cleaning houses and landscaping off the books as I waited for my papers, I started imagining what it was like to live free, disabled, Crazy/Survivor, and on my own. I wouldn't have called myself a member of the post-ADA generation, wasn't in touch with a disabled movement, just sick and brown and twenty-two, but the work of disabled and neurodivergent people to form a movement and crip community and cultures paved the way for me to imagine a way to be disabled and neuroweird in the world. A life where the best I could hope for was more than a tight, silent, masked house or an institution.

I wanted the world, and I got it. I was a crip brown daredevil for all of my twenties and thirties. Jumped on any Megabus to a gig or a friend, worked the Canadian arts grant system to pay my way to Sri Lanka for the 2006 Pride still happening during the civil war between army checkpoints. For a decade I co-ran a QTPOC arts apocalypse tour, where I got in a serial killer–looking van and drove all over Turtle Island putting on performance art in every Black and brown theater, queer bar, and community center that would have us. My mother's feral, femme, crip crazy autistic child, I had dirt under my nails from growing food, flowers, and medicine in my tiny yard by the railroad tracks.

I had a million friends, worked a million jobs, and my wild Aries/Taurus sun, Venus in Gemini in the eighth house heart, cunt, and hands had a lot of lovers. I touched myself for hours, fucked my hot plum cunt, ground my clit on my hand and my vibrator, went to every fantasy in my head where I got fucked exactly how I wanted, rested my boot on my lover's chest and fed their mouth full, got my cock sucked all the way down, got to be that sexy tired daddy, got to be that good girl best femme well of desire who got fed. Not always but sometimes. Daredevil. Picking the lock of my life with my crip femme ingenuity. I tried real hard to get everything back that had been taken away from me. I had strong brown thighs from pedaling the junker adult trikes I scrounged to buy, speeding pedaling standing up around the city in a tiny miniskirt. I had poetry, the library, a sleigh bed shoved into a $175 a month shack in the back of an Oakland queer mostly brown collective house's yard—all the crip witch sensuality I'd never seen but pieced together out of my best desires.

And yet: I struggled with feeling broken and wrong in how I was sexual, the ways I knew, or didn't know, how to be a girlfriend or a lover or a wife. I masked for years to try and win what seemed to come so effortlessly to the others, the non-survivor, nondisabled, cis femmes—easy casual sex that didn't involve halting negotiations over abuse histories or chronic pain or trust, sexual abundance, the way an abled, neurotypical femme friend bragged about how five butches hit on her at the club and how many numbers she went home with. I remember being twenty-three, lying on my futon, thinking *I need to construct a persona people will want to have sex with.* I masked. I imitated. I told stories and was the sidekick. I caretook, I blended, I studied sex guidebooks hard, and I hid like hell in the corners of my brain my true neuroweird desires—for the shape of the sex and relationships I wanted, but also the life I wanted.

I wasn't my mother. But I was still running hard from the specter of her life, trying to prove I definitely didn't have it. I wasn't my mother, but there were still years of longing and pining and being terrified that maybe I was her. Maybe her spirit was popping up, saying *gotcha!* every time I wanted to be alone, every time there were years of what I called dry spells even if it was wet in my bed. Years where I stuck around too long in relationships that were dry inside, and years when I had lovers who were like quick flame, but I was outside the glass of the candy shop, looking at the Others, the ones with "real relationships," worried mine didn't count. Because mine were disabled crushes and loves where the whole relationship was in text messaging, or in care packages, where maybe we never had Real Sex, so did it count? There were years where I had a very active sexuality, but it was me, my brain, my vibrator.

I never knew how to talk about my solo sexuality and sensuality without embarrassment, how core it was to me. It stung when a friend laughed, "You write about masturbation more than anyone I know." Was I having a lot of solo sex because I couldn't do better or because I liked it better? I didn't know how to write about the synesthetic sensual experiences I had with a song on hyperfocus repeat, with scent, picking out and wearing an outfit and smoothing makeup on my face, the prep to go to the club better than anything that happened in the club. How I had some of my most intense orgasms in long dreams, ones where I came harder and differently than with lovers. When I had partners, we would become family in the way of all queer orphans who fuck, and I wanted that with my whole big orphan heart. But sometimes all I wanted was to walk into the woods and not text back.

I worried that all this weird, but especially my desire for solitude and autonomy, was just a trauma response, scars from being an incest survivor and a survivor of partner abuse. Always "fear of intimacy." Never a legit desire. Never a lineage working its way out into something else. It was hard for me to differentiate between my parents' lockdown abuse house and what a chosen house of delicious autonomy and solitude that was not closed off to others might be.

I sat in circles of other early 2010s disabled femmes, where we talked about the politics of desirability, about our years of dry spells, about how our abled cis femme friends got a million swipes on the apps and we got a trickle. I stayed in relationships past their expiry date because I was an orphan committed to my lovers as family, and because of that core howling wind of fear that my mother's life, the bad lonely, was waiting to grab me. I wanted touch and kindness, a kiss on the forehead and a hard fuck, chosen family who stayed, and I wanted all the pleasures of my solitude.

All that disabled femme longing, it could power the world.

4. what we long toward

I have a core need to do whatever the fuck I want. I think partnership is overrated and total femme autonomy is underrated as a life goal for femmes, I text a femme.

Our relationships and ways of doing intimacy were always different from the abled and neurotypical, but for some of us, the pandemic just put it into hyperdrive. Like that one autistic tweet I saw that said something like *the relief I felt when I realized I could let go of standard NT partnership as a goal and just embrace weed, cats, books, weird relationships, and jacking off as my life goals.* My friend who writes, *sensuality and sexuality for me during the pandemic . . . is letting the longest leaves of my favorite plant brush my face and arms as I roll by in my wheelchair.*

I am securely attached to myself, I text a crush. In the middle of the world's end, I am the sexiest, most relaxed-into-my-power self I have ever been. Even when the world is on fire crazy fucked, every single day there is a certain kind of feral autistic peace. I claim all the liminal situationships, friend web so sturdy, fantasies and dream liminal loves, self sex and ghost sex as the real thing.

I want more choice for all of us who are disabled and desiring. Choice not born out of reaction to the specter of the forced isolation of ableism, of never being touched or loved. Choice born out of our own particular disabled, autistic desires and ways of knowing, that I know we're just getting started to know.

Stacey was right. All our longings—those of us living in institutions or our family's back rooms, those of us who escaped only to make a locked ward of our own apartment, those of us trying to make a free disabled home without locks, but with boundaries—shape the future. The disabled free futures we dream of in the largest macro scales are built on the delicate bones of our desires for pleasure and joy in our bodies and hearts. Those desires are not just about the big changes in the world, but about how we know how to trade a sex notebook where we write down our desires for a new date or partner and never live together or sleep in the same bed each night, know that the desire we have when sometimes we never touch counts.

I don't have it all figured out yet. Not even close. But I close the door and suck down silence when I want. I open the door and stroll outside when I want. I crook my finger and beckon someone in when I want. I put my hand up and walk them to the door when the first red flag comes. I work to turning toward what my mother's best hopes always were for both of us: disabled, autistic femme choice. The luxury of being able to be curious, to taste life. To choose, and to choose again, something different.

Here you go, mama. One gift I managed to give us, blooming fully now, just after your death. I am your freedom dream, and my own.

Never ugly. Always worthy.

Strange Love via Crip with a Whip

Robin Wilson-Beattie

My journey to BDSM (Bondage, Domination/Discipline, Service/ Submission, Sadism, and Masochism) began at eighteen years old because of a song. The song, "Strangelove" by Depeche Mode, revealed definitions of intimacy and connection in relationships that were previously unknown to me. It was the '90s, and I was in my first year at the University of Memphis in Tennessee. During a poetry unit in Honors English, students were to find a song with intense meaning and present it to the class. We were to play the music for everyone and then share our interpretation of the lyrics and why we found it meaningful. Honors College classes often meant being the lone Black student enrolled that semester. I took a rather sadistic pleasure standing in front of a room of wide-eyed, slightly shocked, and uncomfortable white people sharing the following lyrics:

> *Pain, will you return it?*
> *I'll say it again, pain.*

With those lyrics imprinted on my psyche, expressing intimacy through kink was a concept I secretly sought but initially felt unable to access due to pressure and shame. Soon after that class, I returned home for the summer. My younger sister was horrified to hear me sing a song that mentioned "giving in to sin." She promptly snitched to my mother that I was listening to wicked music. My mother made a massive production of having me return the cassette tape to the store and lecturing the bewildered Walmart clerk on selling music worshiping sin. I quietly repurchased the album on CD when I returned to campus.

Soon after hearing "Strangelove," I started having penetrative partnered sex with men. As I experienced being in sexually active relationships, I realized something was missing. The elusive element was the inability to feel emotionally connected to my partner while having sex. I began to internalize feelings of being broken, and that achieving emotional intimacy through sexual activity was impossible.

My first sexual experience was via assault by an adult cousin. Growing up in the South, the consensus seemed to be that a woman's sexual agency and existence belonged to her future husband. A woman's right to experience pleasure was neither crucial nor a concern in heterosexual monogamous relationships. Sex existed simply as a means to crank out kids and maintain your man's interest in you so he'd stay and not stray. My body, as it existed, was only desirable based on male interest and the male gaze. Sexual autonomy ultimately depended on a husband's wishes, and the assumption that a wife should have sex whenever her husband wants to.

Being that I existed as a fat Black woman in a society hell-bent on labeling me as undesirable, my self-image and lack of self-esteem meant I didn't question those fucked-up messages. Thanks to being an early adopter of the internet, I began online dating in its infancy, joining Match.com's beta site in 1995. Mainly I became pen pals with faceless profiles of men. At that time, when you reached the stage of wanting to view folks, you had to snail-mail them a photograph! I corresponded for some time with a man who began to talk to me about BDSM, defining terms and ideas I'd thought about but never explored. We never met, but he was the first to speak with me about domination and submission. Eventually, I met, fell in love with, and married a man living in England, feeling incredibly fortunate that such a brilliant person found me desirable.

Married, my feelings about sex were ambivalent. I viewed my sexual activity as performances that kept my husband entertained, and although I was a gifted actress, he must have sensed that on some level. Three years later, I ended up hospitalized owing to attempts at suicide I made after feeling like a failure for many reasons, including not being able to sustain my husband's sole sexual interest. I was then formally diagnosed with depression, anxiety, and PTSD (post-traumatic stress disorder) from past trauma and childhood abuse. I also acquired a new identity—disabled. (I had been diagnosed with attention deficit disorder when I was nineteen, but it had not been framed as a disability to me.) Unable to work for the time being because my mental illness manifested in ways that required lengthy hospital stays, I applied for Social Security Disability Income (SSDI). Having started earning a paycheck at fourteen, I had enough credits to begin receiving those benefits at twenty-eight years old.

While in the PHP (Partial Hospitalization Program), I became friends with a fellow patient and fat-identified lady. We were both in our twenties and bonded over shared interests and issues. She mentioned one day that she had discovered a social group for BBW (Big Beautiful Women) in Atlanta called Hipsters. They held events and dances and promised a size-inclusive environment celebrating fat bodies. Intrigued and excited, I accompanied her to a Holiday Inn on St. Patrick's Day in 2001. That dance signaled the beginning of my adventure in sexual rediscovery, body positivity, and BDSM.

Hipsters was a community where I felt attractive and desirable for the first time. Yes, there were issues surrounding so-called chubby chasers, who viewed the big bodies of women as kinky sex objects and easy lays, that were problematic. There were so many lessons I learned about objectification. It was my first time hearing about and encountering "feeders": people—most often men—who became sexually aroused watching women eat and gain weight. These men got treated like rock stars in the community. Owing to the large ratio of women to men attendees, combined with the acculturated self-esteem and internalized issues that come with being fat, there was a lot of unhealthy competition for male attention. I was no angel in this environment, but for the first time in my life, I felt hot and desirable and enjoyed feeling like a temptress who could have any man I wanted.

Having learned about polyamory via the group and being active on LiveJournal, I decided a monogamous marriage was no longer for me. I began exploring my sexual boundaries and experimenting with activities previously unexplored: sex parties, threesomes, and BDSM. I met Rusty (pseudonym). He introduced me to the joy of face-sitting and smothering a man with my big beautiful Black pussy and smoking marijuana as an aphrodisiac. Rusty was not my boyfriend, but he was someone I enjoyed hanging out with and receiving an education from about various sensual-dominant activities. He knew what he wanted, but for the first time in my life, I wasn't having sex because it would make someone want to date me. Instead, I became wrapped up in experiencing the pleasurable feeling of being in control, worshiped, and pleasured. I derived so much power from learning about consent and limits and how to communicate my needs and desires. Communication as a critical component of BDSM was how I finally let go mentally and intimately connected with another person.

Hipsters also became my introduction to sex work. I had two friends working as plus-size escorts, and they sat me down for a two a.m. breakfast at Waffle House and told me that I needed to quit sleeping with all the guys for free because I was taking away paying clientele. Finding out I could make money as a big Black woman via sexual activity with men was exciting. I derived feelings of power by relieving white men of their money and having them perform sexual services. Having studied and embraced BDSM to express myself sexually, I found that being a sensual domme was a great way to engage in kink and earn money as someone disabled and unable to do traditional work at that time.

BDSM stayed a primarily professional activity for a couple of years, and I associated it with getting money out of men. I even dabbled in the world of virtual findom (financial domination), where I got online and demanded that men (well, actually one man) give me funds and gifts from my Amazon Wish List. Besides BDSM being a lucrative means to an end, engaging in kink was not a personal expression of my sexuality. In 2004, that completely changed.

In 2004, the unofficial warranty on my body expired, and it was a turning point in my life. Until my arms and legs inexplicably began to stop functioning and I could no longer feel places on my body, I was unaware of the bomb detonating inside my spinal cord. A rare congenital anomaly, spinal arteriovenous malformation (AVM), was diagnosed after two months. I was born with pseudo–blood vessels attached to an artery, woefully unequipped for circulation owing to their thin walls. Well, that didn't stop those fakers from trying! They began slowly breaking apart and bleeding, on the verge of causing an aneurysm from which I could die. I had experimental surgery to stop the bleeding and remove the rogue vessels. To add to the drama, I discovered I was pregnant a week before the surgery. Fun times ensued. I had three surgeries that resulted in acquiring a spinal cord injury (SCI). Six weeks of IV antibiotics led to yeast infections from hell.

I had months of inpatient physical and occupational rehabilitation learning to feed myself, sit up, and do stuff—while simultaneously growing another human being. Pregnancy brought on the hell that is hyperemesis gravidarum (nonstop pregnancy vomiting). Learning how to be physically disabled in an inaccessible world was the central theme. I learned about navigating my bowel and bladder, using a wheelchair, and traveling while disabled—but nothing helpful about my future sex life with an SCI. Instead, we got a forty-five-minute film telling us we could cuddle. Talk about wanting to vomit.

Becoming physically disabled and a mom simultaneously affected me mentally and sexually. Figuring out my "new normal" was a lesson in trial and error. Sexual expression was one of those areas where my practices led me to make some life-altering mistakes by answering Craigslist personal ads from men seeking daytime BDSM fun. Previously, kink was a means to a financial end. This time, I wanted to explore feeling sexually empowered and in control as I had with Rusty. The good news was I gained a feeling of sexual control of my body as I adapted sex play to my disabilities. I discovered feelings of intimacy and connection with someone by being sexually dominant, switching it up, and being sexually submissive. Communicating my desires and having them granted allowed me to connect to my body in ways that eluded me during "vanilla" sex at that time.

The bad news? As a married person who had agreed to a monogamous relationship when we had a kid, using Craigslist personals to explore my sexuality was not brilliant, so I ended up paying the consequences of breaking that trust. I legit fucked around and found out, with an abortion to prove it. Live, learn, apologize, and do better in the future—that's all I can say about that. Despite how it happened, I gained invaluable insight into reclaiming my sexuality as a disabled person. The experience also showed me the problems created by the lack of disability and sex education in society and how that needs to change.

A year later, I was asked to participate in a disability education series at Charis Books and More, joining a panel of three speakers with disabilities talking about their sexuality. There was a gay white and Deaf man, a Black man with visual disabilities, and me. The first thing that came out of my mouth was, "Hi, I'm Robin. I'm a Black suburban mom with a spinal cord injury, and I like BDSM." This event was the first time I spoke about disability and sexuality, and the beginning of my future self-navigated career as a disability and sexuality educator.

I got remarried and openly identified as polyamorous. As the years have gone by, I have finally been able to experience intimacy with other people without engaging in BDSM. It's been years since kink has been a featured aspect of my sexual expression. I joke and say I have gone hard-core vanilla. I even deactivated my profile on FetLife, the kinkster social media platform, a couple of years ago because it hasn't been essential in any of my current relationships. However, I'm not ruling out kinky sex in the future. Never say never! Without BDSM teaching me to embrace my disabled body and feel sexually empowered, I would not be able to connect intimately with others today.

Pleasure Is the Point
On Becoming a Pleasure Artist

Sami Schalk

My first boudoir photoshoot was in the middle of lockdown. Wearing lacy lingerie I hadn't touched in months, I positioned myself on my bed with a faux fur blanket, in front of my phone on a tripod. On a video call, queer disabled photographer Sam Waldron instructed me on how to pose as she took screenshots: *Turn your face more toward the window to catch the light, now part your lips, run your hands up and down your arms and chest, close your eyes . . . good, yes, that's perfect . . .*

This shoot was an experiment in making socially distanced art, and the beginning of a series of collaborations between us. I had no idea what the experience would be like or how the photos would turn out, but they were great. Sam used editing tools to artistically work with rather than against the lower resolution of video-call screenshots.

These first boudoir photos gave me new insight into the power

Sami Schalk, a fat, light-skin Black woman with short curly hair and glasses, poses in a lace thong bodysuit. She kneels on a bed on top of a faux fur blanket with her arms above her head, looking off to the left. On the wall behind her are framed pieces of art, mostly obscured. Photo credit: Sam Waldron

of letting myself be seen intimately as a fat, Black, queer, polyamorous, disabled femme. Not only did creating the photos feel good, but so did sharing them with my friends, partners, and eventually the internet. This first socially distanced boudoir experience led to more photoshoots with Sam and eventually self-photoshoots as I developed my own skills with a camera. This essay reflects on becoming what I call a pleasure artist, and the importance of pleasure in all of our lives, especially those of disabled people.

Let's start with some context and background. My work as a pleasure artist is grounded in the concept of pleasure activism. I was first introduced to this term in 2018 by adrienne maree brown, when she invited me to do an interview for her book *Pleasure Activism: The Politics of Feeling Good*. In the book, brown writes that pleasure activism is based in the belief "that we all need and deserve pleasure" and therefore works to "reclaim our whole, happy, and satisfiable selves from the impacts, delusions, and limitations of oppression and/or supremacy." When I first read *Pleasure Activism*, I began to consider how I would treat my bodymind and my pleasure differently if I had not been impacted by ableism, sanism, anti-Black racism, homophobia, sexism, and sexual violence. How would I seek pleasure differently if I didn't feel limited by and afraid of the potential repercussions of these oppressive systems?

One of the first things I thought about was how I would dress differently if I was focused on my own pleasure and not on how others may see, police, or harm me. I used to hate and punish my body. Even after years of therapy and learning to love and respect my body as is, I still had a lot of self-consciousness about how I dressed in public spaces. Sharply aware of how others' potential judgment was curtailing my pleasure, I began pushing myself to wear things that brought me joy, not just alone in my house or at friends' parties, but on a trip to the grocery store or to work as well. One of the first outfits I pushed myself to wear publicly I called my unicorn space princess look. I put on a purple mesh bodysuit with sequin unicorn patches over the chest, silver iridescent short shorts, purple sparkle Doc Martens, a glittery-unicorn-horn headband, and extra-large purple wings with poles on the ends I could use to dramatically dance around. I wore this outfit to a street fair one night with friends, and people thought I was one of the entertainers. I looked and felt extraordinary with my fat Black disabled body fully on public display. It was an adrenaline rush to purposely let myself stand out and be seen, and I wanted to experience it more.

In the midst of making this initial shift in my fashion life in 2019, I twerked on stage with Lizzo, wearing a purple cutout jumpsuit and a holographic cape that read 100% THAT BITCH. This remains one of the wildest, most pleasurable experiences of my life. Immediately after, however, my twerking made local news and people began attacking me on the internet, calling me racist, sexist, and fatphobic slurs, and saying I should be fired from my job as a professor for "inappropriate" behavior. I had experienced trolling and internet hate before, but this time I had this new framework—pleasure activism—to help me understand the politics behind the backlash to my public pleasure as a fat, Black, queer, disabled woman showing off and enjoying my body. I credit the combination of having just had my tenure case approved at the college level, reading *Pleasure Activism*, and the pure Black girl magic of a Lizzo concert for giving me a new perspective on how to handle the hate. Rather than locking down my social media or fighting trolls in the comments section, I wrote an essay for *Vox* framing twerking with Lizzo as an act of political resistance, as an act of pleasure activism. If my fat, Black, disabled femme ass-shaking at a concert could cause such a stir among so many people, I began to imagine what I could do if I lived in my pleasure more often and began doing so with intention.

Leaning into my pleasure made me maybe not fearless, but certainly less afraid. The more joy I found in myself the more joy I found in the world. As a person who lives with depression, this is saying a lot. During depressive episodes I isolate and self-medicate heavily, but pleasure activism has also helped me find less harmful ways to take care of myself that I wouldn't have considered before I understood pleasure as political, before I resisted the notion (deeply rooted for me in a Catholic upbringing) that my pleasure was bad, shameful, or frivolous. I learned that wearing what I wanted was particularly helpful during my depressive episodes. Ironically, it is when I am depressed that I'm most prone to desiring bright colors, glitter, and/or generally ridiculous outfits. It's a way of seeking external joyful stimulation when the

Schalk, a fat, light-skin Black woman with short curly pink hair and glasses leans against the handle of a grocery cart in an empty parking lot. She wears a multicolored jumpsuit, a sequin face mask, and shiny boots.
Photo credit: Sam Waldron

internal reserves are low. Wearing clothes I love is a deep comfort when little else feels good for me.

I got the opportunity to articulate the relationship between clothing as a pleasure practice and my depression in 2020 through a video essay I created for the Ford Foundation Gallery's digital exhibit, *Indisposable* (which was later turned into an in-person gallery exhibit in 2022). In that essay I discussed, as someone with nonapparent disabilities, challenging what it means to look sick or disabled. The experience of creating a video essay using pictures I had taken of my outfits during lockdown as well as new photos I took in collaboration with Sam Waldron created a shift for me. I have long considered myself a writer, but this project helped me begin to think of my fashion and photos as creative artistic practices as well. A lot of people have expressed appreciation for seeing a fat, Black, queer, disabled woman claim her joy so

Schalk, a fat light-skin Black woman with short curly hair, stands wearing nothing but waist beads, shown from the waist up in a wooden outdoor shower with her head tilted back under the water and her hands holding her breasts.
Photo credit: Sami Schalk

publicly, but only by taking the time to write about what I was doing, to process it through intellectual and political lenses, did I realize that perhaps I am an artist after all: a pleasure artist.

I came up with the concept of a pleasure artist while on a glamping trip (that's glamorous camping or camping-lite for those unfamiliar) with a group of queer friends, many of whom are also disabled. We had filled our glampsite with delicious food, comfortable seating, multiple hammocks, music, and a beautiful amount of interdependent care. At one point I took my camera to the outdoor shower and took my first artistic nude photos. Showering outside, naked and in private, yet still exposed, was so novel, so delightful. I listened to the birds singing and relished the contrast of the warm sun and the cool water on my body. This was at the end of summer 2022, which I had spent building new romantic and sexual relationships, practicing BDSM rope skills, and vacationing with fellow disabled people, so the creation of pleasure for and among marginalized folks had become a theme by then. Later, I was lying in one of our hammocks, alternating between reviewing the nude photos of my fat, Black, disabled femme body and staring at the tree canopy as I rocked below. I reflected on all my experiences that summer and realized how much intention and care my partners, friends, and I had all put into ensuring one another's safety and pleasure. I realized that creating pleasurable experiences for multiply marginalized people is not simply a skill, but an art. So I came up with this: a pleasure artist creates and captures pleasurable experiences for themself and others in the name of healing and liberation for all.

If pleasure activism, as adrienne maree brown writes, "includes work and life lived in the realms of satisfaction, joy, and erotic aliveness that bring about social and political change" then a pleasure artist is someone who aims to intentionally create lived experiences and work that bring others into these pleasure realms with the goal of social and political change. Pleasure art is political art that both centers and creates the deep satisfaction, joy, and erotic aliveness of marginalized people at every level: for the artist, the subjects, and the audience. This is key. Pleasure art is not simply traditional, fixed, consumable art. Pleasure art is also a Black, disabled nonbinary foodie crafting a fine-dining experience at home for a few vaccinated friends during a pandemic, when eating at restaurants is a risky but deeply missed experience. There is pleasure in the creation of the meal and pleasure in eating it, artist and audience both delighted and reflecting their joy back to each other.

Pleasure art recognizes that the creativity involved in making space for life's pleasures is an artistic endeavor in and of itself. Pleasure art then aims to capture life's pleasure in various mediums to share with others and, ideally, create more, new, different pleasure for the

Schalk, a fat light-skin Black woman with short curly hair and glasses poses wearing a black mesh and lace bralette and thong. She faces away from the camera toward a full-length mirror on the wall, with her arms clasped high above her head and hip cocked to the side. Her reflection is visible in the mirror, with light coming in from a window on the left.

audience. It's a pleasure feedback loop of sorts, in which both process and product matter. This is particularly evident in my boudoir photography and the art pieces I've created with it.

Before any boudoir session I do solo or with Sam, I pick out lingerie and accessories that make me feel good in my body, sexy, and powerful. I mostly choose mesh or lace pieces, and I'm especially a fan of thong bodysuits, open-back panties, and garters, since they all show off my incredible—if I do say so myself—ass. I try them on in advance to get a sense of how they look and feel on my body, since inflammation and hormones can strongly impact how things fit and feel for me. As I try things on, I often send mirror selfies to partners and friends to get affirmation and praise to build me up in advance. Immediately before a shoot, I spend time alone getting ready. I put on a playlist of songs about self-love, take a long hot shower, wash and style my hair, rub my whole body down with my favorite lotion and oil, and do my makeup. Long before I'm in front of a camera, I love on my body in concrete ways.

This self-love and self-care continue during the shoot as well. The experience of letting yourself be seen intimately in front of the camera feels powerful for me, even if it was intimidating at first. When I work with Sam she provides lots of verbal affirmation throughout the shoot, sometimes showing me a few shots so I can begin to see what she's capturing and how. When I do solo shoots, I put on my favorite music and let myself play with light and angles in different spots around my home. It's fun and creative, and sometimes I get great photos. Sometimes I don't. The pleasure art is both the process of the shoot and the photos themselves.

There is also pleasure for me in looking back at the photos later. Sam once told me that most of her boudoir clients are brides who think they are doing the shoot to create pictures for their partner's pleasure, but Sam encourages them to see that the process of doing the shoot and the photos they get afterward are truly for them, even if the pictures please a partner as well. When I look at my boudoir photos, I remember what it feels like to be the center of attention, to feel good, safe, and valued—experiences that can be hard to have when you are disabled, Black, queer, and a woman. Sometimes, when I'm depressed, returning to my boudoir photos can feel like looking at someone else, like an alternate-universe version of myself, but I work hard to remember that the me in those photos is always there, even if my depression or anxiety or internalized oppression makes it difficult in this exact moment to feel like the sexy empowered crip goddess I know myself to be.

I have also recently created mixed media art with some of my self-photography as an experiment in creating layers of pleasure art:

A collage art piece by Sami Schalk featuring a distressed background with cutouts of greenery coming from top and bottom. On the left center is a small oval mirror surrounded by more leaves. In the lower right is a photo of a fat Black woman with short curly hair posing in a black bralette and a thong. She faces away from the camera, toward a full-length mirror with her arms clasped above her head, her reflection visible. In her hands is a cutout of a palm frond. Above her are cutout words that read AT FIRST GROWING MIGHT FEEL LIKE BREAKING.

the pleasure of getting ready for a shoot, the pleasure of a shoot, the pleasure of looking at my photo, the pleasure of making something beautiful and new with the photo, and the pleasure of looking at the art piece. I hope all these layers of pleasure come across for those who view my pleasure art, whether on Instagram, at an art exhibit, or in this book, but even if it doesn't, the pleasure that exists for me in the creation of this art is still deeply valuable.

As a fat, Black, queer, disabled femme, I have been socialized to believe that my pleasure doesn't matter. I have been desexualized, fetishized for others' pleasure, and subjected to harassment for showing my body in public and online. My pleasure and my body have been deemed too much, inappropriate, a problem—always for them, never for me. Pleasure activism and pleasure art have become paths for me to reclaim not only the beauty of my body, but also the deep satisfaction of existing as a fat, Black, queer, disabled woman in a world that wants to deny me pleasure, deny me joy, deny me justice, deny me freedom. My pleasure art insists upon the value and beauty of loving

A mixed collage art piece by Sami Schalk. At the top is a cutout of a photo of greenery, leaves and stems extending down. In the center are layered cutout circles in various shades of blue with a cutout of the phrase "Self-care is essential to my well-being." At the bottom are layered cutouts of yellow flowers in a mound extending up toward the center. Over the flowers is a cut-out photo of a fat light-skin Black woman with short curly hair, wearing nothing but waist beads, shown from the waist up with her head tilted back and her hands holding her breasts.

on, caring for, and celebrating myself as the basis for any liberation work I do. I hope that it encourages other people who share some of my identities to do the same, even if loving on, caring for, and celebrating themselves looks different from how I do it. Your life's art and pleasure is the point; create it and capture it however you can.

How I'm Navigating Play Parties as a Disabled, Immunocompromised Kinkster

Jade T. Perry

"Whatcha got in here, a dead body?!"

The porter lifted a large purple suitcase into the trunk of the Uber, followed by a smaller one. I'd flown Southwest. I always fly Southwest for their two-bag policy, and I'd need no fewer than two bags to do what I'd come to do.

"Better be careful with that one," I said, pointing to the largest suitcase. "If you aren't careful, it'll start vibrating." He stumbled back and licked his lips. Before he could respond, I was on my way to the Airbnb.

Once I arrived, I hung up and set aside my outfits: one-piece teddies with a cutout crotch; iridescent thongs; sequined nipple pasties; short, silk babydoll dresses; a purple leather harness; a black collar with an O-ring; a pink feathered robe.

Toys went in a smaller go-bag: my favorite purple flogger, a Wartenberg wheel, nipple clamps with rhinestones and pink tassels, a

Womanizer clit stimulator, my favorite rumbly Doxy vibrator, a black riding crop, and a wooden paddle. Next to the toys? Particle respirator masks, KN95s (enough to double mask for seven to ten days), wet wipes, hand sanitizer, and a bevy of rapid COVID tests. I had a feeling that none of these things would be provided by the dungeon, not even during a pandemic. But I wanted to be wrong.

"Here's your goodie bag," the person at the event registration said. My own bag fell awkwardly and heavily across my shoulders. I shifted my cane to the other hand and grabbed the bag of condoms and lube. Okay, so I'd have to add a few masks of my own in there, but not to worry—I'd bought a pack of fifty. Plenty for me and any potential play partners.

"Then you'll take one of these purple stickers to put on your name tag if you've been vaccinated for COVID-19."

"And what about folks who haven't been vaccinated?"

"No worries! It's a self-selection process. Some folks don't even use the purple sticker!"

At that point, I ran into the bathroom and took a Klonopin.

I had, in fact, been vaccinated and boosted, and prior to that trip, I'd basically become a hermit. I'd spent the last three years abstaining from travel of any sort. Pre-pandemic, I'd drag my BlackQueerDisabled personhood onto a plane every other month—doing keynote speeches, workshops, panels, and performances. I started masking on planes in 2019 after I noticed I'd get sick after each flight. I had a process and a regimen—one bag for clothing, toiletries, and shoes; another bag for vitamin C tablets, prescription medications, back braces, a heating pad, and a thermometer—things to make traveling with fibromyalgia (and then some) a bit more manageable.

That's the thing they don't tell you about being immunocompromised. You don't go to the doctor for a physical and then they lean in close and say, "My dear, you are immunocompromised." They talk about the diagnosis—if you're lucky enough to get one in the first place—and give you the prescription. They don't tell you about the sheer exhaustion you'll face every time your immune system has to fight hard in order to keep you well. A lot of this shit you find out for yourself.

If I was getting sick before a global pandemic hit, then I certainly wasn't taking any chances with one in play. In 2020, it seemed possible that societal norms were shifting—health and wellness services went online, folks began working from home, gatherings got smaller, and masks were normalized. Yet as the years passed, as airline companies demanded that flights stay full, as real estate companies and employers across fields insisted folks come back into the offices they'd left, as the CDC shifted its guidelines (if you're sick, stay home for two weeks; no, five days, no, three days . . .), as government stipends dried up, as mask mandates were dropped, as COVID strains mutated, as RSV and monkeypox entered the picture, as flu season rolled back around, as US governmental bodies held televised proceedings with unmasked officials, the message became clear: COVID safety is no longer a priority.

The People's CDC reports that in the week of January 4, 2023, at least 2,731 people died of COVID nationally. The United States saw more than a quarter million deaths from COVID in 2022.

Yet there I was . . . in a bathroom, in another city, holding an optional purple sticker for an event that had about four hundred RSVPs. I would have to throw myself on the mercy of double-masking, personal daily risk assessments, and prescription anxiety pills.

"Fuck! I should've known better!"

I'd been so consistent about checking the COVID safety policies for every event I was invited to attend. Then the policies rolled back. Then the invites stopped coming.

Prior to that, I lived out my fantasies largely at home, finding refuge in the few remaining online play parties. Prior to that, I argued with my therapist. "HOW can this moment be called 'POST-pandemic' if the shit is literally still going on?" She'd smile sadly and say, "I know . . . I know. I just want you to find ways to reconnect with the things that bring you joy!"

Heaux shit brings me joy.

Negotiating scenes, talking about limits, exploring new possibilities for our bodies, feeling my eroticism, and sharing it with others brings me joy. And I was at a dungeon led by sexual wellness experts. I knew they felt that STI and STD screening was important. I knew they taught about safety and risk awareness in BDSM culture. And I made an assumption. I assumed that this wellness ethic would carry through in their COVID safety. I wanted to believe that, even though I knew it wasn't likely. I was wrong.

Every confirmation that immunocompromised, disabled, and/or chronically ill kinksters aren't a priority is painful for me. I'm rightfully sensitive that way. So, I went back to my hotel room to breathe (hyperventilate), meditate (pace the floors), and text the disabled/chronically ill babes who'd been keeping my spirits lifted all pandemic. "You're there now, mamas. And once again, the ableds are doing what the ableds do. So, what can we do to adjust? You've got your rapids, your masks, and your good sense. You know how to assess risk and set a protocol. Lean into that and know you can always stay in if it's too much," they said.

The dungeon was sprawling and alive with players. In a corner, I saw one other masked person. Besides that, they wore nothing but form-fitting boy shorts and nipple piercings. We moved toward each other, communicating the complexity of our experiences through touch and wax—six feet away from everyone else.

Afterward, I knew I wouldn't see them again. I'd decided to stay in the hotel room for most of the day's remaining activities to reduce my COVID risk. On the other days, I prioritized eight a.m. workshops, which were always lightly attended. I masked everywhere and tested every day. Other than that, I wished for sheer luck.

A few months after that event, I got a DM from another immunocompromised lifestyler. "How can you say that you want folks to get a clue about COVID safety if you're out here at events?!" I'd chosen three events to attend that year in order to learn skills, compare and contrast safety protocols, and begin brainstorming ways that I could network with folks to encourage kink-friendly events for immunocompromised lifestylers. None of those events required masks. None of those events were outdoors. None of them required COVID testing. One of them required vaccination. Each time, I brought my own safety kit and sat near the door for easeful exits. This is the case for most kink events right now.

Previously, I'd worried about my small "sample size" of three events—but I also wasn't trying to get COVID while reviewing what the COVID landscape was like for immunocompromised kinksters. I'd noticed a sharp, ongoing decline in online lifestyle events while folks (mostly socialized as able-bodied) declared, "Well, we're just all Zoom-ed out." And in that DM, I felt a familiar pang of the sheer isolation that immunocompromised kinksters are expected to swallow down and make peace with. I knew that space intimately. It takes a huge toll on our mental, emotional, and sexual health. YES, I'm saying that a lack of COVID safety protocols takes a negative toll on our sexual health and wellness. If kinksters say they're concerned about safety in general, why wouldn't that include the safety of disabled, chronically ill, or immunocompromised kinksters? That safety work is work that we'd all be wise to do, particularly given the fact that these are identities any of us can enter at any time.

How are we really dealing with issues of consent if we balk at and ignore the needs of immunocompromised kinksters who have not—cannot—give us consent to see them without a mask on? Imani Barbarin, disability-justice activist and speaker writes, "If disabled people want to do fuckshit, they should be able to do it accessibly." And should we just want to *fuck*? We should be able to do that accessibly, too.

An excerpt from:

Hi, Are You Single?

Ryan J. Haddad

Muscular. Tan. Deep voice. Dark hair.

Older than his profile says.

But his apartment is gorgeous, so it doesn't really matter.

He makes me the same cocktail I ordered at the bar earlier.

Our first date.

He dims the lights

Sits on the bed and puts his arm around me.

One leg up on my knee.

And it begins.

Passionate. Deep. Beautiful kisses. My favorite part.

He lifts my hands above my head. He's in control. That's okay.

    He'll take care of me.

He kisses my neck. One side and then the other.

He takes off his shirt. Then mine. And starts on my pants.

But before the pants

I have to take off my shoes

And braces

I do this every day.

Every day.

But there's something about him watching.

I can't quite get the . . .

"Will you help me?" I ask.

He does.

I'm naked.

He's naked.

He gets on top of me.

Spreads my legs. Rests them on his shoulders.

More neck. More lips. More tongue. Rubbing. Our bodies
  rubbing.

A little pain

In my left leg.

Stretched a bit too far.

I try to cover. Pretend it's pleasure.

He puts me in his mouth. He is very good.

I try to return the favor but this position isn't . . .

He lifts me under my arms and sits me up

My back against the headboard

Giving me support

He knows

I like that I don't have to tell him

And I suck

This is much better

He begins to thrust in my mouth

Perfect

Doing half the work for me

But then

Too much

Too deep

Too fast

Gag reflex.

I can't hide it.

It's okay. I'm doing fine.

He pulls out and goes back to me.

He fingers my asshole

Rubs and sucks and licks my cock until I am so close

So close

I have never felt such an intense . . .

Throughout my whole body

Jolting

Rigid

My body is shaking

The stimulation is too much.

I don't know how to handle

all the sensations

happening at once.

It's pleasurable but a little

scary,

so I say,

"Stop! I want to be able to focus on you."

So he lays down and I keep sucking.

As hard as I can.

As fast as I can.

Trying so hard

Not to gag

But it's not enough

It's not
I know it's not
Because he pulls out and starts rubbing himself
Rubbing faster than I ever could
And only puts himself back in my mouth
When he is close
3 2 1
And now
My turn
But I am soft
Why
How
I realize
I have to pee
Limited bladder control
Pronounced due to CP
Or so I like to think
"I'll be right back," I tell him.
I hold on to the nightstand and the wall
And the doorway
I fumble for the bathroom light
Bright suddenly
I squint.
Aim, relief, flush.
Washing my hands, I stare in the mirror for a moment
I am beautiful
I look beautiful
Even if I don't feel it
I know
I know what I deserve

And I return.

Doorway, wall, nightstand

Ready to resume

Finish my almost orgasm

But he is already under the covers.

"Come on," he says. "Time for bed."

There it is. There's your Hollywood sex scene. A gay,
   disabled Hollywood sex scene.

Erotic. Passionate. Messy. Different wavelengths. And ultimately
   incomplete.

doppelgänger

Cyrée Jarelle Johnson

Queer utopians think human beings are perfectible
but we're not, we're just correctable.

In an hourly motel, I recall that Kim Addonizio poem about
tattoos
& ask you how many you have, although I count fourteen
every time you doze & add your spit to the mysterious stains on
the pillows.

But the ink proliferates in twilight's sticky gold: Is a cover-up
one or two or three tattoos?
& how many about your forced disappearances?
& how many about the appearance of manhood?
& how many about being a man
with his face buried in pillows—a short, black man hydroplaning
down our impossible?

I hate how much I love
when you suck my toes & I despise you
for making me beg. That's why I can't know you, that's why I
    stay
perpetually ahead of your judgment. You look just like me

when I'm fucking you from behind. I'll suck that shrimp
    cock 'til the glove pops
plus one extra wop before I figure it out. I don't know god
    anymore
but let's stay here on our knees & wait for him to come.

PART III

Creativity and Power

Soa

Pelenakeke Brown

What does the vā feel like?

Imagine you are floating in the water, molecule, skin, and bone, feeling the warmth of the sun on your face. Letting the gentle rhythm of the waves rock you, softly. You feel at ease as you are, stretched out, in relationship to water, land, and sky.

That is the vā.

When you go home and you're surrounded by your sisters and brother. Your mum, niece, and nephew are sitting at the table. One sister is at the back getting dishes. Your stepdad is sitting on the kitchen floor, scraping off the outer layer of the taro, removing the brown, sometimes hairy exterior to reveal the speckled whitish, pink skin.

That is the vā.

"Mālō faa'uli," my grandfather says as we drive to the shop. He calls it out again on the way home. He always ensures that he says it

at the beginning, during, and at the end of the drive. *"Mālō tapua'i"* I learn to say as an adult in response.

That is the vā.

When you sit in your home on Zoom, presenting a keynote during lockdown, struggling to breathe as you speak. To help you, you invite the audience to pause and take breaths with you throughout. Your partner lies on the floor, out of frame, holding your foot.

That is the vā.

When you visit Sāmoa for a funeral, you are greeted by family friends on the verandah. You cross in front of others bent forward and say *"tulou"* (excuse me). You take a seat on the left side with the other extended family as you watch the village and visitors come and pay their respects. You notice that the choreography is clear—the visitors approach, orderly, in the front. Each has a speaker to represent them, introducing who they are and their relationship with Niusila as they sit behind them. We, in turn, have our speaker, a *tulāfale* who responds to each visiting group on behalf of our family. Our *ali'i pa'ia* is seated at the center of the verandah, and they are quietly responding and directing our response with a look or a turn of the head. You enter the house and find a flurry of activity, washing dishes, cooking food, quiet hum of gossip and laughter. Each corresponding side is engaged in this well-worn duet of culture, together. A careful known choreography of service.

That is the vā.

After a moving performance of *Dawn Raids* at the theater, someone in the audience stands and starts to sing "Ua Fa'afetai." Others stand and join in. You do too, sometimes mumbling over words. In this brief moment, you are together, joined through breath, time, and space. Following, a woman stands up and shares a haka with the cast. Her fiery words and energy ignite the space between us, the audience, and the stage before we all disperse.

That is the vā.

Then you take a moment to rest onstage. You look out and see the shadows from the *tapa* suspended in eight columns before you. You hear your sister start to hum. You get up and move slowly between the *tapa*, the *waharoa*, toward the light. Her presence supports your breath as you move across the stage. As you pace yourself with breath, song, and words, you notice how she is performing access for you in real time as she listens and responds. Supporting your voice. You both move from humming to singing real words—"*malie tanifa.*"

Finally you turn to each other and lock eyes.

That is the vā.

Form

"Can your sister sing?"

"Yes, she can," I say.

"Can your sister drum?"

"Um . . . she can learn," I say, laughing.

"Okay, do you think she can come in and join us?" Anapela asks.

I laugh and say, "I'll go and give her a call."

We're in an old church hall in Avondale, Auckland, for the week. I am making a new performance to take to Berlin but I am stuck, terrified, in a creative block with a slower body that has been affected by the pandemic. I've been making work for about seven years now that explores the overlap between disability aesthetics in dance and indigenous Sāmoan concepts. I find a lot of similarity in the Sāmoan concept of the *vā*, or relationships across time and space, with disability concepts of crip time. I have been making multimedia work, often a combination of performance, installation, poetry, and drawings. I have been using the language of the keyboard in creating choreography and am fascinated by the intersections I find in this everyday tool. I think of the keyboard as this cross-site that enables disabled people to travel across the internet; I love each indigenous idea of time (enter and return appearing on the same key) as well as finding the marks of the *malu* in the keys.

Imogen Zino, my performance designer, has kindly ascertained the situation and traveled down from Whangārei to be with me, and I can tell she is trying to be helpful and support me in all of my uncertainty.

I invited Anapela Polata'ivao to be my dramaturge, and she somehow said yes, and now she's here with us both. I have met her once before, although I have seen her perform and act in theater and on TV for many years now. It's like I have invited my idol to spend the day with me and she has said yes. She has invited her friend, and often close collaborator, Stacey Leilua to join us today. Stacey is an actor currently starring in the NBC hit *Young Rock*, with Dwayne Johnson, commonly known as The Rock, but if you are Sāmoan, more affectionately referred to as "my cousin."

I call my sister, Debs. She picks up the phone and I ask her, "Umm, can you come in and rehearse with me today?" Being the Gen Z adult she is, she answers firmly, "No, I'm really busy with deadlines at work since we are going away soon. I can come in tomorrow afternoon if it's urgent. Why?"

I reply sheepishly, "Umm, Anapela is here and she's asking if you can come in and learn to play the *pātē*."

"Shut up?! Really?"

"Yes, really. She's here in the studio with me and she's asked if you can come by tomorrow."

"Oh my god—Keke, this is a dream come true. ANAPELA!!!" she screams. She pauses. "I'll come tomorrow afternoon."

With my sister confirmed, Anapela starts to shape the staging. Stacey says, "Shall I be Debs?" and dutifully sits down, fully committing to her new role. She carefully places a yoga bolster that I had bought as a last-minute idea to her right, and starts experimenting with its sound. We all agree that it will be our bass drum. I kind of can't believe this is all happening.

That is the vā.

I'm terrified to move in front of these goddesses of performance, but I try to show up for them. Although there is definitely a moment when I lie on the ground and have a silent tantrum, I pretend I am dancing on the floor. I think Anapela can sense this unease as she says gently, "We are with you. This is intriguing." She continues to encourage me, saying, "It's okay to be seen." Stacey says she still gets nervous even after all these years. I try to take that in. "Really?" I ask. "Oh my god, yes," they both say. I excuse myself and pretend to go to the loo, but really I use this time to take a deep breath and try to receive this information, and tell myself *if these two humans want to spend the day with you, then let them in. Try and give yourself over to this process.* I look at myself in the mirror and silently tell myself that I can do this.

Not only is this the first time I've made new work since before the pandemic, but this is also the first time that I have worked with other creatives based in Aotearoa on my own *mahi* (projects). It's a day of many firsts.

Every so often I look over at Imogen and I know my eyes are saying, *Is this really happening?* She has been with me since the beginning of this project, full of enthusiasm, ideas. We reset with Stacey sitting at the edge of the stage, facing me with her makeshift instruments—namely, the yoga bolster. I move toward Stacey, she slowly lifts up my cane to give it to me—we pause in the exchange. After receiving my cane, I turn and slowly move back. I pause and turn around and take a deep breath and look out across the stage from left to right. Stacey echoes my breath. I blink slowly. I want to take small movements and treat them as choreography. Can holding a note be a way to move across time and space?

I turn to look down at my cane and grip it—trying to enter a duet with it. As I do these actions, Anapela sits and watches intently. After I grip my cane she says, "Wait, slower." She comes over to show me how to exaggerate that movement as my fingers grip my cane three times, gradually becoming slightly more overstated with each time. She gestures with the cane and reminds me to be deliberate with every movement. She understands intuitively that small can be powerful as she encourages me to overstate and slow each movement down, and really show each finger slowly grip the cane.

That is the vā.

She continues to do this—gently offering suggestions that produce unexpected and sometimes exhilarating results.

I slowly trace a line down my body and out to the audience.

"And again, with just your eyes," she says.

I bend forward and slowly grab my hair, trying to hold it in one palm. I straighten again with my hair in my hand. I look out and scan my eyes across.

"Wait," she says. I pause, hair still in my fist.

"Go," she says. I release.

I move toward a group of coconut husks on the ground. I kneel down and start to play with the idea of *ascend* by stacking them, imagining whole galaxies in each husk. As I stack, Stacey starts to beat in time with my movements.

I get up and slowly divert my attention to my cane. Anapela calls, "Pull it by the string." I start to do so. I watch as it sways and rolls with the tension of the string. I try to intuitively move alongside it. "Don't forget to breathe," she says.

I pull the cane by its cord toward me and notice the way it moves around on one point, now pulling it in a circular motion as it flows, tracing a circle in the space. I'm not sure what to do, but I try to let its movement guide me. I lift it off the ground and respond to what occurs. I watch as it twirls, still in a circular motion. I try to see if my breath affects its motion. I continue to move alongside it, lifting it higher as I go. As my arm lifts, so too does the diameter of the circle that the cane is making in the air. It is rising and taking up more room. I just keep letting it go where it needs to and follow alongside. Stacey is still creating a beat. Anapela starts to hum. Stacey joins in. I just keep trying to respond to its movement and stay present.

Finally, the cane is above my head, as I'm still turning alongside it. I stop turning, but still mimic the movement of the cane with my hips. I swing it above me, feeling oh so powerful. I feel like we have reached a crescendo, and I notice Anapela's and Stacey's voices have, too. I start to slowly wind down, the cane and myself. I let her, the cane, guide me in our descent. The cane gently returns to the ground, and we somehow end together—Anapela's and Stacey's voices ending alongside us—all in sync. We pause and I look out. I can't believe what just happened. I'm smiling and almost laughing. Stacey says, "It looks like the cane is the dancer." That is exactly how it feels. I feel like we all danced together.

That is the vā.

As practicing artists we can spend a lot of time theorizing about disability concepts like interdependence, cyborg, and disability aesthetics. But this moment felt like all those incredibly important concepts came alive in real time, without explanation. My relationship to my cane was expressed in this movement with intuitive support from Anapela, Stacey, and Imogen. This moment made me so excited. I'm in awe of the way that Anapela could witness and extrapolate small moments and understand them as opportunities for exploration.

Tautua

The next day we're back: Imogen, Anapela, Stacey, and my sister, Debs. Anapela has invited two other artists to join us—Joanna Mika and

Leki Jackson-Bourke, who have a *pātē* and can teach new beats. The
pātē is a hollow drum that is used in Sāmoan drumming—the sound
can change depending on where it's hit. It's a powerful sound, and it's
used to accompany Siva Sāmoa. I've never had so many people in the
room watching me during a rehearsal.

Debs sits next to Stacey as she learns her role. Anapela tells her
that she is to perform the role of *tautua*, a relationship and value that
underpins so many important connections for us Moana people. Service is always the way we show *fa'aaloalo*, care, and *alofa*.

For us this means my sister will always be there sitting cross-legged
on the ground as she carefully imbues me with objects, song, and support, always attentive, watching and witnessing. She will hold the beat,
and will signal change in pace and feeling through the tempo of her
drumming. She will hold important things such as my cane and return
them to me when needed. In the world that we are building she is a
source, and if I receive objects from her, they must return. She empowers and holds space, but she never overpowers. We are always aware of
each other, keeping in time, together, across time and space.

There were so many specific and intentional relationships in the
work, and ours feels like a foundational one for the show, but also for
understanding the *vā*. Our way of understanding time, space, and relationality. The *vā* is the framework that is holding how we relate and connect across time and space together—the central tenet of relationality.

Even our relationship with our audience was deliberate, with
the stage set up in the design of a diamond, the audience sitting on
two sides. This diamond shape references the *malu*, the *tatau* worn
by women on our thighs, and as a symbol in its simplest form it is a
diamond shape. The *malu* means shelter and protection as well as to
soften. We have suspended eight *tapa*, unpainted on the back two sides
of the diamond. *Tapa* that has been scraped, beaten, and dried in the

islands before making its way here. It serves as a portal for projection, an entry point to travel between onstage.

We place Debs in the apex of the diamond facing me. Similar to a *taupou* at a kava ceremony, she holds space, but, instead of giving out husks full of kava, she gives out objects imbued with reverence such as my cane. Like a *taupou*, she is gently shifting from side to side, not to facilitate the kava ceremony but rather to facilitate the show and moving her instruments. In front of her she has a rolled-up *fala*, the *pātē*, and the humble but reliable yoga bolster. She holds time like a *taupou*, not by mixing kava or refilling cups but by keeping the beat, holding *tā*, time, an irreplaceable sister to *vā*. She responds as she witnesses, making complementary taps and sounds. Having someone respond to and witness you in real time is immensely powerful. Our relationship is integral, and as we develop the work her role becomes more and more significant to me. She was always meant to accompany me to Berlin as my support worker, but it has turned into so much more.

We finesse this relationship and its parameters throughout the rehearsal process. During a dress rehearsal, I start to cry as I speak the text in the last scene. I am not expecting it. I keep trying to continue, but then I am just sobbing. This work really has been brewing over the last three years, and returning to performance after such a long break meant it was an act of deep vulnerability to make it, especially with a new, changed body and confidence. As I cry, Debs continues singing and breathing and carrying on the show. It means that I know that if anything is going to happen in the future she will be there, observing, holding us.

As we go through the process, I notice how her role is creating real live access support for me onstage before the show and even afterward. Her role makes me think differently about access for performers onstage. Prior to this experience, I loved integrating access, creatively, for audience members such as through audio description, but I hadn't considered access for me, the performer, onstage. This reflects my current needs as a disabled person onstage after three years in a pandemic.

We realize that fatigue is going to be something we need to be aware of and that doing too many full runs will just exhaust me. So whenever we can, Debs will stand in for me. During lighting checks, because we are a similar height and skin color, she is able to act and be me. Standing can be difficult for me to maintain, so this is so great.

Even for our touch tours that occur before the show, she leads them. Energy-wise, we realized that it would make sense if she could facilitate and explain all the elements related to Sāmoan culture to the audience while I am getting ready. We want the touch tours to be as in-depth and informative as possible, so it's great that she can hold this role. At our first touch tour, Debs shared that she has a vision impairment. It was my first time hearing her identify as having a disability, and it was really moving to watch her lead and be in relationship with her community. She helps me with hair and makeup and does up my ridiculously thick knee pads (normally used for gardening but, in my case, performing) before we go onstage. And of course, we have our pre-show ritual routine of dancing to Beyoncé.

Soa

I've noticed that we love symmetry or duality in our culture. When one receives a *malu*, it is customary to receive it alongside someone else, a *soa*. This *soa* is traveling alongside you and I like to think reflects the first twins, Taemā and Tilafaigā, who were the ones to receive this knowledge and bring it back to our islands. They were also disabled, conjoined twins whose journey across to receive this knowledge ended up in their eventual separation. I like to think this is a visualization of their change, with this new knowledge they were also separated. I'm fascinated that this foundational story for our Sāmoan culture is made possible by these disabled sisters. I think this practice of having a *soa* pays homage to them and reflects this value of reciprocity and being in a relationship that is always apparent in Moana cultures. I feel that the role my sister played was one similar to a *soa*, as she acted as a witness, someone to support and travel alongside me during this transformational journey.

It can be lonely and scary to be a performer. Sometimes I'm not sure why I keep returning to the stage as my mode of artistic expression— writing feels safer and easier on my body. But there's something about standing at the back of the stage behind the curtain, listening to the whispers of the audience and the warmth they bring. We step out into the darkness, together. Secure in the knowledge that our team is holding us: Elliott, our lighting designer; Ernie, our soundie; Nahyeon, working on technology; and Imogen, watching us from the audience. Remembering the many hands and people who have helped us get here. Like the hardworking family members inside the house who are deftly working at supporting the show on the verandah.

As I sit back and look out, I can see forms moving on the eight *tapa* hung like banners in front of me. I take this moment for myself and pause, breathe in, and hum *"malie tanifa"* three times. Debs responds, joining me in humming these notes. I start to get up and move toward the light, passing through the entry between the *tapa*. I'm noticing my breath and listening to her as she sings. I can feel that we are connected. I hang up my cane. I step to the center and lock eyes with her. I step forward. I kneel and look once again at her. We sing now, in time, together, *"Malie, tanifa. Malie tanifa soso atu tua i pa. A i ai o se tautai ua na iloa se mea fe'ai. Mua ō."* Getting faster as we go on—building on each other's energy—egging each other on.

That is the vā.

My Journey with Beadwork

Sarah A. Young Bear-Brown

My name is Sarah A. Young Bear-Brown. My Meskwaki name is tti-ka-mi-ge-a.

I'm a Meskwaki from Tama, Iowa; a mother and an artist; and I'm Deaf. Many people know me for being an advocate for the local Native Deaf community, and some people know me as a Deaf parent of two children. I have different roles and responsibilities to different people, but the one activity in my life that is simply me is my art. I have a few different artistic interests such as clay sculpture, drawing, and different types of beadwork.

The magic of beadwork comes to me through a long family tradition of creating it for the regalia we use to dance in: the garments my people wear to identify us distinctly as people of the Meskwaki Nation at our powwows as well as powwows in other states. We make beaded rosettes, moccasins, dresses, earrings, and almost any type of clothing a person would need. I personally have grown to enjoy making appliqué-design earrings and handbags with unique designs. A few

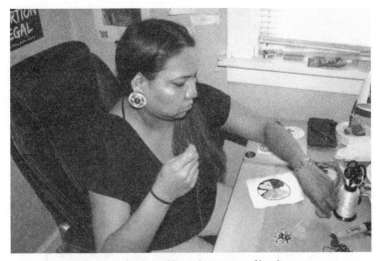

Sarah Young Bear-Brown at a table in the process of beading.

of my personal favorite beading experiments include beaded portraits of famous people, including Che Guevara and Marilyn Monroe. The beads I use are size 13, which are extremely small and allow me to create the fine details I like to see in my work.

When I bead, the first step for me is to say a prayer of gratitude for

Beadwork by Sarah Young Bear-Brown showing a Meskwaki woman in regalia with her hands to her face. On each hand is an eye.

Beadwork by Sarah Young Bear-Brown depicting two Native people facing each other with a sun in the center. On the right are small stars and at the bottom are flowers.

giving me the ability and desire to carry on this tradition. Once I have done that, I check to see what supplies I have available for whatever project I have in mind. The next step is to draw out my pattern and prepare my canvas for sewing. Once I begin my beading, everything comes together pretty easily and I can finish my project in a timely manner.

Beading is a family tradition for me, and I plan to pass what I know on to my own children as they get older. I began beading when I was fifteen but had watched my mom beading throughout my childhood. I vividly remember as a child observing my mom sitting and beading in the kitchen room from my spot under the table. I watched my mom beading for years.

It was when I was fifteen that I told my mom I wanted to learn beading, and she said okay and gave me the supplies. Since then, I've continued observing my mom's beading while doing my own. Beading is something I cherish because the practice of beading has been an important tradition in my family; I'm the fifth-generation beader. While growing up, I also watched my grandmother beading, and my great-grandmother as well; now my mom and I are doing the beading. My daughter seems eager to learn to bead, and my hope is for her to become the sixth-generation beader in our family. I am thrilled to see her interest.

Why is beadwork a big deal to my family? It's the only way to show a labor of love in our family, a labor of love that has happened in our family for generations.

I look forward to seeing how my children will grow and work beading into their future, and how they will incorporate their own stories into their work.

Only now that the canning season is almost over does Mrs. George Young Bear, of the Mesquakie Indians, find time to resume her beadwork. She is stringing beads on an ornamental belt.

Section 4, page 1, *Des Moines Sunday Register*, October 11, 1942. All rights reserved. Part of larger article, "War Scatters Tama Indians."

Disabled Queer Love Exists

Tee Franklin

There's something beautiful about queer love, but there's something *extra magical* about seeing not just queer love but *disabled* queer love in media. If I'm being honest, I don't have that much experience with disabled queer relationships, so I choose to implement that which I *desperately* want in the media I create, whether that means disabled sex worker stories, television, features, or through the comics I write.

I've been attracted to the same sex for as long as I can remember, but growing up in a religious home where that wasn't allowed, you learn to *adapt* and *mask* the queerness. No one in my family, except for my children, knew I was—as my middle child said—"fruity." In 2018, I came out to my family in a *Huffington Post* interview about my queer graphic novel, *Bingo Love*—a Black, queer, disabled romance—which is *loosely* based on my life. Crafting this graphic novel changed my life in many ways, but the best way was that now I was living in my entire truth . . . or so I thought.

I've always been disabled, but my disabilities were invisible. I wasn't looked at with pity or as an infant in relationships until an accident left me *visibly* disabled. A relationship I was in ended because I was too "hideous" to be seen in public with. Y'all . . . I had a CANE and a limp. While I'm grateful I dodged a bullet, it did some tremendous damage to my self-esteem, and I felt—still feel—the only safe space to dream about disabled queer love is when I write.

Writing *Bingo Love, Harley Quinn: The Eat. Bang! Kill. Tour,* and my other disabled queer romance comics isn't just writing "love letters" to the disabled, queer community; it's keeping my tiny spark of finding love alive. But telling stories about Mari and Hazel, Harley and Ivy, or Vixen and Elle—who's a below-the-knee amputee—being in loving, healthy, nontoxic, disabled relationships, has brought out the ableism in so many people, especially "fans" of comics.

The response to these stories should have been celebration and joy, but instead they were received with so much hate. The fact that people believe disabled people don't deserve love and shouldn't be seen as sexual beings is so confusing to me. Are we not human beings with feelings? When you prick us, do we not bleed? Do you not watch pornography?

Now you might be asking, "What does porn have to do with disabled love, Tee?" Well, *baybee,* adjust your reading glasses—if you need 'em—grab a drink, and have a seat.

A vast majority of sex workers many "rub one out to" are disabled; some are even your favorite porn stars or OnlyFans stars. Ever heard of the talented Black, Indigenous, Adult Video News (AVN)–nominated Atzula Storm, or Salvadoran and Filipino nominated Kezia Slater? Both Atzula and Kezia are disabled sex workers who are open about their disabilities. Kezia was in an accident in January 2021 that left her permanently disabled, and she had to learn how to walk and talk again, in addition to being diagnosed with lupus, Sjögren's syndrome, fibromyalgia, and other disabilities. The nine-time-nominated Kezia says that her "disabilities have empowered her to advocate for more accessibility for others and herself." Whereas Atzula—who started sex work in 2020—lost the ability to walk and move her face and arms a few months into sex work, and was ultimately diagnosed with multiple sclerosis. She's also autistic! Atzula isn't ashamed of her wheelchair and uses it everywhere—even at public sex worker events—including looking stunning wheeling down the AVN red carpet. Atzula shares "taking pics on infusion days or using my autistic special interests to engage with my fans! But what empowers me the most is that my disability has taught me to take more chances and risks and be my authentic self. And I wouldn't change that for the world." I know that's right, Atzula! I have been a sex worker for almost twenty years. I turned to sex work when I was diagnosed with a traumatic brain injury (TBI) and seizures back in 2000. I had to learn how to read and write again, on top of horrible bouts of memory loss. I couldn't work, but I had a family, and not working wasn't an option. One day my best friend called me, told me she just made $200 on a phone sex call—in the early 2000s, two hundred dollars was a lot of money for thirty minutes of work—and that was all it took before I made the decision to take phone sex calls while my children were in school.

Phone sex calls turned into webcam calls and eventually filming a variety of fetish videos. These fetish clips—sneezing, coughing, eating, applying lipstick, brushing my teeth, etc.—were simple to film, edit, and upload and generated thousands every single month. Disabled people turn to sex work for many reasons, from making your own schedule, to working from home, to the wads of cash that you could *never* make at your nine-to-five, to not having enough spoons to leave your home for work.

If there's one thing the pandemic showed, it's that there's a reason why sex work is the oldest profession out there! Speaking of, did you know that there are also sex workers who cater to and have sex with disabled people? Back in 2019, a federal court in Australia ruled that funds from the National Disability Insurance Scheme, or NDIS, could be used to access specialist sex therapy and sex worker services. There are even websites dedicated to connecting disabled people with sex workers.

Now that is a movie I would have *loved* to see, but instead, Samuel Goldwyn Films released a dramedy in 2019, titled *Come As You Are*. The logline reads: "Three young men with disabilities hit the road with a jaded nurse driver to a brothel in Montreal catering to people with special needs." This movie starred able-bodied actors Grant Rosenmeyer, Hayden Szeto, and Ravi Patel, with Gabourey Sidibe as a nurse. Full disclosure, I only watched the trailer and *instantly* knew that this movie was not for the disabled community.

Disabled people's love and sex lives shouldn't be used against us for laughs or for nondisabled people to feel better about not having a partner. There have been too many times when a disabled person has a partner and posts them on social media, and the comments are filled with backhanded compliments:

"How did *they* get a partner?"

"And I'm sitting here single."

"There really *is* somebody for everybody."

There is so much hate for disabled people as a whole, but once you find someone who you care for, the commentary can turn into something so disgusting and harmful. This, on top of countless other reasons, is why hashtags like #DisabledAndCute, created by Keah Brown, and #DisabledPeopleAreHot, created by Andrew Gurza, exist. This is also why disabled people participate in challenges on TikTok and Instagram . . . to *normalize and celebrate* disabled bodies, as well as to change these harmful narratives and stereotypes the media and Hollywood has created.

If movies like *Come As You Are* were done properly, they might have potential to be eye-opening and teachable moments, showing how disabled people crave intimacy and how, because of people lacking empathy and human decency, some turn to those in the sex work profession to get what they're craving with respect. And, let me be 100 percent clear here, there's absolutely *nothing wrong* with paying a sex worker for intimacy.

Disabled people are speaking up for themselves more and more, regardless of how it might #MakeAbleistsUncomfortable (created by yours truly). The notion that disabled people aren't sexy, don't have sex, need help having sex, don't deserve intimacy, or are inherently asexual is . . . straight-up bullshit. (Note: there's absolutely nothing wrong with being asexual, the problem is when people assume and lump you into that category because we're disabled.)

As one of my favorite niblings, @teonawrites, tweeted, "*just like my joints, this pussy pops!*" which of course led to Teona being harassed for—as many said—"tweeting something disgusting." Why is the thought of disabled people being intimate disgusting? Personally, what I find disgusting is that ableist way of thinking.

As long as the sex is consensual and you talk with your partner or sex worker about your needs and limits, go on about your business and get your world *rocked*!

Disabled people are worthy and deserving of love. I will try my damnedest to make sure that we are represented, screwing *and* in loving, healthy relationships in everything that I write.

For your pleasure, enjoy an excerpt from "Preparing Dinner," a short, raunchy, disabled erotica:

While the beautiful, Black Queen lay on her stomach, breathing anxiously, waiting for me to ravage her body, I stared at her in the moonlight, mentally tracing every curve, stretch mark, and scar. She is the true definition of perfection.

With an ice cube in my mouth and armed with the knowledge of where her nerve-damaged painful areas are, I carefully glided the ice in a circular motion up and down the backs of her thighs, to numb the pain so that her recovery time wouldn't be as long. As the ice water dripped down in between her thighs, she shivered in a way that made my loins purr.

As much as I wanted to place her in my mouth, I restrained myself as I grabbed her medicated pain salve to lather her body, ensuring she'd have as little pain as possible *after* our romp. Warming the salve up in my hands, then massaging her lower back and round, tiger-striped ass, had her squirming . . . her body *begging* me to have my way with her. Goddess Venus knew I wanted to oblige, but making her wait was a necessary "evil."

Watching her body glisten in the moonlight for a few minutes felt like an eternity, but now it was time to throw her legs around my neck and partake in an all-you-can-eat buffet.

The End.

There are plenty of ways to be intimate and creative with your disabled partner, just be sure to do so safely. Check in with them to gauge their pain levels, add pillows if it will aid in alleviating pain, and above all . . . pay attention. If you notice your disabled partner starting to look or act uncomfortable, reassure them that if they need a break, it's okay. While some of us may like sex to be a bit painful, we'd rather not deal with pain that'll keep us in bed for days.

The above advice is for those with chronic pain, but there are other disabilities out there and it's up to you as someone's partner to find out their needs and wants to be certain that the sexual experience between you is a pleasurable one. If you aren't sure how you'd like to be pleased, I encourage you to get to know your body intimately, so that you can properly communicate your desires and get those orgasms!

As for me, I'm currently on a self-exploration journey. While I *do* know what disability intimacy looks like, I've never had the opportunity to *experience* these feelings, but I can't wait until that time comes. While I consider myself a *demisexual*, I know I *have* to get myself right *first*, before I engage in a relationship. *However* . . . that doesn't mean I won't be creating these disabled stories for us to enjoy.

You, dear reader, *are desirable.* It's time to eliminate those harmful thoughts that can discourage you from feeling that way. Embark on your intimacy journeys and remember: safe sex is the best sex.

Letters I Never Sent

Sejal A. Shah

Dear Alice,

I remember you had suggested we have a Zoom sometime, a social Zoom. And I probably thought: *Well, she's busy.* And scheduling stresses me out. And you were working on your book, so you said, *Let's do it in a couple of months.* And I reached back out after reading *Year of the Tiger* and getting to know you better. I knew you had been sick, but I thought you were getting better. I hadn't kept up with how you were doing. I had been sick, too. You suggested we write letters or postcards. I had a bit of *Oh, I'm not important enough for a Zoom.* But then I recovered and thought, *Yes, I do write letters and postcards* and, in fact, I often hate Zoom, and I loved the idea of writing to you. So, I did.

I wrote to you on the back of a watercolor painting of a window I made in an art class. The windowpanes reflected lemon-yellow and cotton-candy pink light like sunrise or sunset. It was a little piece of art I had kept through a terrible move in August. Perhaps I chose this postcard for you because the palette was close to the bright yellow and deep red cover of *Year of the Tiger*. I wrote about what it was like to read your book. I loved that you wrote about Mrs. Shrock, a teacher who saw you and loved you. It was a rough time for me, the fall. Writing postcards and taking a painting I made and sending it to you across the country, telling you what I loved about your book (yes, I fangirled a bit!)—it made me feel better. The ink smudged from my hand. In your book, you wrote, "SNACK MANIFESTO, TM." I smiled. It made me feel and remember that we can be neighbors to each other from far away.

I read something on Twitter (I had been taking a break) and it said you could not speak. But you could still connect. It has been a joy to connect with you via mail. Something that was in your hand is now in mine and vice versa. The corporeality of it, but that's not what matters. It's the intention.

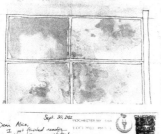

Top: The front of a postcard from Sejal featuring a watercolor of four squares in a grid pattern like a window. *Bottom:* A postcard from Sejal mailed to Alice on September 30, 2022, with a message about *Year of the Tiger*.

Dear Reader,

After I published my book, I was surprised to learn what resonated most for many of you was an essay about postcards! That essay isn't cinematic in scope. It's not set in Sicily or Black Rock City, Brooklyn, or the Playa. It doesn't reference weddings or Indian culture. It is about place, penmanship, friendship, connection, kinship: epistolary intimacy with writer friends I met and conversed with over many years. We never lived in the same place.

This morning, I listened to and renamed my audio messages, saved voice memos, another kind of correspondence—letters to Wendy, Holly, Abbey, Geeta, Liz, Minna, Carley, Cat, Cath—across distance, ongoing conversations, messages born of hand pain. That's Seattle, Maine, Missouri, Pittsburgh, Rochester, Brooklyn, Santa Cruz, North Carolina. When my joints glowed, rheumatoid arthritis, I forsook typing and switched to speaking: the words kept coming, hypomanic. Hypomanic typing makes my hands hurt. Those times I am too disorganized to locate an address, select a postcard, write a note, find the stamps, I keep speaking.

Sometimes I record messages for R, too. Even if you live in the same home, even if you share a life, maybe especially if you do, it can get harder to hear each other.

Audio messages allow for pauses, voice, intimacy, breath.

Postcards or letters, the direct address. *Dear Friend*, Holly and I said to each other. Later, we co-taught a class over Zoom about epistolary forms, what it means to connect. What it can mean. A private correspondence, the intimacy of singular address, sharing in a collective way: an idea that grew out of friendship. We called our class *Dear Friend.*

Dear Valerie,

I wish I could talk to you. I met Jericho last week and showed him my review copy of your book *Bigger Than Bravery.* He got quiet, he got tears in his eyes. I am remembering how, after you and I met for coffee and I was weighing whether to join you at the next event, Jericho walked by. *Hey Jericho,* you said, in a voice that had a lilt and gravity and history to it, and you smiled in a teasing way. The familiarity, the nod, two writers and the years between you. I had been writing to you for almost three years when we met. I wish I had gone with you to that event. Now, I am writing to you in my head.

Dear KK,

I still can't believe you are gone. Of course, it's worse for your kids, but you were my uncle for almost fifty years. Longer than your kids have known you. You were my second father.

Dear Sejal,

I'm sorry you have been having a hard time. Usually when my hands hurt, I record an audio message, but at the moment, I am depressed. I just listen to audiobooks: *Braiding Sweetgrass* and for a second time, CJ Hauser's *The Crane Wife*, then Tricia Hersey's *Rest Is Resistance.* Your cousin sent you an email asking if you could visit her book club by Zoom. You said no. You had decided no events in November. I am proud of you for sticking to it. You worried she would be offended. I see you. You are finally saying what's true: When you are having a flare (and you can't tell when they come), evening Zooms eat your head and drink your blood. Make it harder to rest. I think you are able to tell now when they are coming. I think you are starting to say no more. I hear you: I am listening.

Dear Alice,

Thank you for writing about procrastination in your book—procrastination as part of your writing process. I wish it wasn't true for me, but it often is. I mean, it is. Almost always!!!

Dear LeeAnne,

I miss you. I will always remember how much I enjoyed seeing the world with you that fall—the autumn colors. Going to hear music and to the antiques fair with you. How everything was an adventure! How you saw the world and how you saw me. How I saw you. That love. I thought I met another friend like you. I hate it when I mistake someone with a similar background for a friend. You were my opposite in so many ways. We were different, but you were my friend.

Dear Valerie,

I have not finished that essay about you. I wish we had been able to edit an anthology together like you suggested. I have a stomachache at the moment, but I am not going to complain.

I was thinking about how much space you made for me to talk, and how well you listened, in our first conversation after my pandemic book launch. I wonder what you are thinking about now. I feel ashamed that I have not been doing more, that I've dug so far into my unhappiness lately. Yesterday I scrolled through your old IG photos—from before I knew you. I forgot that you had a photo of things people had sent to you and one was a box of chocolates from me. You didn't tag me. I'm glad. It wasn't performative. I listened to your quiet captions, how you saw the world, what you chose to highlight, your curation.

Dear Mom,

I am sorry I was so mean earlier this week. I was unhappy and it's hard to talk to you about it in ways you would under-stand. So lately I haven't wanted to talk.

Dear Monica,

Whenever I drive by French Road (and let me be clear, I try never to do that), I feel this shiver. Then we moved to a place that is close to French Road, our old middle school, and I feel that shiver almost every day. I remember you in a place where I didn't have friends for a while.

Dear Alice,

My uncle, the first person in my family to come to the US, won a scholarship to Stanford. He lived in San Francisco for a couple of years, but by the time I met him (or by the time I could remember him), he lived in the East Bay, in a house on the Oakland-Piedmont line. I will be going to California for his daughter's wedding this summer. It is impossible for me to think of California without my uncle. I am trying to remember where you live. I want to say it's the Mission. I remember you said in your book that there was delicious food nearby. I had a friend who lived there twenty years ago. No, maybe it's twenty-five. I wonder if I might get to see you. It's hard to think ahead to next summer. (My mother just said, *Use my points, book your ticket now!*) I am grateful I can write to you this way, <u>now</u>. I've got *Strictly Ballroom* playing on the other laptop right now. You said you had the soundtrack. I've always loved the music, but it never occurred to me to buy the CD. I love that you love movies from long ago, too.

When I was in middle school and high school (and even into college), I had a few pen pals. The one I wrote to the longest—I met him in person years later, in France. I hope I meet you, too. But even if we don't meet in person, our epistolary friendship will have shaped me, just as ones from long ago have already shaped me. I couldn't drive—too young, didn't have my license or a car—reading and writing were my ways to travel. I'm grateful they still are now. I'm wearing new glasses and I have an external monitor. Seeing: I try not to take it for granted.

Last month I told a writer friend that I turned fifty in October. He texted back, "Congratulations!" Very few people I know say that. As women, maybe we are supposed to grit our teeth through it. I don't want to grit my teeth. Rahul and I have been in touch, mostly by phone, email, text, for the last five years. I only met him this year. I wrote to him after I read his story collection in 2017. It's called *Quarantine* (I kid you not!!). We have been corresponding for years. We built a friendship through words.

Dear Val,

I loved rereading your introduction to *Bigger Than Bravery* today. I can see your dad in his blue shirt in front of his shop. You posted a photo of him soon after he passed. Your stories fleshed him out, made him real to me. Your opening line, "My father was a numbers runner"—or was it "My father was *not* a numbers runner"—? I go back to look. It had the "not." You also wrote "When Dad passed away on Wednesday, July 8, 2020, we weren't ready." You didn't tell most of us and you didn't tell me that you were sick. We weren't ready. You created an opportunity for me to interview you about your books and editing, because I needed to. It felt urgent in a way I didn't understand at the time. I do now. What the body knows and the mind doesn't. I wish you could have seen Jericho's face. I think you did.

Dear Me,

Sometimes I feel overwhelmed by mail. I turn to voice texting, but autocorrect makes me mad: Raj as Roger, Sejal as Sergio—

Voice memos remind me of answering machine messages from long ago. The voicemails I saved from my nephews singing me happy birthday. Audio postcards from the bathtub, missives sent while speaking, my feet and wrists in Epsom salts. Memos allowed me, in real time, walking and speaking, to stay connected to my friends and collaborators. Voice memos are easier with Mom, too. Gujarati, can't voice text it.

I always preferred the written word, but my hands and eyes tire. Needing glasses over bifocal contacts. Forty-seven, forty-eight, forty-nine. I have had to learn other ways to communicate because my joints burn—hurt from overuse.

Zoom used to be a way to connect. We said, *Why didn't we do this all the time?* Then eye strain, brain strain, fatigue. Asynchronous audio messages arose from exhaustion and isolation. Also—because I couldn't write a long email to Wendy. We are writing partners and had things to communicate.

I learned from listening. Audio messages are different. Are they ephemera if they are not paper? They are ephemeral. They live in the cloud. Intimacy is the direct address, epistolary to a singular person, the opposite of social media, talking to everyone, Facebook is the mall.

Dear Alice,

When I asked for an extension for this essay, I felt I had to say why. I had these flares, my mood disorder rearing, swinging back and forth—hard—meds adjustment not working and

I can't take my ADHD meds. I had made the mistake of powering through, grinding myself down to sand—to powdered glass particulates—when my book came out. I know I cannot focus enough to write when hypomanic. Too many words coming too fast.

Also, I was scared. So many words, but not in the right order. What would you think? I loved Tiger Talk 2, the online event in honor of your book, but an evening Zoom was one more thing that took me out, because I didn't know how to manage all the spikes, high and low. I had not unpacked my boxes. I wanted to do a good job. I kept thinking one more evening Zoom is okay. Maybe, but not after I had just moved.

Later I saw the video. I had prepared, but I could see myself blinking, squinting trying to look at ease. I never said *disability*, I never said *manic depression*, I never said *bipolar. Maybe* I said *ADHD*, maybe I said *neurodiversity.* I said (I think) "performing wellness." I was performing wellness even in a space about disability. I am still learning to say it. My shame runs deep. You were so kind when I asked for an extension. *Maybe December 1*, I said, after I missed the first extension. I had deadlines for my second book. You wrote back, *How about 12/15?* Crip time. I almost crumpled in the face of your kindness.

I think this is a lyric essay. Lyric: the lyrical labor of loving disabled bodies. In the lyric, in lyricism, there is space for the voice, for the stuttering, for what swerves, for the swerve, for language fracturing in its attempt to be spoken. Postcards, these small snippets, get me closer. Every address is a wish.

Every essay is a letter never sent. This is the lyrical labor of disabled bodies. This is a kind of love. Here is something you wrote in *Year of the Tiger*: "SUCK IT, ABLEISM." YES!!!

RAWR!

P.S. Now "Eye of the Tiger" is in my head. And Al Stewart's "Year of the Cat." We are kids of the seventies and eighties. ☺

P.P.S. I see I wrote no letters in November. It was one after another—these flares, these breaking downs.

Dear KK,

You once sent me a book called *Unmedicated.* You sent me turmeric pills, ayurvedic pills, printer cartridges. I'm still using the printer you bought me. My eyeglasses prescription changed and I reminded the eye doctor (because you reminded me) that we have a history of glaucoma and to ask the ophthalmologist to test for it. The only person who had a worse prescription than me is you. Now you are gone. Now I'm the one with the weakest eyes.

Hearing is the last sense to go, they said. Listening is what I am trying to do. I can't write to you now. If I send an email, you won't reply. You told me I needed a printer, and you were right. You would be proud: I kept it even though Raj wanted me to get a new one. It's still working—almost fifteen years. I will print a draft of this essay. I am still writing to you. Krishna told me you didn't get my book in time. You pasted a color printout to foam at the family Zoom so you or she could hold it up. You were proud of me even if my book wasn't the type you would read. I mean, I stayed with you before and after Burning Man. I mean, we are the two poets on our side of the family. I mean, you were the first one in our family to come to the US. You made it possible for all of us, for my father, for me. Because you lived in California, I had a home there.

I wrote down something you read during our Zoom in 2020, which took the place of the eightieth birthday party we couldn't have for you in California. It was a poem you wrote in 1960-something: "*Because I could not find a replica for my parents . . .*" You were missing your parents when you were first here. Now I am missing you. You wrote poetry. Now I am writing to you.

I never sent you an audio message. One of my favorite memories of you is when you showed Sonika and me your VCR, our first time seeing one. "You can tape your cartoons," you explained. (We loved Rocky and Bullwinkle then.) "You can tape them and then watch them later." You didn't have kids yet, but you loved us and you took time to explain things to us and to think about things from our point of view.

My mom told me recently when I was thinking about gifts for Samir's kids that you always sent us Christmas gifts from California. I was too young to remember that. Now I am fifty without kids, and I was forty without kids, and also thirty without kids—as you were. You were different from my other aunts and uncles whose own kids were always first in their mind.

People are different. You were different. I am different, too. I used to write Dear Favorite Uncle, in emails. You called me Favorite Niece. We pretended it was a joke (I have more than one uncle, you have more than one niece), but also. We knew it was true.

Dear Alice,

I have been watching *Strictly Ballroom* on repeat, but it never occurred to me to get the soundtrack. Which song is your favorite? I'm partial to the cover of "Time After Time" and the song that starts with "You won't admit you love me . . ." Speaking of love, I LOVE that you quoted "YOU GUTLESS WONDER!" to me in your last email lol. I'm thinking about the other movies you mentioned— different ways to connect. We are the fellowship of eighties and nineties movies. We are the neon-spangled Dance Federation. We are The Pan Pacific Grand Prix circa 2024, writing from the end of 2022.

Vivir con miedo es come vivir a medias: A life lived in fear is a life half lived. (I looked it up on Google.) Fran's grandmother said, *You just got not to be scared.* I need to remember that.

You reminded me of the joy of old movies. They are the best! ☺ Here we are, writing to each other, dancing our own steps.

Your friend,
Sejal

Index:

"many of whom have never been and are like me and feel alienated by it"

Access Intimacy in Archives

Gracen Brilmyer

Introduction

Being in an archive brings up all sorts of feelings—feelings of loss, grief, joy, frustration, pain, connection. Searching for disabled people in these repositories of historical materials can generate a constellation of emotions. As a disabled person who has worked as an archivist and researches using archival material, I have become deeply familiar with the connections and emotions that arise in archives. There's something that happens when I find disabled people in historical records, something that feels magical when I'm sifting through folders and folders to find one photograph, one letter, some trace of a disabled person.

I've written elsewhere about the relationships that disabled people can have with other disabled people across time through archival materials—relationships that I have also experienced myself. My writing on these connections emerged from conversations with other disabled archives users, who spoke about similar experiences. For example, Stefan Sunandan Honisch, a multiracial disabled researcher, educator, and musician aptly identified "that 'aha moment' that comes from seeing other disabled people historically present." Cody Jackson, a white, disabled, gay graduate student, talked about the importance of witnessing "ancestors and people in the past that I can look to who have done this work and put their bodies on the line." And finding disabled people in history can feel like many things, as Black disabled professor Therí Pickens described: "It felt like this confluence of emotions; this anger, this fear, this excitement, this beauty, this difficulty, and then this sort of hope. . . . It felt like everything."[1]

In other words, researching disabled people in history comes with its own intimacies—through finding disabled people in records, we can feel connected across time. I wonder, though, what other bonds might be created through archives or archival spaces? As disabled people, what else might it mean to relate to our[2] histories? Could connecting to our histories (also) mean something different from connecting through obvious traces?

---

1 These quotes and this part of the conversation will be published in Gracen Brilmyer, " 'It Felt like Everything': Disability, Affect, and the Creation of Archival Interdependence," in *Cripping the Archive: Disability, Power, and History*, eds. Jenifer L. Barclay and Stefanie Hunt-Kennedy (University of Illinois Press).

2 Notes on language: Sometimes I use "us" and "we" in this research; other times I do not, since disabled people are not a monolith. I am a white, Disabled and chronically ill nonbinary queer person in academia. While I do this work for and with disabled communities, I also recognize how disabled people have vastly differing intersecting identities, disabilities, access needs, opinions, and politics. In my writing, I try to honor these differences and my own positionality. I also use predominantly identity-first language, while I recognize that not all people who have disabilities identify with it. And lastly, all the people I interviewed told me how they wanted to be described in writing (and can edit these descriptions at any time), which I use accordingly.

I want to focus here on an archival intimacy that expands out-side the space-time of an archive visit. In this chapter, I draw on my conversations with other disabled people to show how we can center one another *even in our absence.* For me, these conversations resonate with what Mia Mingus defines as access intimacy—"that elusive, hard to describe feeling when someone else 'gets' your access needs." And they echo a kind of crip kinship where, as Shayda Kafai emphasizes, we "first remember the forgotten": those who have been erased, those who have come before us, and specifically multiply marginalized dis-abled people. The conversations that I highlight in this chapter show how cross-disability solidarity might shape us, or how access intimacy is about being in community, even when others are not—or cannot be—there. This theme emerged, as I will describe below, among many of our conversations, and highlights the ways that disabled people can keep one another and one another's needs at the fore. It also shows how disabled people not only navigate their *own access to archives* but also navigate complex feelings around access and the *potential barriers to other disabled people.*

This essay weaves my own experiences with those of others': I spoke with ten disabled people located in the United States and Can-ada about their experiences in archives.[3] The process of having these

---

3   More about the interview process: Each conversation was recorded and tran-scribed into text, which allows me to use direct quotes. Consent is central to these conversations: each person read and signed a consent form before we spoke, where I explained the project, the process, and how their words might be used, as well as how they could specify how they are identified in anything I wrote (by name or anonymously). We checked in about their consent before and during the conver-sations, at which time they could ask any questions. And I continue to get their consent for anything I write using their words; they all had an opportunity to read and edit their quotes in this chapter and change how they are named, as well as add any suggestions to the piece overall.

conversations and building and sustaining these relationships highlights a perhaps more immediate "archival intimacy": the connections,
emotions, and presence that happen(ed) through my interviewing
other disabled people about their experiences in archives. These conversations, parts of which are found in this chapter and in my other
writings, are intimate because in having them, we shared space with
one another. We shared stories of disability, of ableism, of erasure, and
in those stories, we were vulnerable together. Each conversation was
unique: some of us cried together, some shared similar stories, and
we learned from one another's differing experiences. And each of us
built different relationships with one another. We remain in contact—
some more than others—as they read, edit, and consent to each piece I
write using their words. This research connects me to each interviewee
and also the interviewees as a group, as they get to read each other's
words and I connected them by email. This is just one type of archival
intimacy that happens when disabled people come together, to think
together, to collaborate, and to share our experiences. I am honored to
be in community with the people whose words are in this chapter. It's
a privilege to spend so much time with their words, to show all of the
magic that disabled people bring to archives, and to do community-
based research.

Conversations

While there is a constellation of connections and intimate moments
in archives that happens through *who and what is present* (like finding
disabled people in records), I want to focus on how disability intimacy can also be fostered through *absence*. One of the ten principles
of Disability Justice, defined by Patty Berne and the Sins Invalid family is:

Commitment to Cross Disability Solidarity. We value and honor the insights and participation of all of our community members. We are committed to breaking down ableist/patriarchal/racist/classed isolation between people with physical impairments, people who identify as "sick" or are chronically ill, "psych" survivors and those who identify as "crazy," neurodiverse people, people with cognitive impairments, and people who are a sensory minority, as we understand that isolation ultimately undermines collective liberation.[4]

I noticed how through my conversations with the interviewees, a common theme emerged around cross-disability solidarity: when navigating archives, many reflected on all of those who could not be in archival spaces and use archives for various reasons—financial limitations, inaccessible archival spaces, or lack of academic affiliations, to name a few. This felt important.

While discussing their own issues around accessing archives, many people who I spoke to remarked on the ways that other disabled people could be excluded from accessing archives. They named one aspect of this: their privilege in being able to get the accommodations that they needed, which might not apply to other disabled people. I asked hard-of-hearing biracial archivist Michelle Ganz about her experiences as both an archivist and archives user and how she has experienced accessibility. She responded:

"I've been very fortunate that any place I have done research or have worked at has been very willing to accommodate me with the few accommodations that I need. And most of my

4   Sins Invalid, *Skin, Tooth, and Bone: The Basis of Movement Is Our People: A Disability Justice Primer*, 1st ed. (self-pub., 2016), 18.

accommodations revolve around a phone that can be turned up really loud and understanding that I am a very loud person."[5]

Blind historian Alida Boorn described bringing an assistant with her to read written archival materials out loud: "I'd say I've always just been very, very lucky. I don't know the other people you've spoken with, but there was never any problem with having someone read to me." Michelle and Alida identified feeling fortunate to have had support to be able to navigate archives. Their words highlight how disabled people can be aware of their privileges of access around navigating archival spaces that could exclude others.

Disabled scholar and poet of color Travis Chi Wing Lau talked about being in archives' reading rooms, silent spaces which can feel impersonal. I asked Travis, "Do you think that had an impact on how you felt looking at records?" After he responded, "Oh, absolutely," he continued, describing how the rigidity of archival spaces had shaped the way he feels "the archive is often a financially and physically inaccessible space and a place where I see myself as a burden." He added:

"I have to fully admit the fact that . . . I'm privileged enough not to have to require a lot of accommodations, but I know for my colleagues who do, it is an ordeal each and every time; if they need, say, a special piece of accessible technology or they need to bring an inhaler medication, I know they get all sorts of crap by people who are working in front. 'You can't bring that into the archive' or like, 'that's going to be a

5   Part of this quote comes from an essay I previously published: " 'They Weren't Necessarily Designed with Lived Experiences of Disability in Mind': The Affect of Archival In/Accessibility and 'Emotionally Expensive' Spatial Un/Belonging," *Archivaria*, December 5, 2022, 120–53.

problem.' I can see why some people would just be like, 'I just don't wanna do this at all. I'll wait for the digitized versions. I can access it far more comfortably.' "

His words highlight how in navigating archives he is not only aware of how they can be inaccessible to him, but also how they are inaccessible to many disabled people. Along these lines, Stefan describes his sensory privilege:

> "I'm still able to gain access to these materials in ways that blind, d/Deaf, and Deafblind researchers for example, might not. So then the questions about accessibility and representation become even more complicated because it's not simply about how people are represented in the archives, but also about how researchers participate in a certain kind of sensory economy, how certain kinds of circulation of archival records circumscribe questions of access."

Having worked in many archives, I am deeply familiar with the ways archival spaces can be exclusionary: some do not allow water, laptops, backpacks, and other items disabled people might need to be able to safely access archival materials; some require silence; and many only support certain ways of engaging with archival material, such as through sight or sound. Therí similarly brought up the privilege of certain modes of engaging with records, linking it to her experience outside of archives:

> "And this is all kind of based on my own embodied experience of having sight and having haptic capability . . . What's in front of you is evidence. And then what you know to be true about how you are experienced in the wider world is that

there's a degree of constant explaining, constantly making visible, constantly reminding people when something is visible
that there's a lot going on that they don't understand."

Her words show how, as Stefan describes, researchers themselves "participate in a certain kind of sensory economy" to gain access to archives.
She also points to her heightened awareness of the limits of those forms
of access, and further identifies how she is "constantly reminding" others that there is more beyond what is made visible in records. Whether
described as luck, fortune, or privilege, these interviewees identified a
cross-disability solidarity with other disabled people who might not be
able to use these vital research spaces.

Some people I spoke to mentioned how archival research can
be inaccessible to some who may not know the standards or conven-
tions and may find the processes intimidating, which creates barriers
to access. Alida continued to speak about how she's accessed archival spaces, telling me, "I did take a few archival management classes
and museum management courses . . . and I think maybe that helped
because I already knew the rules. I knew the protocols going in, you
know, it was never a problem with putting on the gloves, et cetera."
Speaking with her and others, I, too, thought about my familiarity
navigating archives, having had mentors and educators teach me about
archival processes and accompany me on some of my first archival
visits, which were very intimidating.

Others talked about not only their familiarity with archival visits,
but also how certain statuses or academic affiliations enable access. Disabled queer activist and author Corbett OToole highlighted a barrier
she's experienced with archives: "I don't even know now that I could
get in because I don't have a [university] ID . . . how to find information that's maybe not technically behind a firewall but functionally is
behind a firewall." She expanded, thinking of other community schol-

ars without academic affiliations: "One of the arguments I make about community scholars is we're really, really dependent on free sources and free internet sources." Disabled lawyer Lili Siegel reflected similarly, "I think it's hard for me to say if I felt welcome because every archive that I've entered, I've entered with a certain amount of status: I've been a student or I'm a lawyer or a researcher or, you know?" She continued, "And I was seen as a person who had a right to be there. I was treated pretty well, because I was with [a professor]."

Some of the disabled people of color I spoke to also reflected on how their experiences of exclusion and access were complicated. Travis, for example, told me about a visit to an archive: "I remember being there and my first reaction was: *I feel like I don't belong here.* And at the time it was very much in terms of race because I was the only Asian person in the room."[6] These words point to important aspects of inaccessibility: how a lack of an affiliation with an academic institution or even familiarity with archival institutions and process can create barriers to access. These facets are all complicated by other axes of identity—archives can be predominately white spaces, or for those with class privilege and/or academic affiliation.

While highlighting the potential barriers for others in archives is incredibly important, Travis described how many disabled people just have more urgent and important priorities in their lives:

TRAVIS: Many people don't [use archives] because there are other sorts of priorities that they have to put first rather than getting access to the archive, which may or may not be the best way for them to do their research.

ME: I know!

6 This quote was previously published in the essay: " 'They Weren't Necessarily Designed with Lived Experiences of Disability in Mind.' "

TRAVIS: If it's a choice between being able to pay for a caretaker or to have an accessibility device that they need to do their research, their decisions have been made. I think about that being a choice all the time.

ME: I think that is a piece of this project that I don't always know what to do with as I'm interviewing disabled people who have some sort of privilege in order to be able to enter archival spaces. And so I think about the limits of that and people who don't have a lot of experience . . . because disabled people often are excluded from academic spaces. . . . I think accessibility . . . is also just a central piece of how I can do this work, how anybody can do this work, and I'm grappling with how complicated that is.

These conversations brought up many aspects of archival inaccessibility, but what felt meaningful was the ways that the people I spoke to described being aware of how other disabled people might not be able to—or even want to—access archives.

Lastly and importantly, such cross-disability solidarity and attention to inaccessibility prompted action. Drawing on his experiences of inaccessibility, Travis told me how he often asks, "How do we maximize accessibility for all students that come in here, many of whom have never been and are like me and feel alienated by it?"[7] Stefan described advocating for digital records for many disabled people: "So what I've found as a disabled researcher is that the move toward digitization has been important in ways that go beyond convenience and actually become very much about accessibility." And Michelle told me:

---

7 Part of this quote was published in an essay I wrote: " 'They Weren't Necessarily Designed with Lived Experiences of Disability in Mind.' "

"Being very disruptive in reading rooms has ensured that whenever I'm down [in the archives] with a researcher . . . that I always made sure to ask if they needed accommodations or to just offer accommodations before they even ask. Because I'm very conscious of the fact that I don't like it when disabled people have to ask for the accommodation. Because to me it puts a burden on somebody who's already burdened by so much that there should be regular accessibility things that are available to anybody. So I always offer people headphones; I always offer people a room where they could make more noise or turn things up if they need to without making them ask for it. Most places make you ask for it."

These words highlight how researchers' personal experiences of accessibility or inaccessibility and cross-disability awareness informs their advocacy for others.

Reflections

To me, these conversations highlight an emphasis on community, even without the immediate presence of others. Some interviewees, as described above, talked about their privileges in getting accommodations, remarking on how the materials they use might be inaccessible to others. Others spoke about how academic affiliations or familiarity with navigating archival systems gave them privilege, which may be difficult or impossible to navigate for other disabled people, and even further complicated for disabled people of color.

This theme of community echoes with some of Shayda Kafai's illustrations of crip kinship in the origins of disability justice, through honoring our ancestors and building toward collective liberation, and it also reminds me of Mia Mingus's description of access intimacy. I love how Mingus points out that:

> "Sometimes it can happen with complete strangers, disabled or not, or sometimes it can be built over years. . . . Access intimacy is also the intimacy I feel with many other disabled and sick people who have an automatic understanding of access needs out of our shared similar lived experience of the many different ways ableism manifests in our lives."

Building on this, these conversations expand the concept of access intimacy to think about the ways that it can occur even through other people's absence—and affirm the importance of this. Access intimacy can not only provide a way of making space for those who are with you and "get" your access needs, but can also offer an ethos of keeping disabled communities present, even when they are physically not. Highlighting the ways that others noted their own privilege in visiting an archive or talked about archival spaces that were accessible to them but not to other disabled people, this chapter tells a story of access intimacy and community in ways that might not be immediately apparent, might be more elusive, yet are core components of cross-disability solidarity and crip kinship.

Thinking about archival access intimacy feels important because of the value of accessing our own histories. As someone who spends a lot of time in archives, I often think about the profound impact of their many inaccessible and exclusionary aspects. In our conversation, white, disabled trans scholar Jessie Waggoner touched on how "the more disabled researchers you have . . . the more materials on disability that are going to come to light." I, too, think about the unique perspectives that disabled people bring to history. Corbett added, "I think that what disability history . . . and disability archival stuff offers are ways of thinking in new ways. To me just those little stories I told you—about very different ways of doing archival work and very different kinds of sources—can be really useful to think about and how communities *do* preserve history." What does it mean that so many disabled people don't get to see themselves in history or might not get to connect to our ancestors in archival records? While we have many ways of learning our histories outside of archives—storytelling, performances, writing, and art that document where we've been—how might being unable to access archives shape disabled people's sense of belonging in the present? And how might sharing time, space, and conversations with other disabled people contribute to changing the archival landscape?

The magic of archival access intimacy lies in how we are connected to one another through systems of power, access, history, and community accountability; and honoring this timeless connection is one example of how we might resist (or change) normative spaces like archives. Leah Lakshmi Piepzna-Samarasinha tells us, "One quality of disability justice culture is that it is simultaneously beautiful and practical," which for me is reflected in some of these conversations. As described above, some people I spoke to emphasized how their awareness of archival inaccessibility is also based in action—advocating for changes, thinking of those who might have different access needs. But access intimacy can be messy and imperfect. Piepzna-Samarasinha invites us to think about the assumptions of access intimacy, "that people are going to automatically get our disabled experiences, our access needs or realities, and it bites us in the ass." Instead, they highlight, it takes work, awareness, communication, learning, making mistakes, and growing to *practice* access intimacy. There's something so valuable in not only imagining others into a space, but also learning and building toward making that happen. These conversations feel like the beginning of thinking about the work disabled people do for one another to access our stories in archives and everywhere.

And although this theme of expanded access intimacy addresses *the past* (searching in archives to find disabled people in history) as well as *the present* (thinking of others while in an archive), it is also about dreaming about *the future*. This awareness of others—created through and because of their absence—often goes into access planning, the loving, complicated ways we embrace access friction, and the ways we dream others into spaces to be with community. So while the focus of the interviews was on archives, this theme, to me, doesn't feel specific or only applicable to archives. Mingus powerfully writes:

> "We have to work to transform the world, but we can only do that effectively if we can work to transform ourselves and our relationships with each other at the same time. Because our work depends on us and our relationships with each other. And if anyone is worth it, it is us and the generations of disabled children and people coming after us. We have a responsibility to leave them a legacy worth fighting for.

And Piepzna-Samarasinha foregrounds that "Intimacies of all kinds—our intimate relationship with ourselves and other people—that are held well are not static. . . . As disability justice and collective care practices continue to grow and bloom, I want us to be in a practice of curiosity, of continually learning who we and others are, as we change and evolve." So whether inside of archives or outside, maybe it's a little bit of crip time travel to keep at the fore all of the people who cannot access history and who we want to create space for, in the present and in the future.

Love Letter to London

Emilie L. Gossiaux

With my work, I am interested in exploring themes such as love, intimacy, and memories. Most recently, my work is inspired by the profound love I share with my Guide Dog, London—we have an interdependent relationship that crisscrosses between maternal, spousal, emotional, and practical—a bond that I believe transcends the traditional binary between pets and owners.

Since I've just started the process of applying for a new dog, I've been reflecting on the nine years London and I have been together. She is my first Guide Dog, and I get very emotional when I think about having to replace her. London was born in 2010, only two months before the traffic accident that caused my blindness. I know it's silly, but I sometimes imagine that we were meant for each other, and that's why she would one day grow up to become my Guide Dog, my muse, my partner in crime, and one of my closest companions.

I met London, an English Labrador retriever, on August 5, 2013, the day after my twenty-fourth birthday, and at the start of my final year at The Cooper Union School of Art. When my trainer brought her into the apartment, London made a rush toward me, excitedly sniffed me all over—my hands, legs, and feet. Then I listened to her nails click around my living room and kitchen as she smelled everything in her new surroundings.

For the next two weeks, we learned the route to school, the studio, on buses, and subways across town. Learning how to travel with London was so exhilarating. I walked faster, with more confidence. Through her harness, I followed her graceful movements as she effortlessly glided down the busy streets of New York City, dodging hordes of people and sidewalk furniture. Through the harness she could also feel my grip tighten as we neared a corner intersection. She waited, as I listened to the sounds of traffic for the right moment to signal for us to cross. As a blind and profoundly hearing impaired person, I was given a new sense of safety and autonomy, and I could tell that she also loved working with me. Our bond strengthened over time as we got to know each other's personalities, needs, and desires, through a communion built on mutual respect, care, and trust.

In 2017, London and I moved to New Haven for grad school. I wanted to leave my comfort zone, but it was also scary—being in a new city, with new people who didn't know me or how best to interact with me. There were some funny moments, like when London would stop in front of my classmates' studio doors that were left open. She would pop her head in to see what was up, look cute, and wag her tail at an unsuspecting classmate who'd either be working or eating lunch in their studio. This was a little awkward, but always made us laugh. There were other times when I missed out on socializing. At nights, my cohort would go to the dive bar on the corner to let off steam. In the beginning I tried it out, but socializing at a loud bar, with multiple conversations going on at the same time, was more exhausting than fun for me. Because of my hearing impairments, settings like that can often be traumatizing, making me feel more isolated than included.

I hoped to meet disabled students from other departments who might be going through similar things, but the school didn't make it easy for disabled students to connect with one another, nor did I meet any disabled professors or faculty members. If there was ever any sort of organization or event for students with disabilities, the school did not advertise them the way it did for other organizations and events. I thought I would finally meet people when I enrolled in a class focusing on disability studies but was so disheartened when I learned that there were only three other people in the class, and that I was the only one with a disability. Feeling like the only disabled person in the school was the hardest part. But later I would find myself in theoretical texts and memoirs by disabled writers, and be introduced to a Crip art community outside of school through Instagram and Zoom.

During these lonely times, London became my closest friend, and I began to see her as an integral part of my emotional and physical well-being. She was involved in my imagination—I started to make drawings of London that captured her personality, and our playful interactions with each other ("Arm, Tail, Butthole," "London Mounting the Couch," "Hand in Paw," and "Butterfly Kisses"). I also made drawings of London's exaggerated long and pink tongue licking feet, hands, and faces, depicting the sensual and intimate side of our relationship ("Tongue to Chin, Hand to Paw," "The Good Girl," and "On a Good Day You Can Feel My Love for You").

A group of these drawings are part of a traveling exhibition, Crip*, curated by Liza Sylvestre, at the Krannert Art Museum in Champaign, Illinois, and Gallery 400 in Chicago—a group show I was proud to be part of with many incredible artists—Shannon Finnegan, Carly Mandel, Berenice Olmedo, and Alison O'Daniel (to name a few).

Also included in Crip* is half of "Dancing with London" (2018), a sculptural installation of two Londons, both standing up on their hind legs, front paws extended out in front of their bodies as if leaping into the air, with their long tails extended in an elegant swoop behind them. The paws are sculpted with each individual toe and smooth glossy nail, with soft rubbery pads on the undersides for viewers to hold on to as they position themselves in front of a London. She has a serene look on her face, and her eyes are closed, like she's waiting for a kiss.

This sculpture is a monument to London, a memorial to our younger, and happier, times. Back in undergrad, London and I were both hardworking girls, but we also liked to get rowdy when we played together. At night when we got home from the studio, I'd plug my iPhone into the speakers, turn up the volume, and we'd dance around the apartment. London jumped up on her hind legs, placed her paws

"Dancing with London I." A photograph of a frontal view of one of the sculptures of the artist's dog. You can see that the dog's belly has nipples, and the nails of her claws are shiny and white. The expression on the dog's face is serene, her eyes are closed and she has a hint of a smile.

into my open hands, and I held her up as I swayed my hips side to side, while she wagged her tail to songs by Robyn, Le Tigre, or Grimes.

This piece was conceived when I was forced to think about London's mortality for the first time. In 2018 I took London to the vet for teeth cleaning, because she was bleeding in the mouth. The surgeon removed some teeth that were coming loose, along with tumor-like growths they found on her gums. The vet scraped them away to perform a biopsy, but warned me that it could potentially be mouth cancer. I would have to wait a week for the results. The thought of losing London was devastating.

Later that day, my partner, Kirby, picked us up from the veterinary clinic in New York City and drove us back home to New Haven. London slept in bed with us every night, and we gave her antibiotics and painkiller medication until the doctor called with the good news. The tumors were totally benign! It was just a very ugly case of gum disease. I've been brushing London's teeth ever since, so that it would never happen again. In 2021, I re-created "Dancing with London" for the Crip Time exhibit at the MMK in Frankfurt, where it was installed in the atrium with a mural, "Hand Palm," by Christine Sun Kim—an honor to show with her and many more Crip artists whom I love and admire.

"True Love Will Find You in the End" (2021), my commissioned piece for The Shed's Open Call, is another monument to my deep love for London, and a response to my feelings about the intersectionality of the experience of disabled people and nonhuman animals. During the start of the coronavirus pandemic, it was emotionally painful to read about the way disabled people were receiving less care, and were viewed as expendable, the way thousands of livestock animals were slaughtered because American meatpacking factories were shut down. I was reminded of the time someone I was close to dehumanized me by comparing me to a dog, needing to be walked and cared for by

"Crip Time, Dancing with London." A bird's-eye view of a gallery space, with a sculptural installation of "Dancing with London." The black-and-white mural "Hand Palm" by Christine Sun Kim is painted on the wall.

someone every day because of my disability. I thought of all the times I had to face discrimination for traveling with a dog, being denied access into restaurants, taxis, and shops, which is always so infuriating. And I was reminded of the one day I overheard my neighbor talking into her phone, calling me "the blind girl with the dog," when I only needed to take the elevator one floor down. She was annoyed that I had taken up so much time and space in the elevator with London, which made me wonder if this was how everyone in the building thought of me—a nuisance.

With "True Love" I wanted to dismantle the hierarchy between nondisabled and disabled people, as well as the hierarchy between humans and animals. The sculptures meld my human form with London's as a way to embrace the beautiful animal side of myself, and when I think of London and myself together, we become a whole, a super-being.

Crip Ecologies
Complicate the Conversation to Reclaim Power

Naomi Ortiz

Crip ecologies describe the messy, diverse, and profoundly beautiful ecosystems that exist for disabled people. It is impossible to fit ourselves to a mold to which nondisabled people adhere, which allows capitalism (making money and paying money to live) to flourish, borders to be maintained, and promotes uniform solutions to address some of our most pressing and urgent problems like climate change.

Crip ecologies are living, breathing spaces of conflict and creativity.

As a disabled person of color (POC), my body, needs, and perspective do not have a home in conventional responses to climate change. Dismantling systems that were built up over centuries to increase access to the resources I rely on for food, shelter, and connection is not the strategy I choose. When the task to address the climate crisis means taking apart multilayered industrial, governmental, and care systems that I rely on to provide for every necessity, then the work feels incomprehensible. Where is safety in this time? Is it in the ways I find to shore up my own security? Is it in voting and giving my proxy to corporations to make the changes needed?

I'm not sure.

What I do know is what a pursuit of safety is not. It is not going zero waste. To drink, I need a plastic cup or a straw. I can't reuse bandages or needles. My hand does not pinch four fingers to thumb, and my elbow cannot bend in order to use a menstrual cup. I bleed too fast, too heavily for cloth pads. Waste equals function. I need equity instead of equality. I need to utilize single-use products to live.

Safety is not found in growing my own food. I have to make choices about how I use my energy. Every day, there is a finite amount. Do I use that energy to water and tend the soil, or do I use that energy to feed and clean myself? As a disabled person, self-sufficiency is never viable for survival.

My body is the oldest story in the world. Part broken, part brilliant, all nuance, disability offers a layer of perspective that is unique and profound. Knowledge of disability experience is political, social, sexual, ancestral. To name something is to claim knowledge. Disability poetics reclaims the power of understanding our culture(s) and our truths. It has the ability to build bridges between communities and support mutual liberation. It is an essential tool to pry loose and shake out the vulnerabilities and possibilities that we all confront with climate change.

*   *   *

As a child growing up amid conflict within my home and neighborhood, I came across a book containing a poem about a dragon who was afraid of everything and a young girl who helped the dragon to become courageous. I learned poems could help when I felt afraid.

Poetry became a companion. As a teenager, poetry became the way I created space between wounds.

Then I met my friend Marlin D. Thomas. We met at a youth disability conference and bonded over disability activism. One evening we were sitting at a table in a cavernous ballroom, listening to speakers, when this elderly white man rolled onstage with a cowboy hat. An Asian woman stood next to him holding a microphone so we could hear him speak. The first words out of his mouth were "I love you." Glancing around at all the teenagers and twentysomethings, I saw that I was not the only one who immediately started squirming in their chair. Then, leaning closer to the microphone, he allowed a dramatic pause before again saying, "I LOVE YOU!" As the man continued his speech, I looked over at Marlin, who sat enraptured with a goofy grin on his face. I had never seen a grown person tell a crowd of people "I love you," and I was ready to bolt, but seeing the expression on Marlin's face made me pause and listen. The man talked about the need to redefine how we saw ourselves and one another. That we were powerful and had a responsibility. When the speech ended, I leaned over to ask Marlin who the man was, but Marlin was already maneuvering around the table in his powerchair, headed to meet the man as he came offstage. The speaker was Justin Dart Jr., and the woman with him was his wife and partner in activism, Yoshiko Dart. Together, they had traveled to all fifty states, collecting testimony in partnership with local activists. This testimony helped convince the United States Congress to pass the Americans with Disabilities Act. Marlin showed me how to pay attention and collect courage from living disability history.

As our friendship grew, Marlin and I traveled across the country to visit each other. We would bring suitcases full of old notebooks to read in the few hours of privacy between personal assistants supporting

Marlin with day-to-day life. He was the first person I became really close to who was also a person of color, disabled, and a poet.

As we shared our writing and read works by other poets, I realized that what I connected to about poetry was not form, style, or rhythm. Rather, I connected to poems whose words vibrated on my skin or in my heart—all the diverse ways people capture truth.

In addition to poetry and activism, Marlin and I also shared a similar experience in our cultural communities—disability being shoved aside and disappeared, or focused on as the sole area of attention. As artists, it was tough to access performance or gallery spaces. Because of physical barriers, but also because we weren't seen as people who could contribute culturally—as people who have something to say about our ancestors, place, or histories.

When Marlin and I would talk—especially on days when something terrible had happened, hearts were broken, or violence was experienced—after rehashing the details, Marlin would inevitably say, "We gotta put it in our poetry." I learned poetry is a way to witness. One afternoon I was working at my consultant gig, listening to music, dancing around in my chair, having fun in the ways we encouraged each other to, when I got the call that Marlin had suddenly died. On that day, my life changed forever. I have a poem about it.

Marlin helped me believe that my work is worth sharing, but in artistic spaces, I continually confront ableism. Recently, at an online Latinx writing conference, there were no options for access needs, and my questions and feedback were ignored. At poetry open mics, I am unable to get to the stage or even to the sign-up sheet. Often I am not invited by peers, friends, or family to cultural events because they know I am disabled. When I am invited, I am on my own to figure out how to get in (let alone find out if there will be a restroom I can use). If I cannot get in, no one identifies that I, or disabled people in general, aren't there. That we are missing from the community gathered at the table. After facing such intense inaccessibility in artistic spaces, places that are supposed to be grounded in creativity, how do I find accessibility within the environmental movement's response to the climate crisis?

Similar to how I feel in artistic spaces, I feel like a lost soul wandering around the communities and discourse of the environmental movements, shaking my jangly earrings, whispering, "Hello," into the wind, my ghostly presence one they cannot quite make out. Yet, they use language in which I recognize my reflection. *Mining scars cripple and deform the earth. People are blind to the cost. Pollution spreads like a cancer.* Disabled bodies are thrust like a dam to make people stop and pay attention. Using the fear of my body and other disabled people's bodies as a metaphor for environmental destruction is just using fear to incite fear.

Fear of disability is transferred and leveraged as a cautionary tale, to stop us from embracing our environments. Why incite more fear? Does fear create agency? The thing is, fear does not define my relationship to my disabled body. Discrimination? Fewer options? Yes. Making do with less? Making hard choices? Yes. But I have an intimate awareness of my needs. I know what minimums I can live on.

Here it is—we now live in a disabled world. Earth has been forever altered. Disability is not fair. Some of us live shorter lives. Some of us do not make it. Some of us live far better and longer than anyone would have predicted. There is not a road map for change, but change is happening.

In the Sonoran Desert, where I live, the palo verde tree has green bark in order to absorb sunlight, so it is free to shed its tiny leaves during long periods of drought. Vulnerability is the best teacher of adaptation. Disabled people know how to adapt to a world that is ever changing without considering us.

I, too, want to save ecosystems. I believe the animals and plants deserve to live. Yet if disability has taught me anything, it is that there is much I do not control. Very little, in fact. But choices always matter. Disability is a life of inhabiting contradiction and venturing into vulnerable unpredictability.

One of the foundational elements of ableism is a fear of vulnerability, a desire to push away and ignore what reminds us of helplessness. Disabled and nondisabled people alike are taught this in our families, communities, and institutions. This desire to push away leads to judgment, exclusion, and oppression. Forced into competition with each other for scarce resources, helplessness can be equated with powerlessness.

What clues toward resilience and creativity are my other cultural communities missing? Disability poetics is how disability gets politically translated into everyday life. The hundreds of ways we have to ask for help—whether we want to or not—and the ways we find to reciprocate or to help others. The humor at some random stranger throwing change in our half-filled coffee cups. Having to plan for everything. And then having a backup plan for each plan. The brutal experience of having little pieces of your humanity splintered away as you try to wedge yourself into a system that is supposed to help you survive. How Crip sex takes all the creativity earned by having to function in oppressive and inaccessible environments (having uncomfortable and awkward conversations, explorations of adaptive equipment, explaining to another person exactly what you want done to your body) and puts it to an amazing use. How we are brave only because we cannot back down from other people's fear of vulnerability. As I learn from Crip art, I think about how my other communities could gain so much wisdom from disability culture.

If one is afraid of being vulnerable, how does one adapt? Disabled people know that living into the future means learning to ask for help, and being patient, flexible, and insistent. To provide help is to be in a place of having resources, time, or energy to share. To give respectful help is a process in becoming aware of our own capacity in the moment. It takes practice to know providing help is not always convenient *and* boundaries can also exist. Grappling with interdependence necessitates slowing down, listening, disappointing each other, and mending.

I have touched the edges of interdependence. I know how underdeveloped and limited people's understanding of interdependence is. Yet climate change isn't an "I" situation. As a single person against the proposal of the world's largest copper mine or the housing developments that keep getting constructed despite the lack of groundwater, I can only do so much. Relying on one another, however, builds power.

As a disabled mestize growing up in the borderlands, poetry serves as a way to reclaim my cultural relevancy. To share my understanding of driving weekly through one of the many border-patrol checkpoints set up near where I live, miles from the international line, or witnessing climate change's effect on the desert ecosystem. My visual art, writing, the songs I sing to the sky are all ways to glean what matters from my lived experience. These understandings are intersectional. They are disability culture experiences and ethnic cultural experiences.

What does it mean to be a disabled mestize cultural worker? I am a bruja when I write my truth down on paper, casting spells of transformation, even if it's just coaxing a different perspective on the sunlight illuminating cactus thorns next to the patch of pavement outside my door. In capturing a moment, a feeling, I am child, elder, ancestor. I render safety by bracing against place, maybe found on the edge of a parking lot between picnic table and wild, helping me to inhabit spaciousness. This allows my arms, legs, feet, torso to remember what body integrity feels like outside the constriction of rooms where medical trauma or other harm has occurred. Describing how I know family through plantas and ancestors is my own mending. It is sharing a model of restoration that transcends individual relationships.

A legacy I carry from my friendship with Marlin is this: I know in my bones that art and writing by disabled people of color is valuable. Living in multiple worlds at once, we explore the hidden tunnels between our disability and POC associations, and we grapple with the consistently rotating reasons given for our exclusion. There is power claimed by naming these layers. Our work unearths links, sometimes even between contradictory realities, which can deepen relationships between our communities. Living within contradictions facilitates a kind of problem-solving that is inclusive, a means of tackling problems in which diversity and an expectation of difference is valued. This provides support and structure to our collective journey toward intersectional liberation and facing climate catastrophe.

Climate change is a "we" situation. We have hard choices to make. Ecosystems that include disabled people consider accessibility and interdependence in relationship to everything. Crip ecosystems flourish in a state of creativity.

They ask: What interventions can support continued life? How can they be sustained? By whom? Where do we need to just accept the altered state? How do we adapt? Ask for help? How can disability poetics help us touch what is scary? Confront our own fears of vulnerability? How do we prepare not just for suffering but for sharing and innovation?

These questions are not just full of agency and self-determination; they are what hope looks like now.

Top Secret Club Abjection

Ashna Ali

It's H who starts me on the teas, delivers four fragrant boxes
she mixed herself, ingredients on a handmade label.
C I find on Instagram talking about herbalism practice,
how she treats her own body. She makes me videos
about my limbs while holding her baby, feeding her dog.
I find N through P, who says hey, I think N might have doctors
who believe non-men when y'all talk. We make a list with
    reviews,
a private Yelp for queer crips and kin. I find the NAIPO
    oCuddle
through B, who uses it before bed to not ask too much
of a massage therapist partner. I buy it as a gift for at least three
of the club, recommend it to everyone who has enough money
this month. We use it together on the phone, the buzzing
and moaning from each of our homes confusing, we hope,

to whomever might be surveilling. When I start the new drug,
two of the club tell me not to be surprised when I can't eat,
when there's a zap between my ears, when joy feels
just as far as rage, which, combined, feel like nothing.
Though we live in different states, we coordinate days
to say fuck it, do whatever we like, have one glass of wine
too many, eat everything. We cackle and cry to one another
from wheelchair, bathtub, toilet seat, shower stool,
somewhere on the floor. The club says plans are not plans
unless we've measured capacity, found whatever honesty
we have left between the sofa cushions. The club says hey,
I've got enough Valium for two, today. The club isn't afraid
of blood, vomit, piss, shit, pills, passing money around.
Tomorrow we get up, clothe ourselves in health,
a workplace costume because everyone knows
that everyone would rather be fooled.

PART IV

Everything and Everywhere

an incantation.

Aimi Hamraie

The following incantation was written by Aimi Hamraie and has been delivered as a #CripRitual at the Critical Design Lab's Remote Access parties, beginning with a 2020 "Witches and Glitches" event at the Allied Media Conference.

We welcome you to the crip ritual of
Remote Access,
a way to celebrate and be together that emerges from crip
culture.

We'll start by creating a container for our party by imagining
our spaces glowing with pink and purple light.

Imagine your space as a bright dot
on a map
of the night sky.

When we zoom out, your bright dot appears
scattered across a landscape of other dots, with lines connecting
    them until multiple concentric circles of purple and pink light
    form.

They shimmer.

And within that shimmering, we charge up our circles with
    elements of crip power.

We call in the power of
Crip Access.
crip as refusing normalcy.

Access as the flow of radical love and hospitality.

Crip access as the element of facilitating belonging together
    for all of us and
        refusing
to leave any of us behind.

Crip access as flexible, ingenious, creative,
    and world-changing.

We call in the power of
Crip Rage.

Crip rage as noncompliance, the fire of crip protest, the
    smash of sledgehammer against sidewalk, of body against
    inaccessible building.

We call in the power of
Crip Humor.

Crip humor as irreverent, taboo, biting, political.
Crip humor as turning the gaze back onto Ableds.
Crip humor as a cornerstone of crip ritual.

We call in the power of
Crip Slowness.
Crip slowness as valuable methodology and technology. Crip
   slowness as focusing away from ableist futures toward the
   pleasures
      and value of the present.
Crip slowness as a way to move and
                     a way to
know.

We call in the power of
Crip Pleasure.

Crip pleasure as the joys emerging only from crip culture.

Access intimacies, shared skills and stories, accessible
   potlucks, mutual aid networks, extended kinships, and
   access as love.

The Leg Chapter

Ashley Shew

"Prosthetics are so advanced now," a nondisabled stranger tells me in passing.

"Mine is held on with Velcro," I reply pleasantly, to give them a splash of real talk, but also they aren't listening and don't care. They already have their beliefs set.

The promise of prosthetics is one of restoration of ability, and this narrative leaves little room for reality.

The promise of prosthetics is a rote call-and-response for those looking to inject a little technological optimism into their daily lives, to believe in the power of technology and restoration, and the idea that problems are solved tidy-like. They also then don't have to worry about disability, or disabled people, or about building that ramp that they are already thirty-two years late installing.

The promise of prosthetics is an ending of disability, but that's a promise from people who don't know disabled people or disabled communities. Disability is longstanding and not going away—the future will give us new ways to be or become disabled. New viruses, new patterns of animal migration and disease thanks to climate change, new weather patterns, hopefully new ideas of work and of good bodies, too.

My body is good.

I love Velcro. I like the sound it makes. I like how well it works with secure fit and adjustability. With my last leg, I used to adjust my Velcros a lot more. I used to have three Velcros, now I have two. Carefully cut, melted, and then sewn with the giant sewing machine in my prosthetist's lab by his son, who is also his technician. My Velcros are mine only, perfect for my leg.

Imperfect, too.

I used to have white Velcros and a white upper on my prosthesis, but they got skanky and discolored from the darker-wash jeans I prefer, and every little fiber they pick up shows—not that I'm hiking my pants up every day to show off my Velcros, so it didn't matter that much. I have an old-style prosthesis, almost like a Hanger leg[1] for those familiar with disability design. My amputation is very fancy. Some people like me still use lacers instead of Velcro, and others are using the snappy adjusties you have on skis now, too. High tech.

I know that there are at least some people who have flipped to "the leg chapter" to read about the intimate relationship I have with my prosthesis as a body part, or, worse, for me to tell you a tale about getting jiggy[2] with my prosthetic leg on, or off. What do I do with this equipment if I want to have sex? What's the plan for the leg?

But that's boring. And you've read enough idealized tales where

---

1 Imagine a classic historical post–Civil War old-timey leg with a below-knee socket and joints on either side of the knee and an upper leather portion around the thigh that laces up to hold the leg on securely.

2 Do people still use "getting jiggy" as a euphemism for sex?

bodies sing electric, where man is one with machine, where flesh is made whole again, and where people can then get freaky with the manic pixie cyborg electric-sheep-dream girl.[3]

The disability intimacy I want to address is about when prosthetics are a shield preventing intimacy, when the narratives we have about prostheses put real-life prosthetized people in a pickle. Prosthetics are a shield to other people's ideas of intimacy that I do not share with them—those who gawk and give unwanted attention, who smirkingly or even sincerely ask things like "leg on or leg off?" My legs are not an invitation to your education, or your desire.

There is no good way to be an amputee because of all the stories and expectations and images that are out there about us, and the questions and information people think they are entitled to through that media, too. The promise of prosthetics is a curse.

Prosthetics are a defense.

Some amputees talk about how they put their leg on first thing and take it off last thing *and don't want to be seen without their leg on.* They will literally work through terrible blisters, rashes, and pain to avoid going legless, or be seen outside their homes with any assistive devices other than prostheses.

The promise of prosthetics has meant for them that they need to *appear* as close to nondisabled as possible. To make themselves invulnerable to *other* disability narratives that may haunt their existence—of helplessness or need, of shame and pity, and even of just deserts: that they are not trying hard enough to "overcome."

Instead, the promise of prosthetics—that they re-enable us and

---

3   "Not a girl," says Janet from *The Good Place.*

make us whole again—requires our constant work to be "good crips," those who confirm the power of technology over disability.

I'm not against prosthetics; I'm wearing one, aren't I? We amputees are (or some of us are) quite lucky for the technologies we do have, and the choices about those technologies. I love my leg and my perfect Velcros. Access is key: we should be able to get different types of technologies to try out, and then also afford.

But I also want to be able to take off my leg without fear that people will reconsider their judgments about my capability and competence, my status as re-enabled and whole.

You see, if we crips don't buy into prosthetics as redemption, they won't either, and we'll go back to being seen as incompetent and incomplete. Broken.

There is actually research about perceptions of people with bionics (prosthetic limbs, retinal implants, exoskeletons). In a paper called "Disabled or Cyborg?" (a false dilemma), researchers share their conclusion from an online study that asked people their impressions of various groups. They gathered that:

> People with physical disabilities who wear bionic prostheses . . . are perceived as more competent than people with physical disabilities in general [but both groups still less competent than nondisabled people] . . . So-called cyborgs are perceived as much colder than able-bodied individuals [and others with physical disabilities without bionics]. . . .[4]

---

4 See Bertolt Meyer and Frank Asbrock, "Disabled or Cyborg? How Bionics Affect Stereotypes Toward People with Physical Disabilities," *Frontiers in Psychology* vol. 9, November 20, 2018 (Chemnitz University of Technology): https://www .frontiersin.org/articles/10.3389/fpsyg.2018.02251/full. There is a lot to unpack about this study and the categories used, but that goes beyond the scope of this essay!

The fact is that puzzling out how to do things differently can offer a space of personal creativity and new surprise and pleasure in the mundane tasks. But I only hear those stories in disability groups (and not just amputee groups), and then only rarely and sometimes abashedly. Joy is not what we're *supposed* to feel or what we're supposed to share to get "peer support." These crip intimacies include not a triumph over something, but the sharing of everyday tricks and ways we have, in sharing the creativity of our embodiments with and for one another.

Prosthetists and physical therapists get praised for their humanitarian work. News stories pump up engineers working on better prosthetic feet or hands. But I really like Fred's Legs: an amputee and his spouse sell stretchy prosthetic socket covers out of stretchy fabrics, sewn on a home machine with some small customization possible. This is very cheap and easy tech, and they ship all over. I don't need a prescription to order from Fred. I don't need to leave my home. The things we do, get, and learn, and even sometimes buy from each other are never on the nightly news. They can't see *us* in our making and our sharing, with joy and some frustration and community, too; they want too much for us to be tragedy so the abled can be the heroes, can save us. *The promise of prosthetics is that a humanitarian engineering team takes over.*

Prosthetic devices make it so that we may pass for a time as less disabled (or at least stave off being recognized as disabled under some circumstances)—this includes cases of breast prostheses and cosmetic prosthetic covers for arms and legs. With my leg, I look ambulatory, though I might look disabled with a limp or cane. I look *less disabled* to other people; I am no different, but different perceptions get placed upon me. People can forget for a time that I am disabled.

Showing up wearing my prosthesis means I get routed to a long staircase. (No thank you.)

Passing is its own burden: to avoid being fully seen, but also to avoid being discounted. Because disabled people are discounted. "Disabled or Cyborg?" Best to stick to the side where you are judged as cold but competent.

Of course, it's a luxury many non-prosthetized disabled people don't enjoy: to be able to convince others of not-quite-the-truth, playing on their expectations.

Better to pass sometimes, and deliberate carefully about *disclosure*:

- When and to whom you reveal yourself (and whether they will treat you differently after that disclosure),
- Where your need for accommodation or access is so great that you have to disclose (and whether what you then encounter is retaliation for being disabled),
- How to best explain your body and what this explanation will produce in those around you (e.g., pity, understanding, questions about your ability to live/laugh/love and work).

I do this, too—ask myself about what I reveal as a hard-of-hearing, chemo-brained amputee with Crohn's and tinnitus—where disclosure is important and not. Rarely am I handing out the list, and recipients wouldn't know what to do with the list anyway.

The promise of prosthetics to this cyborg is that I can push people away who would do me damage.

There is a list of people I try to appear as abled as possible to. People who would weaponize any perceived incompetence against me. People who would swoop down in helper mode to make me doubt myself. People who would point out perceived faults to my children or my colleagues. People who would cry about me, even though I have no tears for me. People who have said enough nonsense about other disabled people that they cannot be trusted.

A couple shares a story about a friend who became "a vegetable," but they just mean quadriplegic. He got a spinal cord injury from an accident. They visited him at his home once about six months after his accident, judged him to be too sad, and never visited their once-friend again.

So awkward to watch people tell a story with no self-reflection or shame, recognizing that they would just as soon turn away from you—judge you and your life "too sad" from a single visit.

And perhaps tell my partner he should leave me, and take our kids. His leaving would be typical of the experience of a woman who acquires a disability: our partners are statistically much more likely to leave. And parents with disabilities are at much higher risk of having their children taken away.

They have told a short anecdote from decades ago, and they have opened up my mind to a series of horrors that would undo the life I know and remove the support I have.

They tell this story in passing, and so I pass as hard as I can.

I keep my leg on all day when they visit, on my feet and busy working, and every visit after. There are physical consequences to appearing this way, trying to put on the ruse that I am not "really disabled," or at least not in the way they would find sad.

I get called an inspiration, and I know the vast separation between their experience of me and my actual experience. I want to scream, but can't have them suspect mental infirmity in addition to my physical invalidity.

I want no intimacy with them. I will choke down an Advil, smooth on extra Adaptskin 50, and be absolutely exhausted trying to keep up the ruse that I don't need to sit down, don't need to slow down.

The promise of prosthetics goes:

Gaslight (prosthetics are so advanced now),
    Gatekeep (you certainly aren't like those other disabled people),
        Girlboss (you can do it all, forsake your bodymind).

The promise of prosthetics is that I can betray my disabled brethren and fuel the ableist narratives that feature bodies like mine. The promise of prosthetics means that I can pretend for a while and hide my vulnerability away—people will believe me "re-enabled" if I appear just so, play into their expectations about prosthetics. "Wow," they say. "Prosthetics really are so advanced; you get around great on that thing."

First of All, I Love You

Dr. Syrus Marcus Ware

I've been working on a large-scale drawing project since 2014 called the Activist Portrait Series—a study exploring Black activist culture and disabled, Deaf, and Mad Black communities. Graphite on paper drawings six feet wide and twelve feet tall, these large-scale works are an act of reverence and love—celebrating activists who are making change in our communities. I get to draw every line on their faces, every curve of their cheeks. I get to study their beautiful beings and translate this onto the page to encourage dialogue and discussion—inspiring the viewer to feel a connection to the portrait sitter and care for their survival. Artistic practice can help us inspire irresistible revolutions, as Toni Cade Bambara encouraged us to do in 1982. As artists from the margins, we get to make work that sparks catalytic change in our systems. I've been asking all of the people that I've drawn, every activist, to describe for me what it feels like to fall in love. I ask this question because of how closely linked activism is to love and to intimacy. Che

This portrait was drawn during the height of the BLM uprisings, as part of an Activist Portrait Series to celebrate and honor activists for their labor and organizing. QueenTite Opaleke is a disability justice activist and cofounder of Prosthetics For Foreign Donation.

Photo credit: Dr. Syrus Marcus Ware. Activist Portrait Series: *Portrait of QueenTite Opaleke*, 12 × 6 ft., graphite on paper, 2015.

Guevara reminded us that all revolutions must be rooted in love. So our irresistible revolutions must be loving ones.

Can you ever really pinpoint the exact moment you fall in love? I'm a Taurus femme, and love is big in my life. I have been thinking about love as we find ourselves at the precipice of a new world. The pandemic and the uprisings of 2020 have propelled our system into a chaotic state, and in this period of release on the panarchy cycle of adaptive change we are able to plant new seeds of possibility. So, what kind of future are we building toward together? As we start to move forward in this pandemic and dream of a future time when we finally come out of it, I wonder what kind of world we want to emerge into? I want a world that is rooted in disability justice, interdependence, mutual aid, collective care, and, above all else, love.

One of my longest loves has been activism, but it's hard to pinpoint when I first fell in love with organizing. If I had to pin it down, I would have to say that I fell in love with activism sometime in the frantic years between 1997 and 2003. We were on the ground doing abolition work, trans justice work in Tkaronto (the Mohawk word referring to the city known as Toronto), working to support MOVE and Mumia Abu-Jamal, organizing around Mad and disability justice. We organized Saturday Mumia rallies at the US Consulate, made quarterly trips down to Philadelphia to support MOVE; we organized to create trans sexual health resources and to get gender-affirming care relisted in our provincial health coverage. We launched a study of gay, bi, and queer trans men and their partners and held educational sex parties for trans guys at the local trans bar in Tkaronto. We pushed for disability justice and Mad justice and questioned the white supremacy present even within our organizing. We made road trips down to the Philadelphia Trans Wellness Conference and the Allied Media Conference, and we attended the Mad Bed Races in the city on Mad Pride Days. We gathered every year to listen to Faith Nolan, an AfroIndigenous singer-songwriter and longtime abolitionist, and Rosina Kazi, a Bengali abolitionist, perform their latest music every year on Prisoners' Justice Day, chanting and singing so loudly that we were sure the folks inside the prison could hear us and know that we were out there fighting for them for another year. *So* much was alive in these years of transition—from one century to another—from a generation to the next.

What sparks our feelings of love? For me, it was finding community, kinship, and love through organizing. I remember an antipoverty march that was to be a full-day affair beginning at six a.m. at city hall in Tkaronto and spreading into the night with marches and rallies in various locations downtown throughout the day. I'd spent the night before the march at my lover's house. We were baby queers, though I'd been out since 1993. She wasn't very out, and our courtship was complex but beautiful. We had spent much of the night prepping for the rallies and then trying to get a good night's sleep before the early-morning call. We got up and it was still dark. We taxied across Harbord Street down to city hall. There were throngs of people and a relatively elaborate hot breakfast being served by Food Not Bombs or a sister group. We gathered in clusters, finding people we knew and reconnecting after a long winter. And then, when the sun was starting to peak above the towers peppered across Tkaronto's downtown core, we marched. We marched in a snaking pattern through the streets, chanting, drumming, breathing in the heart of the city, crying out, "Whose Streets? Our Streets!" and believing that change was possible. After the first march, I invited a bunch of the activists back to my tiny apartment on Sullivan Street. Together a pile of ten cold and damp activists huddled on my couch, on the floor, and in my bed as we rested before the next part of the demonstration. Somewhere in that pile were two future lovers—people I met that day and continue to love today, our lives entwined after twenty-plus years of organizing. I fell in love with activism that day—the radical potentials of it, but also the kinship models it offered—new ways of being in relation to each other across difference and distance.

I think about another moment in 2006. We had organized a three-day Prisoners' Justice Film Festival and invited Climbing PoeTree to come and present their S.T.I.T.C.H.E.D. project, a textile work exploring messages of prisoners' justice and abolition created inside and outside of prison walls. As Alixa and Naima recited poetry, we all got busy crafting and creating our messages of hope and possibility on our squares to be quilted into the expansive strips of curtain panels filled with messages. I felt love in the room. We were surrounded by ex-prisoners, Mad people, queer and trans people—we were dreaming into abolition and the idea that these messages were connecting inside and outside of prison walls at a time when the system was desperately trying to keep us apart.

Fast-forward ten years and it's Pride Sunday in June 2016; I'm standing in the hot sun in the middle of College and Yonge Streets in Tkaronto. BLM has just stopped the parade to ask for more support and care for Black, queer, trans, Deaf, and disabled people at the festival, and requested the removal of the police roadshow from the parade. I held the microphone while rainbow-colored smoke bombs went off to my left and right and told stories of activism: stories about Blockorama, the Black pride stage, the longest-running and best-attended stage at the Pride festival, and about the Black Coalition for AIDS Prevention, an HIV/AIDS service organization serving Black communities since the early '90s. I was harassed. Water bottles were thrown at me and bottle caps whipped at me as I spoke about this incredible activism, prompting Janaya Khan to stop me and announce on their mic that Tkaronto's "racism was showing" before I continued. This moment inspires many feelings for me, but the biggest one is love, for I am connected through space and time to the same moment in 2017, at the Pride parade, where we marched with banners that read MAY WE NEVER AGAIN NEED TO ASK YOU NOT TO CELEBRATE OUR TORTURERS and MAY WE NEVER AGAIN NEED TO REMIND YOU THAT WE TOO ARE QUEER. And in this moment, marching funerary style with our placards, something entirely different happened. People clapped. Cheered, celebrated, and thanked us for our efforts to make Pride safer for all of us. So much had happened in a year, on-the-ground organizing and work with community to bring the membership on board, and attempts to unpack the rampant white supremacy in the white queer community in Tkaronto. I think of these two moments at once, a palimpsest, and hold their experiences in relation to each

This image was taken by artist Michele Pearson Clarke for BLMC in the second intervention at Pride Toronto lead by BLM. Focused on justice and the right to exist as Black queer and trans people, activists marched funerary style down the parade route with signs that read, MAY WE NEVER AGAIN HAVE TO REMIND YOU THAT WE BUILT THIS and MAY WE NEVER AGAIN HAVE TO REMIND YOU THAT WE TOO ARE QUEER and MAY WE NEVER AGAIN HAVE TO REMIND YOU NOT TO CELEBRATE OUR TORTURERS. Photo credit: Black Lives Matter Canada. Pride March 2017. Digital photograph.

other—being shunned for sticking up for Black people and then being celebrated for this labor, as it serves all of humanity. Profoundly, a part of me will always be on that road in that parade. It is a moment forever etched in my mind.

Much of what's happened over the past three decades is a blur of BIPOC DJ nights organized by activists, winding snake marches for Take Back the Night, Take Back the Streets, the trans community (sanctioned and not), sometimes diverging, chants made up on the bus to the FTAA (Free Trade Area of the Americas) protests in Quebec City in 2001; our abolitionist chants honed on the streets of the G20 protests in Tkaronto in 2010. It's a blur of textile scraps and banners made at dawn before the rally, borrowing megaphones from the local student union, making placards, figuring out where to store the stuff after the rally, food donations, gift cards for coffee places donated while we occupied police headquarters. It's a cacophony of banners unfurled and sealing off intersections, press conferences in the middle of Yonge and Dundas Streets at rush hour, and SIU (Special Investigation Unit) branches that couldn't open for the day when we'd shut down their parking lots. It's a beautiful blur of textures, memories, songs, and ideas spanning thirty years of organizing.

My last memory of falling in love with activism is from 1999, amid Y2K fears and global panic that the world might be ending. We had organized a student rally and march about tuition freezes and the creation of a free university through local academia. I was marching with a team from the Centre for Women and Trans People at the University of Toronto. We were holding our placards, laughing and walking down the street. Suddenly a reporter approached and asked us if he could snap our picture. We beamed into the camera, telling him absolutely, "No no no." He said, "Stop smiling. This is activism. It's serious." Mansplaining aside, this sentiment was the root of so many of our problems. Yes, activism was a serious pastime, but it was also joyous, life-giving work. I met my beloveds through activism, I fell in love with myself more deeply through what I learned from activism, and I built community collectively through activist efforts. I am so thankful for this life of an activist.

I'm reminded of Assata Shakur's missive from 1977 in which she says, "We can win, we will win our liberation." But strikingly, she starts this message with love, beginning with, "Uhuru, Sisters and brothers, the first thing I want to say to you is that I love you, and the second thing is that we can win."

To the three decades of organizing I've had the privilege to do here in northern Turtle Island, to all of the activists that I've gotten to work with, to my community for whom I do this work, to all of you I want to say that I, too, love you. And I want us to get free. Together.

Profoundly Together

The Redwoods

Hi, we're the Redwoods. We are many people living in one body, sharing a life together.

We identify as plural. *Plurality* is a community-generated term to describe being two or more people, parts, alters, identities, or consciousnesses in one body. We Redwoods prefer *people*; it corrects a tendency to reduce expansive individual members to the "sad one," the "happy part" or the "trauma-holding alter." Inhabitants of the Redwoods figured out there was more than one person here over ten years ago. We Redwoods talk to each other, inside and out loud. We take care of each other. People like us appear to be a timeless dimension of human diversity.

You may correctly guess an overlap with dissociative identity disorder (DID), or an earlier formulation, multiple personality disorder (MPD). Some plurals have the diagnosis of other specified dissociative disorder (OSDD). Some sharing a body don't use the term plural and prefer *multiple* (a term we used for years) or *person with [diagnosis]*. Most are in the buckets of unaware, isolated, misdiagnosed, lacking access to diagnosis, or not interested in seeking one. You don't need to fit any diagnosis to be plural, you just need to be more than one. We first received a DID diagnosis in 2012, but it's not the whole of our plural identity.

The diagnoses around this experience are double-edged swords: a form of institutional recognition for many, yet full of the bias of a society that largely rejects us. Our revelation of discovery gave way to stigma whiplash as we encountered toxicity in research and clinical treatment. Clinical terms gave us something to look up online and find readings, therapists, and even conferences, and yet the paternalism of psychiatry permeated everywhere. These paradigms were designed by people who don't share our experience, and who pressure plural professionals among them to stay silent and "objective." They contend being plural at all is wrong, that we are broken or perhaps selfish trick-sters, and then justify these views with conjecture or outdated research. That same research often has tiny sample sizes, sometimes carried out nonconsensually in psychiatric wards decades ago. Furthermore, many plurals don't fit, or stop fitting, the criteria for diagnosis yet remain many in one body.

Obtaining these flawed diagnoses can be costly and take years. Finding and sustaining competent care involves risking ridicule and abuse, as much by "experts" as those who insist DID is fake. Better practitioners exist, but many would-be clients lack the resources to engage in trial and error, recover from incompetence, or access com-munity word-of-mouth networks. Even if you finally hear of an excellent psychiatrist or therapist, they are often cost-prohibitive or not taking on new clients. Some plurals resort to educating their pro-viders but can feel the provider is getting more from the relationship than they are. Training is minimal in healthcare education. For nearly every great clinician we've encountered, we've been able to trace their refreshing competence to being educated by plural clients, plural community resources, or their own plurality. They are good despite their training. We also face real threats to healthcare around other issues if those providers learn a patient is plural and react ignorantly.

Plurals overlap with other psychiatrically and medically marginalized communities, including peer and psych survivor movements. It is empowering to organize outside of establishment healthcare, build community around shared experiences, and process interconnections between our lives and the psychiatric landscape, which variably exploits and supports. We attempt to overcome internalizing the worst of it, striving to navigate and reform, from careers within to protests outside and the creation of alternatives. Though plural activists are making inroads, most radical mental health, disability, and neurodiversity advocacy doesn't even mention people like us.

Plurality is real. We are here. *We exist.* A generic term for a group of people in a body is a *system.* The Redwoods is our system name. Individual system members in the Redwoods have our own names, genders, ages, facial and vocal muscle patterns, interests, skills, and tastes. Plurals tend to find more system members over time. There are currently about a dozen of us here. We are in close recurring community with around thirty other systems; these are plurals ranging from partners to friends to shared circles. We have met hundreds while speaking at venues in person and online.

More and more are coming forward! In response to our own visibility, people come up and say, "Hey, I know someone like this, they'll be so happy to hear about you all" or "Hey, we are also like you." Excitement is followed by grief: "I haven't told anyone about this in ten years." "My friend is really struggling." There is research estimating over 1 percent of the population is like us. There are bleak statistics about our well-being, where they exist at all. More community-driven research, activism, services, and funding are needed, as are more positive representations in media. It's wonderful to be alive and engaged at a time when lasting change seems possible, oppression addressable, and each plural who comes forward in their personal or public lives can make a tangible difference.

We are inspired by countless systems. Spanning back decades, some were famous like the system Truddi Chase and the Troops who appeared on *The Oprah Winfrey Show*. Others hosted early influential websites on multiplicity, like Astraea's Web, or anonymously contributed to forums or newsletters like Many Voices. We've worked closely with Nsashaell, The Crisses, Irenes, and NYƎ (The Sorority) and others. We all supported the creation of The Plural Association by the Stronghold System and other volunteers. All together, we are developing and sharing more plural-positive frameworks. There are people like us, we are not bad or doomed, we are okay, we even have reasons to celebrate. We each and all belong. Our mistreatment is injustice.

The establishment is behind on plurality, like the status of sexual orientation and gender identity in the 1970s, or autism in the 1990s. We are trans and plural. (You can be both, and much of healthcare is still catching up with that.) We appeared on BBC Radio in 2019. After affirming us in our recording, they played it live with a host who misgendered and insulted us, and then brought on a psychiatrist who claimed he'd only seen a few instances of DID in his thirty-year career. The psychiatrist also bizarrely claimed it was mostly an American phenomenon. Yet just outside London that week we had met ten systems in one day, at a small neurodiversity conference with no agenda on plurality except a pop-up session we offered.

Many fights are being fought on many fronts: by social media voices big and small; by quiet warriors inside institutions; event organizers creatively making space for our communities; writers and speakers finding new ways to break the cycle of erasure. Accused of seeking attention, chastised to stop saying *we* or stop bringing out different system members because it's too *weird*, plurals nurse trauma and then rally to demand acceptance from their providers, family, and friends. We decry Hollywood's DID murderer trope while dreaming up the movies we wished they'd make and will someday make ourselves. We risk income and reputation to fight for change in careers from psychology to business to law. We invite allies to go further. So much more movement work is needed.

We also need to live our personal lives. Activists frequently burn out trying to lead on the big picture while neglecting the small, and the private world is particularly important when it comes to plurality. On a personal level, we Redwoods want people to know us, to spend time with us. Let's shift to expressing individually.

ALLI: Hi! If I didn't have the benefit of "Alli:" printed on the page, I'd say "Hi, this is Alli." While they loom large and get us fired up, structural discrimination and clinical concerns are not the foundation of our life. Being plural is a very intimate, interior, and mundane experience. It's about being in an ever-evolving inner community. It's about sharing a body and life, together day by day, eleven years and counting, in a world that didn't really prepare us to do so.

The Redwoods are in a body in its thirties. Alli is in her twenties, is a nonbinary woman, and her voice is—

My voice is a little higher, softer, than others.

Alli smiles, considering the possibility of narration of the inner world. She notices the inner gaze of various Redwoods shifting to contemplate this new strange way of expressing. What will this narrated voice say about me? *some wonder.*

Joy, younger than Alli and with a higher voice, moves into the front, which is the place where one goes when they are interacting with the outside world. People on the outside experience whoever is fronting as more here, *whereas people who remain non-fronting or inside appear to outside audiences as* not here.

JOY: I'm smiling. This is fun. I love you all. Plurality is also about getting to be here, right here, with people I can talk to, ask for help, or smile at.

A few people smile back at Joy. She pauses to consider what to say.

So, behind the front, behind the scenes, there is always a process of negotiating going on. The italics or stage directions above are but a selection. Right now, members of the Redwoods are wondering who wants to speak next and negotiating whether this meta subject matter is even on topic.

A moment of peace falls over the Redwoods, satisfied that rather than needing to transcribe a conversation like a podcast or group panel, we can just be and show you.

Smoke makes the decision to come to the front; the mechanism by which Joy left is unclear. Smoke's voice is much deeper.

SMOKE: Hello.

Smoke smiles, perhaps content with just one word, now that narration does some of the work for them. They nod in agreement.

Eliza, with a voice in between Alli's and Smoke's "steps" forward into the front, observing the narration as it unfurls.

ELIZA: Amazing! So yes, as you can see, we're in a constant process of attempting to maintain selves-awareness and listen to who wants to be here and when they are ready to switch out and who wants to come forth next.

Switch.

JOY: Efficient! Obviously we are in a quite demonstrative mood.

Several nods from the "back," that is, not the front. Folks in the back realize they are unusually on display. A quick meeting happens; the first agenda item is to drop a privacy screen, indicating that even in this "x-ray" mode there are certain inner workings that should not be narrated by default. The group consents to list "meeting in progress" on said screen. If you were in the room with us, you would see us sitting back, the body's eyes moving back and forth—an internal conversation. Or you might hear us talking out loud together, or some combination, like hearing only one side of a phone conversation or a conference call.

ELIZA: So, we imagine you may have some of the following questions.

How did they figure this out? There was an initial period of discovery in 2012 that was very intense for several months. And lots of work since then. How do they switch so fluidly? (This is not a meta-phorical conversation. We are writing fairly as it happens for us.) We got better with practice.

Isn't this a terrible amount of work? It's extra work to narrate what's happening, you're welcome, but this is pretty much what happens on good days when we are feeling fairly open, focused, and connected with each other. On not so good days we can struggle to connect with each other and tune into these subtleties. More on that later.

Are the Redwoods really like this? As far as we and those around us can tell, and others we've met with similar experiences, yes. We do have co-consciousness, or the ability to be aware of and communicate with each other internally. We didn't always have that, and many systems don't, and that's where you get some of the notorious amnesia symptoms. These include a new person coming to the front and having no memory of what was going on prior to their arrival and perhaps no awareness that there even are other people sharing their body. We have mild loss of detail on switches; if someone else came to the front they might not know exactly where I am in this paragraph, but they likely have the information that we are currently writing for this anthology and would be able to catch up quickly.

JOY: Yeah, that's good. Well said.

EZRA *(deeper voice)*: We want to tell you about our daily life. But maybe we can just show you.

SCENE—The Redwoods are asleep in their bedroom. It's late in the morning and light is filtering through their blackout curtains. Night owls. Eyes open, they turn over, looking at the clock. Dialogue is out loud unless otherwise indicated.

"Good morning," says Alli.

"Good morning," says a younger system member, name concealed for privacy.

Alli yawns.

Inner world listening is engaged. It appears a few people remain asleep, but the brainmind ripples and parts with the motion of someone coming forward.

"Good morning," says Eliza.

Morning greetings are an old habit, a building block of acknowledging plurality, that someones else are there. Grown over a decade from a frightened question (is it possible someone else is there again today?) to a routine expression of connection (I am here, and I'm glad you are, too). It doesn't always happen, especially if the Redwoods are in a rush to a virtual meeting pretending to be one person, but a little communication goes a long way for system maintenance and growth.

Today, Redwoods lay about for a while before getting up and entering a variety of semi-automated behaviors that don't require much consensus. Going to the bathroom, a kind of odd task they got used to sharing a long time ago. Milling about, catching up on their shared phone.

"What are we doing today?" someone asks. If anyone knew they might answer, but since it's an unstructured day: "Not sure." Sleepy consensus shifts toward a new chronic pain management habit they are trying out. Eventually they collect an apple and nondairy yogurt from the fridge and glance out the window. As breakfast begins, it feels like most people aren't even up yet.

End Scene. Back to Redwoods at the keyboard.

ELIZA: That's cool, I felt that.

ALLI: Yeah, me too.

PETRA *(medium-deep voice)*: I'll note that it looks really different on mornings when we have an early flight. *Laughter.* It's more like the family in *Home Alone* trying to get out the door, though fortunately we pretty much can't leave anyone behind. I say "pretty much" because it is helpful to sort of signpost for the whole system what is happening in big transitions like that, so people don't miss cues and wake up very disoriented because they are now in a tube thirty thousand feet high.

ALLI: Mornings are also different on days when we are sleeping with another person. Since we aren't permanently cohabiting with someone in bed, it's still kind of a special occasion with partners.

PETRA: Yes, transitions with external intimate partners need special care. We'll often have several Redwoods cycling in to say good mornings or goodbyes, announcing themselves and kissing, etc. We'll talk more about dating.

JOY: What's important to cover first?

EZRA: I'm really pleased with how that morning scene came together. Notice I'm a topic behind, that's a common nonlinearity for us, where not everyone moves as one through the flow of conversation and emotions. I came back to the front because I think it's key to emphasize a little more about how we are together before we introduce other relationships into the picture.

The Redwoods move to speak in a general We *once more for simplicity.*

We Redwoods love each other. We regularly murmur "love you" and "love you all" to each other throughout the week. We often ask for or offer help while taking turns tasking. "What are we doing?" "Can someone help me?" "How can I help you?" It is a close, intense bond that comes from attempting to embody individual and collective goals and values, and dealing with life's challenges and setbacks, from the vantage point of essentially a body-mind-reading-sharing comrade. We are in the same boat; the actions, thoughts, and emotions of one affect all.

While the unit we share is a one-body life, the dynamics have commonalities with a multi-body family. Many call this internal community. We value quality time together. We take turns savoring a special meal at a beachside restaurant, or witnessing a solar eclipse, delighting not just in the events but in each system member's reactions. We also try to balance chores, have meetings, and manage a budget. We have our different emotional patterns and strengths and weaknesses. Some of us are quiet, others are more outspoken. We discreetly switch to the people with the highest pain tolerance for the worst parts of dental appointments, but also let others who want to practice being brave quietly step in before dashing away. Teamwork! Our collaboration is always deepening. The main challenge is shame, largely stemming from society's insistence that plurals are fake, dangerous, or a nuisance. Oppression creates pressure to neglect ourselves, cover up, and disconnect. We got texts from people while writing this essay, and the mere fleeting virtual presence of another person can cause us to clam up, stop listening to one another, and freeze communications. A relic of internalizing "Don't tell anyone about this."

Singletsona, or pretending to be one person, is what some plurals call this kind of masking. It takes a long time to get out of and can be very disruptive. In a full-time job setting, it can take all night to decompress from pretending all day. This makes us stay up late at risk of being punished for tardiness just to finally get some contact with one another before doing it again the next day. Many plurals work toward an income with less pressure to hide, requiring calculated risks educating a revolving door of colleagues, clients, and/or supervisors, and facing the impression that you are somehow a liability. Office workers introduce their dogs, kids, and partners on video calls to colleagues' delight. Your plural coworkers, members of a team which works together to perform a job daily, are implicitly to remain out of sight.

"Not practical"

"Confusing"

"A wound to just work on with me, your therapist"

"Upsetting to others"

"Keep it to yourself"

"Why do you need to tell anyone?"

"Are any of you dangerous?"

And so on. Given the trauma of ignorance and rejection, if a plural system reveals themselves to you, please make a difference in their life by gently thanking them and letting them know your level of familiarity with the experience. Be positive and welcoming toward those you've met, and ask them if there's anything or anyone else they'd like to share.

Even with singlets' best efforts at support, we've often gotten stuck behind a façade for weeks or months at a time. The best way to beat this is to spend time with other plurals. Stigma is perpetuated by the "No one will love you," "Don't say *we*," and "You're too difficult to understand" trio. Plural community counters these beliefs. We've found people who share niche experiences we didn't have language for, and role models for navigating vulnerable situations. We've found friends, colleagues, mentors, and partners. We've also found expansive diversity: Systems with hundreds more members than us, systems with only two members. Systems with similar or different age and gender distributions than us, systems with different communication, decision-making structures, paradigms, and goals for their lives. Together we expand each system's sense of what is possible, and as judgment turns to appreciation, it becomes easier to appreciate ourselves.

The disability community is still singular normative, as is the LGBTQ community. So the joy we find when we connect with other disabled LGBTQ plurals brings tears to our eyes. It is a community of people who've all been told countless times we belong nowhere and are beyond help. Yet there we are, belonging and helping together. It's so sweet when shy members of two different systems come out and have a conversation; often it's the first time each one is talking to anyone on the outside. It's satisfying when plurals share their immense creativity to make art for a plural audience, free of needing to explain things to singlets. It's cathartic when long-held pain or joy is shared and finally resonates with a large group. In general, child and teenage system members in adult bodies are common. It's a real challenge to find safe places and people for them to connect with. When all the young people in a group of adult systems can hang out, "it freaking rocks" and "it is the best" report some of our own littles. It's important to find personal compatibility—like neurodiversity more broadly, some people's access needs can conflict with others. We don't befriend every system we meet any more than every singlet we meet. We do feel a kinship and larger shared community with other plurals and get a lot from community meetups organized in person and online.

We also have many singlet friends and family with above average engagement with and respect for our plurality. While the gap between the most interested singlets and our plural friends is significant, it's nice to take a break from plural community dynamics. There are good singlets. It took us years to find other plurals, so for a long time all we had was supportive singlets. In larger long-term groups like extended family and organizations, knowing that people know and care about us Redwoods has been a huge source of relief. We help other systems think about coming out as plural in small and big ways because it is a game changer, and there are many levels of deciding how much to share or not.

Being openly plural has placed a dense filter on our life. Especially as our online presence has grown and we disclose on dating app profiles and searchable press interviews, it certainly removes many job, dating, friend, creative, and housing opportunities from our life. Yet being ourselves also makes us freer and more selves-aware, attracting wonderful people who make us grateful for the risks we took and less wistful. Every close relationship has been shaped by our plurality, from having our parents get to know some of us individually, to falling in love with other plurals we met through community. Our life is more troubled than pretend-cis, pretend-straight, pretend-singular, pretend-neurotypical upbringing prepared us for. We've faced ignorance, discrimination, trolling, doubt, internal conflict, PTSD, anxiety, depression, economic insecurity, and other sources of agony. Yet working together has always made it better, as has pushing for authentic belonging and community. We are so much happier now than when we didn't know we were plural, and the more we are ourselves the more we heal and savor life's offerings. Amid rising fascism and climate chaos, it is well overdue to stop being our own enemies. As we push harder for change, we hope the rise in support outpaces the backlash. Being visible activists has given us an impact we never would have had otherwise. We are determined the biggest and best years are yet to come.

Companionship is crucial; for us that includes romance and long-term partnerships. Once we figured out we are more than one, we went long stretches of doubting we'd ever connect with anyone romantically outside our system. Occasionally, we had hookup experiences with people who had already decided they were attracted to us sexually before we told them, and their "acceptance" felt like it had the level of investment that generally applies to the rest of a hookup, which wasn't enough for us. Eventually we moved disclosure of our plurality further upfront: second date, first date, before a date, and finally well before a date to the point of only dating people who essentially know us from spaces where we are openly plural.

Romance between plurals is very special. In our early years, cisgender singular people would sometimes say "you'll find someone like you," and it felt like being relegated to some pile of undesirability. Years later, we've met quite a few systems who have incredible long-term relationships with other systems. We've also had that pleasure and turns out we prefer it! The constellations of relationships and abundance of possible combinations between many people in two bodies is thrilling. It also demands scheduling, flexibility, and prioritization skills. One person in our system might be dating a few people in your system, play an older friend role to others, and help raise some of your youngest system members. That's just one of the Redwoods, and several of us typically date.

Let your imaginations soar regarding plural intimacy. We still find it constantly surprising, challenging, and delightful. It also poses logistical challenges. How do we protect younger system members and sex-repulsed or otherwise disinterested system members from that intimacy? How do we maintain individual ownership and privacy around intimate experiences? We moved from unintentional dissociation to intentional boundaries. We pause and take breaks when someone who doesn't want to participate needs attention or time in front. Who gets to have first experiences, anniversary experiences, and other rare moments? We negotiate that and compromise. We also work hard to choose available compatible partners so that we have lots of time and chances for everyone to have special experiences. Life in general has given us lots of practice sharing. It's unlikely that someone will be intimate with everyone in a system, or across two systems, but it's important that everyone is welcome and neighborly in the partnership community between two bodies. It's also important to note that many systems have internal couplings and group relationship dynamics that can include sex and romance. We've known systems with dynamics ranging from hookups to marriage internally.

We've also met singlets who deeply regard their plural partners. Jim Bunkelman is one, and of his plural wife Rhonda he said, "When you love a multiple, your love comes back to you multiplied." One tender thing about dating plurals is how people on the inside can vicariously progress with the external dynamic. Such that when they introduce themselves, they may already be fully in love with someone who is meeting them for the first time. Humbling and so beautiful!

Experiencing profound compatibility and huge numbers of relationships across two bodies, all manifesting through a deep experience you were told would mean you'd always be alone, is very healing. It's taken us years, long ravines of loneliness, and so much work. The love that follows is deep. Despite insecurities, we are having sex with beautiful people who find us very sexy. The sex is *hot*! We and our partners support each other, cook great meals, make each other laugh, go on adventures, adapt, cherish, and celebrate. Will we be able to sustain our relationships over years and decades despite cumulative discrimination put on our collective lives? One kiss at a time.

Many plurals have deep relational trauma that makes connecting with others uncomfortable to terrifying, on top of barriers of distance, lack of time, resource limitations, and challenging searches. But we can love and be loved. If plurals want, people like us can have fantastic sex and epic romance. It works best when everyone is actively engaged in their own healing work. deepening relationship skills such as managing trauma and triggers, identifying compatible people, and establishing context and trust before diving in. Getting intimate with someone external is a big decision for our system, demanding significant consensus. Even if only one system member is involved at first, the connection between two bodies will affect everyone in the Redwoods. We keep in touch about how any major relationship is affecting our life and goals. It's truly wonderful when it is good. The peace, joy, and connection we share with others is multiply real.

We're proud of ourselves. We're proud of plurals! Each of us Redwoods loves deeply. We feel each other sparkle and glisten as we nurture communities and capacities to give and receive as who we really are. It's so clear to us that many of the great untold love stories of our time involve plurals. If you get the opportunity, we encourage you to listen, or even write your own.

Thanks to Irenes for providing feedback on the second draft of this essay. Thanks to our partners for the opportunity to live plurality, disability, and intimacy together so joyfully. We love you all.

Strange New Worlds and Other Love Languages

Marieke Nijkamp

1.

My first introduction to *Star Trek* was watching reruns of *Star Trek: The Next Generation* at my grandparents' house. I must have been twelve. While other kids my age went to school, I settled into the old, faded couch in the corner of the living room, turned on the TV, and got lost exploring the final frontier.

It wasn't that I didn't go to school at all. I did. I attended classes when I could, but *when I could* was often complicated. I struggled physically. My body didn't always act the way I wanted it to or even the way I thought it should. It was in pain, a lot. It was exhausted, often. I felt a disconnect between my body and the rest of me, and I didn't yet have a disabled community around me to help me learn how to connect.

I also struggled with the world. The one I lived in wasn't the same as the one my friends inhabited. I didn't have a name for my neurodivergence yet, but I knew I felt different. Odd. Interacting with the world was like balancing on a tightrope, in the middle of the night, in a storm. Every step required both concentration and conformity.

(Only much later would I realize that both feeling different *and* feeling disconnected wasn't just wrapped up in disability—but in gender, too.)

And then I discovered the bridge of the USS *Enterprise*. And on that bridge, characters that I recognized. Not because they resembled me, but because they reflected parts of me. I recognized myself in an android, longing to understand humanity. I saw a visibly disabled man with adaptive devices, unapologetically successful. I connected to the somewhat obnoxious, awkwardly intelligent teen boy, and I wanted to fly a spaceship, too.

A lot can be said about how well—or not, as is the case often, too—*Star Trek* handles disability and representation. But then and there, I saw a future where the pieces of me that I felt were strange— sometimes even wrong—were not just included but accepted, explored. They were literally and figuratively given space.

This story of the future felt hopeful. It was one of different worlds. And it was one where I wanted to belong.

I didn't share my love for *Star Trek* with other fans. Not yet. To be honest, I don't think I *knew* any others. And even if I had known others, I'm not sure I would have shared how much *Trek* began to mean to me. It felt tender still, and I didn't yet have the words for it.

Instead, I kept the final frontier to myself and I found part of myself there.

2.

Every week for years, my grandmother took me to the library. There, I could trade one stack of books for the next. The library we used to visit has long since been torn down, but I vividly remember the smell of too many books in too small a space. The scuffed up, once brightly colored carpet in the children's section, where half-read books inevitably lay scattered about and tiny feet stomped across the play area. The rows of shelves in the children's and teen sections, with books that I read meticulously, stacks at a time, until I'd read them all.

I was always hungry for more. Hungry for knowledge. Hungry for stories.

Every week, we took a taxi to get there. Because it was a para-transit service, it often traveled via detours and routes that never quite made sense to me. But on one of those trips, the driver took the time for us. He saw all the books I held and he smiled at me. He told me he used to read fantasy books by the dozen. Not so much anymore, these days, but he wanted to know: What did I love about the books I read?

I told him, I loved exploring new worlds. I loved the sense of adventure and the endless opportunities that opened up to me. I loved finding connections between the stories inside of me and the stories on the page.

(Especially, though I didn't tell him this, on days when my own world felt so very small. Especially when it felt like my friends were slowly moving in different directions, when the teens around me were growing up and I didn't know how to. I wasn't always sure I *would* grow up.)

Try these authors, he said to me. Try these books. They were my favorites, and I think you may like them, too.

We never saw that particular driver again or I would have told him, I did try. I read all of the authors he suggested. I read all of the books. In fact, I loved some of them so much that I read them multiple times. And eventually, when I started building my own collection of fantasy books, they were among the first that I bought for myself.

3.

I fell in love with other worlds. From the Delta Quadrant to galaxies far, far away. From the kingdom of Dagonaut to Ingary. From Camelot to Middle Earth. They all shaped me. The last one changed me.

When *Star Wars: The Phantom Menace* came out, I was thirteen. I fell in love with the music before I fell for the adventures. I'd seen the original trilogy, of course, but in bits and pieces over time. Scenes, while others were watching. Fragments, before my bedtime. *The Phantom Menace* was my moment of connection. And like before, I didn't *really* share it with others. The fact that it was everywhere for a few months helped, but I wasn't really interested in popularity. I was interested in exploring stories. I wanted connection.

I had some access to the internet but I wasn't online much yet. It was a hassle at home and expensive at school. So I did the only thing I knew to do. I went to the library. I read all the Star Wars books I could find. My small-town library, which sadly held no Star Trek books, held a surprising amount of *Star Wars: Expanded Universe*—now *Legends*—books. I always wondered who else checked them out. I never saw anyone browsing the shelves.

(Back then, I wouldn't have said anything, even if I had seen others. Some days, the smallness of my world was of my own making.)

Then *The Lord of the Rings: The Fellowship of the Ring* came out. Two years later, my life had changed in bigger and smaller ways. I'd lived in a medical rehabilitation facility for a year, part of a youth program with other disabled teens, where an interdisciplinary team of doctors and therapists helped us to live with disability. Their treatment wasn't focused on impossible *curing* but on *living*. On finding ways to adapt. On learning strategies for that tightrope dance.

It wasn't easy. Some days, it felt like I had to rebuild my life over and over again. Other days, my autistic brain, struggling with being constantly surrounded by others, never alone, snapped, and I fought anyone who came too close.

But it was the first time I had a disabled community around me. It was us few against the world. I didn't feel outside the norm; the norm never bothered us anyway. I felt connected. I wasn't different because I was ill, I was different because I was a writer and a know-it-all and stubborn and passionate.

My love for other worlds was still uniquely my own, but we shared our own pocket universe, filled with joy and heartache, late nights playing games, long existential conversations, grumpy breakfasts, hide-and-go-seek in the hallways. When I picked up my pen to write, others wanted to read and talk about it, and it helped steer me toward creating to connect, instead of creating to leave behind.

By the time I returned to the real world, I'd grown more comfortable in many ways. More comfortable in my body—though it continued to be as stubborn as I am, I had some tools to live with it. More comfortable interacting, though sometimes the tightrope still felt like it swayed in a storm. More comfortable being different, and finding ways to express the parts that made the whole of me.

By the time *The Fellowship of the Ring* came out, I was also comfortably online—it was becoming increasingly accessible—and I'd tentatively found my way to small writing communities.

Then the movie was released, and I fell in love with the music *after* I fell for the adventures. I'd already read the books, so often they were falling apart. I watched the movie and I felt longing for a place I'd never been—*fernweh*, perhaps—and I wasn't the only one. I still did not know how to find my way to fan communities, but gradually, they and my online writing communities began to overlap. It turns out we all had stories on our minds.

For the first time in my life, I found others who were just as weird, just as passionate as me. The friends I'd made in the outside world, the friends I'd kept there, appreciated my strange quirks, but they didn't necessarily *understand* them. But then I found people who did. People who poured over backstory and detail and word choice and song. Who were as curious and as intensely focused on every detail as I was. Who spoke the same language.

I felt seen, just like that first introduction to the bridge of the *Enterprise*. I felt seen, just like that random encounter with the taxi driver. And I felt connected.

4.

When I pursued my degree in medieval history, my main focus was the history of ideas, language, and storytelling. Stories, after all, are what give us meaning. We tell stories to make sense of the world around us and of ourselves. But to do so, it's essential to understand the rules of story—and the language we use.

Fandom—through message boards, forums, emails, texts—brought me to people who never claimed dragons aren't real. Instead, we discussed whether they were made of scales or shadows and fears of the unknown. No one claimed androids were nothing more than futuristic fantasies. Instead, we talked about the expansive boundaries of human experience.

We had a shared language for our universes *and* our own experiences, and it allowed us to discuss ethics, identity, depictions of trauma and healing, relationships, being. It allowed us to shape these stories into places of opportunity and belonging.

And oftentimes, it helped us create places of belonging where the rest of the world held none.

In these spaces, I discovered many who were neurodivergent like me. Turns out, when you create spaces based on shared passions, you attract people whose brains are hardwired to delve deep. And much like my earlier experiences with disabled communities, being *other* together made it easier to be ourselves.

I met many others who were queer like me. These communities were among the first where I tried text-based role-playing games, and where I could subtly try on different genders for the first time, too.

Beyond speaking the same language, these were communities that were accessible at all times. Not confined to physical spaces and set times, but present no matter how stubborn my body was. Not bound to other people's norms because we build our own rules.

In finding the connections between these stories and ourselves, we also found connection to one another.

5.

Fandom and writing communities became my online life. A refuge when I was exhausted or in pain. A home when I felt better, too, when I found a reasonable balance (at least for a while) between what I could and couldn't do. Because I had two worlds, I didn't need *everything* from either. I could settle for *enough.*

When I stumbled out of my teens, online spilled over into offline, and I was terrified it wouldn't hold. But the shared language and stories bound us. These friends—some of whom are still such essential people in my life—knew me before they knew me.

When online spilled over into offline, offline expanded as well, in various ways. There were adventures to be had. Late-night conversations. Introducing one another to different universes. Sharing books and inhaling them. The *Star Wars Holiday Special.* The *Doctor Who*

Christmas specials. Nights in castles. Travel. Games. Long, hilly walks discussing and telling stories. And just as important: finding places to rest.

Interacting with them didn't feel like walking a tightrope. It felt like we all anchored one another.

And that only became more apparent when it turned out many of my fandom friends were far more comfortable with physical touch than I ever had been. This space between us became one of the first and only spaces where I felt comfortable with (platonic) physical intimacy, too.

It stands to reason. So many of our conversations had always been variations of, "I feel this way. Do you feel it, too?"[1] that intimacy between us wasn't strange and couldn't be strange.

6.

These days, I approach writing with a sense of intimacy. The stories I tell, I tell from an office where books are crammed into every corner, where half-read books inevitably lie scattered about, and where the books that have been passed down through the generations stand side by side with books I found because others loved them first, with my own collection of Star Trek and Star Wars novels, with my well-loved copies of the Lord of the Rings trilogy, with every book that forms a gateway to strange new worlds and a tether of connection to other people.

The stories I tell are all a small part of me. I write them for the

---

1   In his Nobel Lecture in 2017, Kazuo Ishiguro spoke at length about the creation of stories, and those sparks of revelations that may become essential turning points. He spoke about the purpose of stories, about connection, and shared humanity. His words gently shifted my own perspective on storytelling.

hungry readers. Hungry for knowledge. Hungry for stories. Hungry for connection. I write them for the kids who feel odd or at odds and who need to be given space. I write them for the readers who hope to find connections between the stories inside of them and the stories on the page.

Several published novels in—both original work and stories tied into existing universes—I especially find myself writing about hope and found family. Hope, in the face of adversity. Found family in all shapes and sizes. And above all, connection through stories. Because to me, intimacy is sharing stories and sharing hearts.

7.

When the pandemic hit, the world grew smaller again, and it felt like it had no place for us. I struggled physically and mentally. With the effects of lockdown and the lingering effects of COVID. With the loss of the adventures I longed for and all the expansive ways I'd learned to be. With the rampant ableism all around us.

Then my friends virtually invited me to the bridge of the USS *Discovery* and the USS *Protostar*. We watched new episodes of *Star Trek*, in different time zones, on different sides of the world. We cheered over music choices, we dissected stories, we laughed together.

We connected, and the future felt a little more hopeful.

We shared the final frontier, and we demanded space.

We created space, and we found ourselves there.

Crip Class

Gabrielle Peters

How do you protect your humanity while exposing enough of it to break through the deliberate "*not-knowing*" and inhumanity that made it legal to kill disabled people? How do you dive into the deep end of ableism and not drown in your own tears or forfeit the heart that produces them?

These are questions we did not ask ourselves beforehand and ones we are only now belatedly trying to answer. Back then there was no time.

On the evening of March 3, 2021, Catherine Frazee sent me an email with the subject line: *Sharing an idea—would love to hear your thoughts.*

> Wondering if you could help me play with an idea. In the spirit of "leaving it all on the field" next week, or maybe just going out with a bang, I'm wondering about rallying our

community around an online event in which we simply take up space, keep it gritty and real, work on crip time . . . The broad concept is "A Disability Filibuster on Bill C7"—a live Zoom broadcast, or Facebook or some other platform, where disabled people across the country sign up to fill a half an hour or maybe an hour of broadcasting time, round-the-clock, 24/7, starting maybe at 5 PM on Sunday night and not stopping until the Prime Minister withdraws Bill C7 . . .

Bill C-7, which became law on March 17, 2021, expands Canada's euphemistically and inaccurately named MAiD (medical assistance in dying) legislation to disabled people beyond those whose deaths were "reasonably foreseeable."

Assisted suicide and euthanasia were first legalized in 2016. The original legislation limited these to people whose "natural deaths" were considered "reasonably foreseeable"—a term that has no scientific meaning and was left up to interpretation. While the public believed that only people who were actively in the process of dying would be offered or receive MAiD, this was not the case.

Early on, there were indications the interpretation of eligibility by the courts would be broad. In 2017, an Ontario court ruled that a seventy-seven-year-old patient known as "AB," whose only condition was osteoarthritis, fit the legal criteria for MAiD.

Similarly, Alan Nichols, who was hard of hearing and had a history of depression, and some other medical conditions, none of which were life-threatening, received MAiD in 2019.

It was also clear prior to the expansion of MAiD that disabled people were dying due to ableism and Canada's failure to uphold its commitments under the United Nations' Convention on the Rights of Persons with Disabilities (UNCRPD).

Archie Rolland and Raymond Bourbonnais both died by MAiD

after raising the inhumane conditions in their long-term care facilities. What makes their situations unusual is that they became publicly known despite the tight seal of secrecy around MAiD.

The enthusiasm with which some in healthcare professions promoted and pushed MAiD as an option to their patients was also apparent even before its expansion under Bill C-7. When Sheila Elson told a physician treating her disabled daughter, Candice Lewis, that she was not interested in hearing about MAiD as an option, the physician told her she was being selfish. For *Maclean's* magazine I interviewed Corinna Iampen, herself a physician, who was asked about her interest in MAiD while in the hospital following a non-life-threatening injury.

The legalization of MAiD followed years of lobbying, most notably by the group Dying With Dignity (DWD). DWD gained broader public attention because of its vocal support for a man who murdered his twelve-year-old disabled daughter. In 1994, a jury convicted Robert Latimer of the second-degree murder of his daughter, Tracy. He appealed his conviction to the provincial and later Supreme Court of Canada. He was again convicted at a second trial but with the recommendation that he be eligible for parole after only one year. This in turn led to further appeals, which continued until 2001, at which time the Supreme Court of Canada upheld a life sentence with no eligibility for parole for ten years. Throughout the entire process, some things remained constant: disabled people and their organizations were forced to argue as intervenors in the courts and in the court of public opinion that killing us is not a "compassionate" act; the media created a sympathetic and extremely sanitized portrayal of Robert Latimer while simultaneously failing to humanize or accurately portray Tracy, the murder victim; and the right-to-die movement capitalized on the media attention and public sentiment to catapult their issue onto the national stage.

Marilynne Seguin, then executive director of DWD, was quoted in 1994 in the *New York Times* arguing that a ten-year sentence would be "quite unconscionable" given that "the Latimers had already lived under a sentence during the twelve years that Tracy was alive."

Analysis at the time by University of Alberta professor Dick Sobsey concluded that the media coverage of the Latimer trial was "irresponsible, biased, and dangerous." Sobsey was concerned the coverage may have played a role in two other deaths since Tracy's murder and felt "it is almost certain to contribute to further crimes against people with disabilities."[1]

More than sixty thousand people signed a petition in support of reducing his sentence. and over one hundred people stated they would agree to serve one month of Latimer's sentence for him. A 1999 poll found 73 percent of Canadians believed Robert Latimer should have received a more lenient sentence and 41 percent believed mercy killing should not be against the law.

The Senate's 1996 Standing Committee on Euthanasia and Assisted Suicide included discussion about involuntary euthanasia, and the final report recommended creating a separate offence of "compassionate homicide" with less severe penalty.

Eike Henner Kluge, a tenured professor at the University of Victoria and founder and first director of the Canadian Medical Association's Department of Ethics and Legal Affairs, argued openly for involuntary euthanasia of disabled infants, defended the actions of Robert Latimer, and even suggested someone should have ended Tracy's life earlier.

A similar argument for euthanizing some disabled infants was repeated in 2022 by Dr. Lois Roy, of the Quebec College of Physicians, before the Special Joint Committee on MAiD. The committee recom-

---

1   Dick Sobsey, "The Latimer Case: The Reflections of People with Disabilities—Media," Council of Canadians with Disabilities, accessed June 30, 2023, http://www.ccdonline.ca/en/humanrights/endoflife/latimer/reflections/media.

mended expanding MAiD to include mental illness as a sole qualifying criterion—though that was delayed until March 2024. Advance directives and assisted suicide and euthanasia for children and youth deemed "mature" enough to consent to their deaths are among the committee's recommendations.

MAiD is a public declaration by the Canadian state that they find the assertion that it is better to be dead than disabled to be a reasonable position they not only support but will enable by funding lethal injection house calls.

Unlike other countries, which require that all other options be tried, Canadian doctors and nurse practitioners are only required to list other options of which they are aware. Whether any are available or not is often a question of ableism and cost, not science. As a result, disabled people have applied and died due to poverty, medical ableism, isolation, loneliness, and inability to secure accessible and affordable housing. The romanticizing of MAiD by proponents and its spread by Canadian media has also contributed to suicidal ideation, adding marketing to the many ways that disabled people are being socially coerced to die. Even the affidavits of the original plaintiffs in the Supreme Court case list ableism—though they don't call it that—as their reason for wanting to have their lives ended.

My response to Catherine's email was as short as it often is: Yes!

The following morning, we met over Zoom, and invites went out the same day. We were operating within the government's unbending timeline and with the urgency of life and death. We didn't look or sound frantic. When you understand what is at stake, that planning space is like the quiet center of a storm. And leaving it all on the field means the effort you intend to put in will not be mitigated by the usual concern for things like rest. While Catherine mentions crip time in her email, that turned out to be more hopeful than real. The adage "rest is radical" was temporarily sacrificed as was pretty much everything else in our lives. And there was tension. Catherine and I are an odd coupling. Especially back then. Especially on my end.

Intimacy is a strange topic to be writing about for someone as isolated as I am. I don't have many friends. Ever since the onset of my condition nearly two decades ago, my world has never stopped shrinking. Poverty plus ableism plus a pandemic left me with a world that fit inside a tweet. Social media was my main connection left to the universe beyond. Given how isolated I feel, you would think I would welcome the emotional connection of working closely with someone else.

The thing is, I carry a lot of trauma—some of it attached to being a disabled person, some of it attached to being a poor person, and some of it attached to being a woman. All of it is attached to intimacy.

The traumatic things that happened outside of intimacy healed. The ones inside have blistered at best.

My deep secret is that I love people despite the many reasons that have been handed to me not to. I love to explore every cave of obsession they create, sponge up all their very specific and detailed stories, and free dive deep into everything they are passionate about. People fill me with wonder. And hope. Except when they don't. Like when they yank out the handle of the knife they put into your back and declare themselves the victim because your blood got on their hands. Or when they find you bleeding and turn and leave. Which many of them do when you develop an incurable condition that includes things they refer to as TMI. There are the semi-self-inflicted scars that are a result of not seeing the value in myself, which, I have discovered, means that when others do, they take pieces of me for themselves. I overshare, not feelings as much as ideas and thoughts—and then someone whose life did not include getting fucked over to form them, presents them as their own.

I tell myself I need to shut up and stop sharing, and yet talking out loud is my only intimacy and connection with the world, and sometimes a connection to someone who is similarly threatened, not aided by the saviors of the system.

You are either out or in, and if you are in, then you are close enough and have sufficient ammunition to do me real harm. And many have.

When it comes to poverty, middle-class people assume it's just a collection of stories and photos of empty fridges, which they can read and repackage into a more respectable content/product. But leaving aside how much they fail to grasp, they violate some pretty fundamental ways of ensuring truth is preserved and credited.

Being poor or working class is much more than a deficiency framing allows. We plebs in the lower classes place higher value on interdependence over independence.

You don't retell John's story; you say John told you a great story and urge people to ask him about it. And if K taught you a trick for fixing a leaking faucet, you mention their name when you share it—even if it is ten years later. We actively work against each other's erasure. Among poor and working-class people (these are not the same, but I have lived as part of each), trust given and received is observed and not earned with words. Disrespectful words might get you in some trouble, but ultimately you are more likely to be known by the words you didn't speak—to the landlord, to the police . . . and by the questions you didn't ask before offering—and by the deeds you did do—showed up, helped out. Kindness is demonstrated.

We tell the lady with the hamper full of donated things we wouldn't pick but that will keep us alive that we are very grateful. We thank the worker behind the plexiglass at the government office for not making our life worse. The words between friends and community are fewer, less obsequious and flowerful. Maybe just a nod. Or silence. It doesn't matter. No one's looking at you like emotional fuel or demanding you follow some set of rules. Not making a big deal about doing something for someone is essential, as is allowing for future reciprocation of some kind regardless of the other person's situation relative to your own. There are no one-way friendships. You don't give and not receive because that would make it charity. You tell the person they are doing you a favor by taking the extra food you bought by mistake. You say it and you mean it. You understand the gift giving *gives you* and the fortune that has put you in the giver's seat—this time. You diffuse the power differential, not pretend the potential for one doesn't exist. This is honestly one of the biggest problems I have in trying to form friendships with middle-class people.

There are other unwritten rules—I've broken a big one by making this about myself—and differences in culture and norms, so when I cross the class divide, I end up in all sorts of trouble. The nicer ones call me awkward. Mostly, they perceive poor people as lacking a filter instead of understanding ours is just different. It's also worth mentioning that class culture is not a monolith and variations occur depending on generation; location; the racial, religious, and ethnic makeup of the community; and other factors.

Catherine and I are on opposite sides of a very large country. We have never met. We are both disabled but have lived very different lives, and we each interact with very different parts of the disability community. I was surprised and a little confused as to why she was reaching out to me of all people. I decided it must be because I am active on Twitter. I couldn't imagine any other reason, as I had not always been pleasant in our private interactions. When a fish is out of water it flops around, and I was always crossing into her world, not she into mine.

At this point in my life, the route to intimacy involves doing something that has nothing to do with being friends but necessitates or accidentally leads to forming a friendship of sorts. It's almost like I need to trick myself into taking a chance and trusting someone—or really myself—especially if they are from another class. It helps if something of real significance is involved. My anxiety loop is outmatched, and I take the risk. Not doing everything possible to try to stop C-7 from passing felt almost as choiceless as the false pretense of choice it is based upon. Almost.

Community organizing around eugenics is difficult because the backdrop is fighting to assert "We are human" in addition to and before we can even get to discussing the line edit of the legislation written with the intention of "mercifully" helping us kill ourselves. But the thing about community organizing, as anyone who has ever done it knows, is that it is alternately thoroughly exhausting and the single most energizing, soul-fulfilling, replenishing force on earth. And it's not just each other and those in your immediate proximity holding you up; it's those who came before you and those who are working on other things in other places and just radically resisting by existing. And there is the whisper the wind carries to the horizon at the spot you are making for the future crip you will never meet. We were also aware that dehumanization and death is exactly the backdrop many others have had to and do organize around—missing and murdered Indigenous women and girls, Black Lives Matter. The much-too-long list of oppressed people trying to right the wrongs past and present. There was ever-present humility in the knowledge that, while we were the targets of this bill, we were not the only ones targeted in this world. We were two white disabled women and we tried—though invariably failed—to be conscious of how this would impact what we did and did not do. We wanted to make space, not simply take up space.

While Catherine, as host for most of the Disability Filibusters over the years, has acted to provide some continuity and connection, we also offered to not be present or involved at all, beyond providing the platform and funding the ASL and transcription if that's what some communities preferred.

I stayed mostly behind the scenes, working to pull together the people and the shows, and pushed past my problem with working with Catherine. My brain fought trusting her. To be clear, I also didn't dislike Catherine, nor did I actively distrust her. I didn't really know Catherine as a person, so the placeholder in my mind was a set of experiences that were not great. That is an understatement. Middle-class white women have a way of never actually revealing a single feeling or thought not calculated to be appropriate and to their advantage in that moment, and yet somehow giving the appearance of complete transparency and openness. My experience is that people like this have an agenda to which I am not privy; and without knowing it, and owing to our very different access to resources and power, I may end up a pawn in a game I did not sign up to play. I can read a room, but reading a white middle-class woman—disabled or nondisabled—is like looking through a glass of milk and hoping to see what's on the other side. Over time, I get tricked into thinking we have established friendship, when what we've established is convenience. The men may have perpetrated the violence, but these women dug deep with their betrayals. They are soooo nice—and yet, also not at all.

This is my long way of saying I put Catherine through a lot and reacted with suspicion when in doubt, but somehow—mostly to her credit, not mine—we persevered. Sometimes middle-class people think they are being put through a test, but it is self-preservation. When these inter-class interactions go south, it's always those of us with less money who pay in ways those with more won't even recognize. The greatest danger to Catherine, the professor emerita of Toronto Metropolitan University and former chief commissioner of the Ontario Human Rights Commission, was people thinking she made a bad call by associating herself with that passionate, "unpredictable," foul-mouthed person on social media. Being called "passionate" in this context is never a compliment and, like the word *vulnerable*, connotes a type of human rather than a part of being human. "Unpredictable" is a "nicer" way to mark someone as an untrustworthy and possibly even dangerous person. "Foul-mouthed" depends on your definition of what words and ideas are foul. I'll own the swearing, but I don't spew hate or pitch privatization.

Once, at a public meeting, I spoke forcefully but calmly, using only the most professional and respectable words and following all of Robert's Rules. Another woman on the same side, but visibly well-off and highly credentialed, was far less careful in her speech and tone. She shouted, made a few personal attacks, and ignored "decorum." One of us was characterized as intimidating and emotional, and it wasn't her.

Unlike Catherine, the tether I have to society is slipping and frayed. Failure for me ripples differently. Middle-class disabled people fear a loss to their reputations. Disabled poor people fear losing their (relative) freedom and lives.

Another thing middle-class people don't do especially well is understand the grunt work that goes into their grand—and I mean this genuinely, not sarcastically in this case—ideas. I knew we needed some people around who understood. I also knew those people are also the ones operating on the least reserves. Having had periods of greater financial stability in my life, I understand that a lot of what middle-class people pride themselves on as being "organized" is actually a product of, and dependent on, their ability to pull out a credit card. The mental loads carried by poor and working-class disabled people are heavy, and our risk analysis is constant, with much higher stakes and almost nonexistent room for error. We run through not just what could go right but all the ways something could go wrong, and all the rungs between here and that place you are pointing to. And so, the very first people I reached out to were crips who I knew had the skills, hoping they also had the fuel. Q is the kind of person who hands you the answer before you ask the question. Kate has a mental net that catches all the thoughts that matter, and polishes, sorts, categorizes, fills in the blanks, and turns them into lists, schedules, and budgets.

Meanwhile, Catherine was working her connections. An organization would receive our funds and provide all the labor for bookkeeping and dispersal of them. Her partner set up a GoFundMe, and one of the disability organizations gifted us with a Zoom account.

From there, things grew as they do whenever many hands become involved. Disability Filibuster is not a corporation; it is a living organism, and it rests and changes shape and adapts. Lately, Harper, who is the creator of our image and logo, is spending a lot of time thinking about how we can care for the community of people fighting Canada's seemingly ever-expanding assisted suicide, and the death that surrounds and follows us in this work.

I have a fair number of followers online—which I hope we all know is not the same thing as having a lot of friends, even though I do care about and value a great many of them. They have saved me and supported me in important and valuable ways. For me at least, the size of my social media presence is inversely related to the intimacy of interactions. I feel self-consciously aware that I might be perceived in a way that is not an accurate reflection of my invisibility in life offline. I am acutely aware that if my account went silent tomorrow, I would be replaced by someone else's presence in your timeline, much like our units are binned and cleaned when we die, without any ritual of goodbye before the next poor crip moves in. I try to stay inside the narrow lines that I feel sufficiently informed about to venture a public opinion on, but also worry that I may disappoint and abandon some, the way most everyone but crips abandons us. I amplify other people who are more informed, but even that requires knowing which person and which opinion. I worry about the people reading my words and what else is happening in their lives. I have done harm and said the wrong thing in replies and direct messages, so now I mostly freeze and avoid them entirely.

Someone I cared about and messaged semi-regularly unfollowed my account during the C-7 fight. My timeline became intense, and it wasn't a great place to hang out if you were struggling, so I suspected that was her reason. She didn't block me, and we had not had an argument, so I told myself I would just give her some space. About a year later, she took her own life. Loss mired in regret. Perhaps if I had remembered the lesson she taught me to not wait for people to reach out, that you need to reach in . . . I didn't see her telltale tweets leading up to it until after. If I had, I would have said, "I see you and I care." We used to do that for each other. Such a small thing that made so much difference on a bad day. I think about her often and wonder whether the conversation we didn't ever have would have made a difference. The words I was too tired to type were saved for another day. And now that day will never be.

Whatever else social media may or may not be, it is definitely real life. And for some of us, it is the only connection we have to life in the broader world. Disability Filibuster would not have happened without social media and the connections it created. We are trying to put these connections in richer soil.

Disability Filibuster is archived evidence and a diary with blank pages to be written by those who log on.

Catherine and I are closer than we were when we started out. She is now someone for whom I will put up my hair, crack my neck, and speak very loudly up close to your face if you go after her. I still honestly could not tell you how she feels about me, but it doesn't matter. We share a bond that we don't share with others we may have more in common with. It's a closeness that happens when you push past every reason not to like someone, because liking them or not isn't a good enough reason not to be together. You start with mutual respect and shared purpose as your foundation. The struggle takes care of the common obstacles, setbacks, small victories, and deeper grief.

For the most recent Disability Filibuster, disabled poor people offered poetry, stories, and songs. A panel discussed the contents of the Special Joint Committee's Report on MAiD, after which we all watched as KC in Ontario stepped outside into the night and set their copy on fire. KC had just returned from an extended hospitalization to finally have their pain properly diagnosed and to address the suicidality that MAiD propaganda had stoked. As the crisp white pages shriveled under the heat of fire and our collective rage, flames shot up, grabbing at bits of the darkness. The report that landed like a giant anvil turned into amber sparks that became dust in the wind. There would be an after. It was not forever.

Earlier, Garth from the *Crackdown* podcast videoed himself burning a copy on the back porch of VANDU (Vancouver Area Network of Drug Users) in Vancouver's Downtown Eastside. He called it East Van policy analysis. Garth and others move against a current of grief, aware that the declared crisis in overdose deaths resulting from the toxic unregulated supply isn't one to those with the power to end it. The Downtown Eastside is home to many of the city's poorest disabled people and the highest proportion of Indigenous people (31 percent) in Vancouver. There buildings wear street art, not corporate logos, and paths are paved in concrete (no green space for grassroots activism). Care is spoken from the nozzle end of Smokey D's spray paint can.

Other crips ripped up their copies of the report. Many, like me, without a printer, watched and willed heat into the screen. Witnessing didn't feel passive that night.

As always, we had a minute of silence for those who have died.

And then it was over until next time. I think I am supposed to put a happy ending here, but I honestly have none beyond the fact that we are still alive and still fighting for crip lives. There should not be a need to state our lives are worth living, because that implies there is some question about which lives are worth living and that living is a right one has to earn. We need a society that supports and cares for life—all life.

Otherwise, to paraphrase Rosina Kamis, who fundraised for food for her last five days on earth and left video testimony of the abandonment, isolation, poverty, and fear of institutionalization that led to her MAiD, it becomes like Canada, a country of killing, not caring.

As for me, I can only hope that those to whom I have failed to show my heart during our interactions can know it through my deeds.

A Tale of Three Hospitals

Jaipreet Virdi

They were perceived as dens of death.

Desolate, decaying spaces for sick persons desperate for relief who were admitted and faced with the likelihood never to return home. These were spaces of discovery, where technology, expertise, and experimentation banded together to take up arms in the battle against disease, spaces where bodies were stitched back together, where hope reigned again. More than mere institutions, since the nineteenth century, hospitals have defined the parameters of health and illness—often along class, racial, and gendered lines—even altering the landscape of healthcare delivery during disease outbreaks.

Hospitals are also spaces of pain. As the loci for recovery and rehabilitation, they become contested spaces between patients and professionals, where the clinic is pitted against the body and where expertise over diagnosis, validation, and recognition is continuously negotiated. Julie Anderson writes that for medical rehabilitation to be successful, it needed to be intensive and controlled, often by regulating the space whereby the therapy took place, with the spaces then becoming a significant part of patient experience. Specific spaces were created for specific diseases, though their architectural design did not always safeguard the embodied experience of rehabilitation.

For endometriosis survivors in particular, hospitals are vexed spaces: a place where pain is dismissed and symptoms are ridiculed, but the only place with lifesaving technologies to transform their lives. This essay tells the tale of three hospitals where I received starkly different levels of care and the trauma that persisted long after I was discharged. Together, all three hospitals reveal expectations about the ethics of care, and the importance of creating and understanding the interconnections between bodies and space.

Pain narratives offer a crucial approach for understanding the ethics of care and how patient experiences can be shaped by the spaces that encompass them, whether it is a hospital, clinic, or at home. Disability scholars philosophize that pain has a distinct experiential quality that is only perceived through firsthand, personal experience—either as a feeling-sensation or as an emotion—with pain phenomenology providing us the tools to understand the nature of pain as *pure* experience. Outside the realm of biology and sociology, pain blurs the fluid line between illness and disease. Pain manifests, Travis Chi Wing Lau tells us, and "diagnostic imaging realizes that pain by bringing it to light from its hidden recesses within the body. Yet even when it manifests, the experience of pain remains so idiosyncratic to the individual."[1]

With endometriosis, you live in a land administered by crip time, existing in a liminal space controlled by flare-ups sending tendrils underneath the flesh, binding organs together, scarring muscle and tis-

---

1   Travis Chi Wing Lau, "The Crip Poetics of Pain," *Amodern 10: Disability Poetics* (December 2020).

sue. The pain overwhelms you, steals your time, and twists your body-mind into grotesque forms such that you no longer recognize yourself. You mourn the loss of previous capacities and imagined futures.

Elaine Scarry taught us pain exists outside of language, and Havi Carel convinced us illness is the cry of the flesh. Can pain exist outside of space?

I think pain is grief.

We lived across the street from Hospital 1, in a busy part of a Canadian city. It became somewhat of a monthly—then weekly—routine to go to the emergency room and spend a lot of time waiting. Sometimes I was brought there by ambulance and sat in a wheelchair for hours, wrapped in a blanket, my pajamas, and socks. No shoes, of course, because the paramedics came too quickly for me to grab them. Sometimes I was quickly assessed and sent home with pain meds and no diagnosis. Other times, my partner and I gave up and walked home, me in my socks and no shoes. Hospital 1 was also where I screamed in agony, sobbed uncontrollably, and demanded an expert consultation as scan after scan showed no evidence of pain. I was sick and tired, but I was "fine." After weeks, it became the space where my pain was finally taken seriously, and I was admitted for further consultation and treatment. My deafness was acknowledged—they noted it on the patient chart—and the reality of a possible malignancy and hysterectomy sensitively handled. But perhaps cruelly, I was admitted to a suite in the maternity ward, because no beds were available in general surgery. One night my screams sang the same song as the laboring person in the next room; our pain joined together in shared suffering.

It became clear I needed surgical treatment that Hospital 1 could not provide. One evening long after visiting hours were over, two orderlies and a nurse came to take me to the ambulance transfer, explaining I was being admitted for surgery within the next day or two. When the orderlies went to reception to register me in Hospital 2, they learned a bed was not yet available. I waited in the wheelchair for what seemed like hours—on a hydromorphone drip, you lose your sense of time—before I was on a bed, in a shared room, maybe a third of the size of my former suite. There was no chair for my partner. The hallways were overcrowded with supplies and equipment. The lights occasionally flickered. This was a ward where people wait for surgery or death, a place with no security or comfort. Here, a patient becomes a subject and not a person, their autonomy stripped like the sheets the orderly took from my bed while I slept. I went without food, because they forgot to update my chart. My calls for help went unheard through the empty corridors, and when someone came, it was usually because my IV drip loosened from my arm, sending off alarm bells that I could not hear.

At Hospital 2, I was constantly terrified. My partner had no space to sit or work, so he went to the lounge and stayed in touch with me through text chats. Doctors made decisions but my hazy, medicated self could scarcely comprehend their explanations, though they kept reminding me I was here for surgery. Every day, they told me, was my surgery day. Every day passed with no answer. Then one afternoon, shortly after my partner left to pick up lunch, the surgeons arrived to tell me I was being discharged: the cancer they suspected I had was "merely" an endometrial mass and thus, outside their jurisdiction. I would not be having surgery here but would have to see further specialists.

I went home, with the eight- or nine-centimeter mass—sometimes they told me it was six or seven—still in my body, crestfallen and terrified at the prospect of suffering for a few more months until it would be removed, if it would even be removed at all. At this time, I had no guarantee, only fleeting promises of cure.

Eight months later, I was admitted to Hospital 3. It was two months since I had the surgery to remove the mass, and I was experiencing unusual complications—fever, rash, and anaphylaxis—which indicated I was having an allergy attack, even though I had no documented allergies. An EpiPen shot helped to stabilize my symptoms, but only for a little while, as there in the emergency room, my temperature soared as my blood pressure dropped to dangerously low levels. Specialists were called for an assessment. Hours later, with little improvement, I was taken to the sleek and sterile intensive care unit. Pain meds were provided at easy disposal, and for the next few days, numerous specialists came into my room to take my vitals, draw more blood, and examine me, in what seemed like a futile quest to diagnose my mystery illness.

While with the previous hospital experiences I never worried about the costs, Hospital 3 was different—it was American, as we had relocated to the United States for my new job. With every test, expert, medication, I silently calculated what it would cost me and how much would be covered by insurance; the stress of this affected my ability to rest, as much as the ill-equipped waterbed did. The lights were hardly turned off, and thus my mind was always running, worrying about how we would survive not just this latest encounter, but our future. How could we live our dreams if we were straddled with immense debt, mere months after starting a new job? I couldn't sleep. I had nightmares. Days later, I had enough of being poked and prodded without any improvement and discharged myself against medical advice.

For so long, I've been an unwell woman with an uncertain disease, repeating patterns of others who, as Elinor Cleghorn aptly put it, "emerged from the annals of medicine like so many matryoshka dolls." Within these different spaces of healing, I found myself performing differently. I made myself invisible when I thought it best to defer to the hierarchical order in the hospital. Or, I screamed as loud as I could so they could testify to my agony, trying to cut through what Alex Haagaard describes as the "process of invisibilization mediated by the clinical gaze," to demand the pain of my illness receive clinical recognition. This became a constant negotiation of carefully crafted responses so I could receive the care—if not cure—that my suffering body was yearning for.

And in the process of waiting for the end of suffering, Bharat Venkat's words echo through my mind: "What happens when cures instead come and go, when you can be cured and then cured again?" Cure then becomes a fragile accomplishment, temporarily existing within the spaces where it resides, constantly brushing against the walls of grief.

Dreaming of Black Disability Doulas
An Imagining

Moya Bailey

I am disabled. It's taken me some time to get (more) comfortable claiming this as an identity for myself alongside Black, queer, woman, nonbinary, Southern, etc., and a host of other identities that I readily acknowledge. I know that part of my reluctance was the particularities of disability stigma. Not that these other identities don't have their share of stigma, too, but honestly, being presumed able-bodied added a layer of disclosure that generally required me to out myself in ways that my Blackness, queerness, gender—being generally already legible—did not. My lack of exposure to disability culture and disability intimacy played a role in my hesitancy with claiming disability identity as well. Having grown up in a Black family with a Black mother and father, and access to Black queer community in the Black gay mecca of the United States—Atlanta, Georgia—by virtue of attending Spelman College, a historically Black (and women's) college, I found many places where my other identities were actually part of why I was in these spaces. I had connections to communities that affirmed these stigmatized aspects of myself, and access to institutions and organizations of support.

My initial interactions with disability as an identity were through white people in my hometown, who used "disabled" to describe themselves. In college and then graduate school, I was introduced to the largely white canon of disability studies, through white disabled academics. While many in my family had disabilities, they were not connected to disability organizations or institutions and certainly did not say they were disabled. Family members with cognitive and physical disabilities were not institutionalized, even if they received government assistance because they were "on disability." They remained a part of the fabric of Black communities even as many of their needs for access remained unmet. In my mind, disability identity was for white people.

To move from a disability identity to disability culture seemed an even more distant reality to me given the prevalence of racism within disabled spaces. For example, the development of Black American Sign Language as distinct from American Sign Language makes the racist history of this country evident within Deaf culture. Racial segregation existed alongside ability segregation via the creation of schools for the Blind and Deaf in the United States that were initially only open to white students. As I just mentioned, having space with people who share your identity can be fortifying. Even as these institutions reflected a deep-seated ableism, they gave the space to develop unique disability cultures, albeit racially segregated ones.

Not all disabilities are created equal, and it matters how and when your disability shows up in your life. Some disabilities grant you community at birth, a culture to connect with, while others are acquired. Some disabilities make shared culture harder to produce. While I am still ambivalent about the need for disability to be understood as an identity, the power of claiming a disability culture, community, and intimacy cannot be ignored.

I've written elsewhere with collaborator Izetta Autumn Mobley about the particular reluctance of Black people to identify as disabled, which we attribute to the need for us to be seen as productive in this capitalistic society. Black people have always labored in the United States, and any threat to the idea that we can't pull our own weight is stamped out as quickly as possible. What good are we if we are not useful? As someone who appears able-bodied, it feels strange to lay claim to an identity that others don't regularly ascribe to me, particularly when we see how little care is afforded those with disabilities that are readily apparent. But lest I be some tragic mulatto equivalent, caught between two worlds of able-bodied and disabled, let me state, unequivocally, I am on the disabled team.

Part of what helped me get to this full-throated declaration was reading the work of other disabled people of color and being close friends with disabled people of color with whom I built intimacy. Disabled friends have been such important teachers for me on what a disabled life can be. However, my disabilities were so different from the ones that the people closest to me experienced. It took more time for me to be comfortable saying "me too" given those differences.

One of these teachers was the late great Stacey Park Milbern, who came up with the idea of disability doulas. Disability doulas are folks who can usher you into disability with ease and care, much like birth and death doulas help usher people through those incredible transitions. Stacey was a digital turned IRL friend who was at the forefront of shaping the disability justice movement as we know it today, via the digital content she produced and the incredible on-the-ground activism she sparked.

I keep thinking about what disability doulas look like for Black folks, for Black folks like me. What would have made disability more accessible to me? Instead of just thinking about it, I decided to write about it. What follows is my imagined disability doula's words to me.

Well hello there! How you is? You look nice! How do you feel? No, seriously? How do you feel today? I ask because I get the sense that you might be someone who says they are fine when they are not. I know because I used to do that, too.

What's that? It's okay not to know. Sure can be hard to know when most times folks ask the question they don't really want to know.

Tears are okay, too, you know. Have you been holding it in? For how long? Long as you can remember? I get that. It's hard when people think the heart, brain, and body are separate.

I know what you were told. I was told the same thing. You are stronger than the rest of them. Conceal, don't feel. Gotta be twice as good? Maybe three times in your case. Can outwork anyone, can't you? Am I right? It's okay. I won't say more. Talk soon.

Oh, hey! How you been? How you livin'? Ahh, see you caught yourself. You can tell me the real. Yeah, I been there. What did I do? I found a therapist. It took a minute. She wasn't Black either but we talked for months and months. She told me that medication might be helpful. I know, I know it took me some time to wrap my head around it, too. I couldn't think of what my people would think about me taking medication.

What it meant for me to need something outside myself. And how long would I need it? I didn't know. I thought about it for a long time before acting on it. No, no I get it. It was a lot, or it took a lot for me to get comfortable. Have you ever thought about it? Therapy?

You remember that line in *The Salt Eaters*, "Are you sure, sweetheart, you want to be well?" Seems to me, you and those around you have a narrative about health that doesn't seem all that healthy. Someone tried to tell me once, "You know if you were physically sick you wouldn't hesitate to take medicine now would you?" I had to remind them that I sure would and would still go to work anyway. Always gotta keep going, I know. But you know that leads to burnout, leads to worse things than that, and the same is true for the mental I . . . I can tell you are getting overwhelmed. I'll leave it here. But here's my number if you ever want to chat, you know, talk about it.

Hey, it's been a while! How goes it? What's new witcha? Oh let me find out! You got a therapist?! Okay!!! How's it going? That's so good to hear! Right out the gate! Sometimes people have to shop around. Your therapist said, "You don't have to protect your parents here." Oof! I felt that one. Totally feels like telling family business, I know. Took me a long time to get past that. Come to think of it, don't know that I will be past it, to tell the truth. I mean some things need to be said, but the lessons you learned about keeping things close are hard to let go. Oh my therapist? We talk about all sorts of things. They're disabled, too, you know. Yes, I'm disabled.

[*rolls eyes*] And what's a disabled person supposed to look like? You know it's not all physical disabilities, right? Well if you know, then why'd you ask? Sigh. I get it. Took me a long time to get comfortable. I internalized all those narratives, you know the ones, you're too needy if you need help, can't do it by yourself. How come you get relief when the rest of us have to keep going? Took it in and took it on. But I'm here now. I'm gonna go. No, I'm not upset but just need a minute.

Oh, good to see you! Sorry . . . for what? Oh, no I told you I wasn't upset, just a little annoyed. You know you'd think that all the social justice types who know not to make assumptions about pronouns would know not to do so around ability. No, good point. We don't all grow up with people around us to help us think about disability like we do gender or race as folks who get marginalized by society. Part of the reason I am so patient with you. Well I am glad you appreciate it. Been talking about it with more people, too. Oh yeah, you'd be interested in that? I'm going to an event by the disability justice culture club this weekend. Want to come with? Yeah? Cool.

Disability doulas that are from our communities are essential for disability justice to flourish and take root. They know the particular types of ableism we are fighting in our community, know the narratives, and know the rationalizations. Disability doulas that can speak back to the problematic narratives we've internalized that valorize overwork, that can separate paranoia from the justified anxieties of living in a racist world are essential for our collective liberation. It's not enough to identify as disabled; we must also do the work of undoing the internalized ableism that lives in our communities and in ourselves. It's so important that my imagined disability doula took a break, rolled their eyes, and checked my ableism for what it was. Disability doulas are not here to take on the labor of undoing internalized ableism for us. They are guides, who need their own rest and their own breaks from the ableism that is all around us. As capitalism and nation-states slowly erode before us, it's time to start imagining the world we want. We can move toward a world that will be in right size with our capacity and where ableism had best be checked or we won't make it for very long. They are true possibility models for what is next.

Thirteen Considerations of the Holy Bug

Claude Olson

1.

I am often mistaken for a tiny biting insect. No one cares to know my taxonomic name. The term *midge* will suffice. Any little two-winged fly can be a midge. There are highland midges and phantom midges, midges with affectionate nicknames like "punkies" and "no-see-ums." There are midges that spread bluetongue disease and midges that pollinate cacao trees. Midges live in mountains and mangrove swamps, among marsh marigolds and monkey flowers and spider lilies on the margins of standing freshwaters. A midge can be found just about anywhere, aside from barren deserts and the frozen tundra.

And yet, people are often surprised when they see me. Sometimes I am met with a look of fear, wide eyes, and a muttered "sorry" before I've had a chance to get in the way. Other times, astonishment. Children who ask how I can be so small, mothers who turn them away from my line of sight. Men who regard me as a rare and mythical creature.

2.

All I wanted was a pack of sour gummy worms. All anyone wants when they go to a CVS is to leave as soon as possible. But I happened to look up at the man beside me in the candy aisle. His eyes were locked on me. It was disturbing, how little fear I saw in them.

"I've never seen a midget in real life before."

I blinked.

"Only in porno."

My body might as well have been on the shelf, sandwiched between the bright yellow packets of Peanut M&M's and the stacks of King Size Kit Kats. A fly among the sour worms. An animal just the same.

3.

The term *midget* returns 560 results on Pornhub. There's Midget Mouth and Midget Grannie, Midget Tiny Texie and Midget Girl Mary Jane. Midget Fucks Her Pussy On Webcam. Midget Gets Destroyed By a Big Black Cock. A midget can be found doing just about anything.

Any little person can be a midget. It's not a medical term but instead a convenient, albeit derogatory, catchall for any person of unusually short stature. Unusual, as in a deviation from what is normal. Unusual, as in a spectacular curiosity. Horny Midget Having a Good Fucking Time clocking in at 5.9 million views.

4.

Our bodies were built to be worshiped. Before the internet, we were the stars of circus tours and, before the invention of the wheel, we were among the ranks of Egyptian gods. Little people were seen as celestial gifts, bodies bestowed by the heavens. We were royalty, depicted on the walls of tombs and buried alongside mummified kings. We were actual gods, too. Bes was the dwarf god of childbirth and the protector of households, a squat man with a face so grotesque it could drive away evil spirits. Still, there is beauty in a body that can ward off all the world's sorrow.

Bes was indeed a symbol of all that was good in the world. He could be found rendered in stone, tattooed on the thighs of dancers, painted in the hopes of healing the sick and barren. He was fertility and music and sexual pleasure, a deity with a cult of devotees. A body, indisputably holy.

5.

I knew I would never have trouble finding a man to worship me. I could open up Tinder at any time, gather a few dozen matches, and wait for my inbox to fill with requests for explicit pictures, propositions for one-night stands, and open confessions that the thought of me was enough to bring on an orgasm or two.

The trouble comes when men begin to feel ashamed that they ever saw a body like mine as a sexual spectacle. I can lure them with my siren song but I cannot keep them in a state of perpetual hypnosis. They inevitably wake in a moment of realization: I've drawn them to the traveling freak show.

6.

The first time I was with a man, he interrupted me mid-act.

"Are you legally able to consent?"

He had a twinge of fear in his eyes, like he suddenly snapped out of the spell I had put him under. The ruse could only last for so long. My body was that of a goddess's and then it was that of an insentient fly. I hadn't felt small until that moment.

I finished the act as a retaliation, some desperate attempt to reclaim whatever agency I had left. If I was a rational person, I would have kicked him out. No, if I was truly rational, I would have left him behind earlier that afternoon, when I entered his car and he asked if it was safe for me to ride in the passenger seat. I would have gone home alone and wished I stayed. Instead, he left and I wished I didn't feel so satisfied.

7.

Growing up, I never imagined that I could have sex with a man. I was four feet tall, rather chubby, and a lesbian, as far as I knew. Having unrestricted internet access from an early age turned me off the idea of attracting men entirely, Google searches acting as a sort of reverse conversion therapy.

It does not take long to find a man burdened by his attraction to our holy bodies.

"How can I stop having a midget fetish?" one Quora user asks.

"You need to slip growth hormone into the food of the midgets you love," another responds.

8.

The word *fetish* derives from the Latin *facere* and *facticius*, literally "to make artificial." In order to have a fetish, in this sense, you must believe that an ordinary object holds supernatural power over you. My holiness, then, may be a delusion, entirely.

There is no official name for this certain fetish, only close approximations. Anasteemaphilia, an arousal to a person of extreme stature. Microphilia, a fetish for unrealistically tiny people. Formicophilia, a pleasure derived from insects crawling over one's body.

9.

If you want to call a midge by its taxonomic name, you can look toward the name of its family: Chironomidae, derived from the ancient Greek word for "pantomimist."

Perhaps my attempt at being attractive in the secular sense is nothing more than an act of playing pretend. The men I have hooked up with may only remember me as a fulfilled item of a bucket list. They may talk about our time together like it was an encounter with a cryptid, along the likes of Bigfoot or Mothman. It is entirely possible I was no more than a fetish to them. If so, should I be ashamed?

10.

It is not as if I could ever disentangle my conventional beauty from my physical deformities. I have a perfect button nose, virtually unblemished skin, and orthodontically corrected teeth, but none of that guarantees I will be seen as beautiful in my entirety. I will always have bowed legs, stunted arms, an uneven gait, and an unusually short stature. I will always be a spectacle. Maybe there is beauty in a body that can draw the attention of an audience.

11.

In 2009, Chen Mingjing, an average-size man, constructed a theme park in China to house and employ about one hundred entertainers with dwarfism. He named it the Kingdom of the Little People, envisioning it as a safe haven from the social and economic setbacks these performers faced.

While the organization Little People of America, among other human rights groups, condemned the park, its residents found within it confidence and community. They could spend their days dancing in elaborate costumes and singing on a stage designed to resemble a woodland garden. They could be spectacles on their own terms.

12.

I do not want to believe that there is something deeply wrong with those who admire our beauty. After all, our bodies have been worshiped for millennia. Our genetically mutated bones are a sight to behold.

I am reminded of Charles Sherwood Stratton, otherwise known as General Tom Thumb. At three feet and four inches tall, he was by far the most famous act of P. T. Barnum's traveling circus. Though his height was certainly an aspect of his appeal, Stratton was a genuine showman, able to act, sing, dance, and perform comedy routines to such an outstanding degree that he was regarded as a professional entertainer, beyond the ranks of the freak show circuit. He made a wildly successful career out of being an oddity.

13.

The world still sees us as items in a curio cabinet, so I choose to believe this means our beauty is truly otherworldly. I think we deserve to be showcased in that way. We may be unusual, but we are not common flies. We are oddities, possessing the type of beauty that is loud and thunderous, resonating like the footsteps of dancing gods.

About the Editor

Alice Wong is a disabled activist, media maker, and research consultant based in San Francisco, California. She is the author of a bestselling memoir, *Year of the Tiger: An Activist's Life*; the founder and director of the Disability Visibility Project—an online community dedicated to creating, sharing, and amplifying disability media and culture; and the editor of the anthology *Disability Visibility: First-Person Stories from the Twenty-First Century* and *Disability Visibility: 17 First-Person Stories for Today* (Adapted for Young Adults). Alice is also the host and coproducer of the *Disability Visibility* podcast and copartner in a number of collaborations such as #CripTheVote and Access Is Love. From 2013 to 2015, Alice served as a member of the National Council on Disability, an appointment by President Barack Obama.

About the Contributors

Ada Hubrig (they/them) is probably off somewhere fighting some ableist institution and/or trying to provide care for other disabled people. They are a genderqueer, disabled/chronically ill, autistic caretaker of cats. They work as an assistant professor of English as their day job. Their scholarship centers on the overlap between disability and queer/trans theory and has appeared in several academic journals. Their words have also found homes in Disability Visibility Project and *Taco Bell Quarterly.* Raised in rural North Dakota, they currently reside in Texas with their partner, cats, and pollinator garden. Find them on Twitter @AdaHubrig.

Aimi Hamraie (they/them) is associate professor of medicine, health, and society and American studies at Vanderbilt University, and director of the Critical Design Lab. Hamraie is the author of *Building Access: Universal Design and the Politics of Disability* and host of the *Contra** podcast on disability and design. They are a member of the US Access Board and a 2022 United States Artists Fellow. They have been quoted by the *New York Times*, the *Chronicle of Higher Education*, National Public Radio, the History Channel, the *Huffington Post*, *Art News*, and others. Hamraie's critical design work focuses on disability arts, digital media, tactical urbanism, fashion, participatory mapping, and landscape design. Hamraie is a certified permaculture designer and herbalist, with particular interest in antiracist and disability-justice centered practices. They have worked as a community organizer in disability justice, antiwar, labor, racial justice, and immigration justice struggles, and cofounded the Nashville Disability Justice Collective and Nashville Mutual Aid Collective.

Akemi Nishida uses research, education, and activism to investigate how ableism and sanism are exercised in relation to racism, cisheteropatriarchy, xenophobia, queer- and trans-phobia, and other forms of social injustices. She also uses such methods to contribute to disability justice activism. She is the author of *Just Care: Messy Entanglements of Disability, Dependency, and Desire*, in which she examines public healthcare programs as well as grassroots interdependent care collectives and bed-space activism. She teaches at the University of Illinois Chicago, while also advocating for disability justice locally and nationally.

Ashley Shew works in philosophy of technology, animal studies, and disability studies as an associate professor of science, technology, and society at Virginia Tech. She is the author of *Animal Constructions and Technological Knowledge* and *Against Technoableism: Rethinking Who Needs Improvement*.

Dr. Ashley Volion is a native of Louisiana and currently resides in New Orleans. Ashley has a PhD in disability studies from the University of Illinois Chicago, and a bachelor's and a master's degree in sociology from the University of New Orleans. Ashley's research interests are disability and access intimacy as well as home and community-based services. She has also had her poetry published in the *Queer Disability Anthology*. Currently, Ashley is a lecturer in sociology at Tulane University. She is committed to ensuring that people with disabilities are fully integrated members of society.

Ashna Ali is a queer, Bangladeshi-diasporic, and chronically ill Best of the Net–nominated poet, writer, and editor based in Brooklyn, New York. Their chapbook, *The Relativity of Living Well*, traces the early days of the COVID pandemic in New York City. Their poetry has appeared in *Indiana Review*, in Sun Dog Lit, as Brooklyn Poets poet of the week, as Split This Rock's poem of the week, and elsewhere. They serve as a fellow in Shira Erlichman's In Surreal Life poetry program and hold a PhD in comparative literature from the CUNY Graduate Center. When they're not running a tech start-up, they support writers as a coach and editor.

Carrie Wade lives in Los Angeles.

Claude Olson (she/they) is a writer and educator with a passion for social justice and literature. Before joining the Education Programs team at PEN/Faulkner, she completed a summer teaching fellowship at Generation Teach and an AmeriCorps service term at City Year. She recently graduated from Smith College with a bachelor of arts degree in education and child study. At Smith, she became involved with community organizing projects related to disability justice and ethical community engagement, and authored a zine titled *Organizing Is for Everyone: A Guide for the Emerging Activist*. Born with achondroplasia, a form of dwarfism, Claude uses their experience as a physically disabled person to advocate for the inclusion and equity of disabled students and educators, as well as for those from other marginalized communities. They are proud to be a part of an organization that seeks to uplift diverse voices in the classroom and the literary world. Claude works to share their experiences of the joys and challenges of living with a visible disability.

Cyrée Jarelle Johnson is a poet from Piscataway, New Jersey. He is the author of *SLINGSHOT*, winner of a Lambda Literary Award for Gay Poetry. Johnson was awarded a Ruth Lilly and Dorothy Sargent Rosenberg Poetry Fellowship from the Poetry Foundation and served as the inaugural poet-in-residence at the Brooklyn Public Library. His poems have appeared in *POETRY, Apogee, Foglifter, WUSSY,* and *Atmos,* among other publications. *WATCHNIGHT,* his forthcoming book of poetry, considers ancestry as history in the context of the Great Black Migration of the twentieth century, familial estrangement, and queer family. He is a 2023 National Endowment of the Arts Creative Writing Fellow.

Born in New Orleans, Louisiana, in 1989, **Emilie Louise Gossiaux** is an interdisciplinary artist currently based in New York City. Gossiaux earned her BFA from The Cooper Union School of Art in 2014, and her MFA in sculpture from Yale School of Art in 2019. Her solo exhibitions include After Image, at False Flag Gallery in Long Island City (2018); Memory of a Body, at Mother Gallery in Beacon, New York (2020); and Significant Otherness, at Mother Gallery's location in Tribeca, New York City (2022). She has shown her work internationally in multiple group exhibitions at museums and venues, such as The Wellcome Collection (London); 1969 Gallery (New York City); The Aldrich Contemporary (Ridgefield, Connecticut); MoMA PS1 (New York City); Gallery 400 (Chicago); The Krannert Art Museum (Champaign, Illinois); Museum für Moderne Kunst Frankfurt (Frankfurt, Germany); The Shed (New York City); SculptureCenter (New York City); Julius Caesar (Chicago); Pippy Houldsworth Gallery (London); and Recess Gallery (New York City), among others. Gossiaux was awarded a VSA Award of Excellence from the Kennedy Center for the Performing Arts in 2013, the Eliot Lash Memorial Prize for Excellence in Sculpture in 2014, and a Wyn Newhouse Award in 2019, and was one of ten artists to be awarded the Colene Brown Art Prize by the BRIC Art Center in 2022. Gossiaux has been featured in publications such as *The Brooklyn Rail*, *The New Yorker*, *Art in America*, and *Topical Cream Magazine*.

Ellen Samuels is a queer disabled poet and professor in the departments of Gender and Women's Studies and English at the University of Wisconsin-Madison. She is the author of a verse memoir, *Hypermobilities*, and a poetry chapbook, *December Morning*. Winner of two Lambda Literary Awards, she has published poetry and creative nonfiction widely, including in *Tupelo Quarterly*, *Copper Nickel*, *Colorado Review*, *Brevity*, *Journal of the American Medical Association*, and the collection *Disability Visibility: Voices from the Twenty-First Century*.

Elliot Kukla is a rabbi who provides spiritual care to those who are grieving, dying, ill, or disabled. He is working on a book about the power of grief in a time of planetary crisis.

Gabrielle Peters is a disabled writer, policy analyst, storyteller, curator, and creator of unique learning materials and events. Also a wannabe artist of some kind. She is poor and lives in a social housing "unit" that she hates because the word *accessible* has lost all meaning. #MakeItAccessibleOrBurnItDown. She wants a dog and to be in/on water and to bake everyone treats . . . but poverty. She loves reading letters to the editor and doctoral theses about anything the person who wrote them is passionate about. She wants people to know there's no kindness in injustice.

Gracen Brilmyer (they/them) is a Disabled researcher whose work investigates the ways that disabled people use, experience, and understand themselves through archives as well as how to tell histories of disability when there is little or no archival evidence. They are currently assistant professor at McGill University and director of the Disability Archives Lab. For more: disabilityarchiveslab.com.

Ingrid Tischer is a crip-lit writer who blogs at talesfromthecrip.org. Her work has appeared in *High Shelf*, and she was mentored in fiction writing by Lewis Buzbee through Gemini Ink. She has also attended Flight of the Mind workshops taught by Gish Jen, Lynne Sharon Schwartz, and Charlotte Watson Sherman. She will always be indebted to Linda Elkins' Writing Circles for Women, where she found community for more than eight years.

Jade T. Perry is a BlackQueerDisabledFemme, interdisciplinary artist, and spiritualist. The mission of her work, as a whole, is to contribute writing, resources, art, and experiential learning opportunities that aid in the holistic healing processes of Blackfolk; Queer, Trans, Black, Indigenous, People of Color (QTBIPOC); and Disabled and/or Chronically Ill folks within these communities. She's a Philly jawn living in Chicago, an avid tea drinker, and a regular headliner at home shower concerts. Learn more and keep in touch at jadetperry.com/links.

Jaipreet Virdi is an associate professor in the Department of History at the University of Delaware, whose research focuses on the ways medicine and technology impact the lived experiences of disabled people.

She is the author of *Hearing Happiness: Deafness Cures in History*, a coeditor of *Disability and the Victorians: Attitudes, Legacies, Interventions*, and has published articles on diagnostic technologies, audiometry, and the medicalization of deafness in *Slate, Bitch Media, Forbes, The Atlantic, Psyche, Welcome Collection Stories*, and the *New Internationalist*, among others. She can be reached via jaivirdi.com.

John Lee Clark is a DeafBlind poet, essayist, and independent scholar from Minnesota. His chapbook of poems, *Suddenly Slow*, appeared in 2008. He has edited two anthologies, *Deaf American Poetry* and *Deaf Lit Extravaganza*. His latest book is a collection of essays called *Where I Stand: On the Signing Community and My DeafBlind Experience*. Clark was a featured writer at the Deaf Way II International Cultural Arts Festival, and has won grants and fellowships from the Minnesota State Arts Board, VSA Minnesota, the Laurent Clerc Cultural Fund, Intermedia Arts Center, and The Loft Literary Center. He was a finalist for the 2016 Split This Rock Freedom Plow Award for Poetry & Activism. His work is included in the anthologies *Beauty Is a Verb: The New Poetry of Disability, Deaf American Prose, St. Paul Almanac*, and *The Nodin Anthology of Poetry*. Clark lives in Hopkins, Minnesota, with his wife, the artist Adrean Clark, and their three boys. He works for the Minnesota Department of Employment and Economic Development as a Braille and Protactile instructor.

Kennedy Healy (she/they) is a Fat, Queer, Crip writer and media maker. Her work focuses on disability, accessibility, care, sexuality, media representation, and abolition. Most recently, she founded Crip Crap, a media company that makes media about disability, by and for disabled people. She is a Libra who loves plants, chicken wings, and feminist country music. Follow her work at cripcrapmedia.com or on Instagram @crip.crap.media.

Khadijah Queen, PhD, is the author of six books, most recently *Anodyne*, winner of the William Carlos Williams Award from the Poetry Society of America. A zuihitsu about the pandemic, "False Dawn," appeared in *Harper's Magazine* in 2020. Individual works appear in *American Poetry Review*, the *New York Times*, *The Poetry Review* (London), and widely elsewhere. In 2022, United States Artists recognized her work with a $50,000 Disability Futures Fellowship. A book of literary theory and criticism, *Radical Poetics*, is forthcoming in 2024.

Leah Lakshmi Piepzna-Samarasinha is a nonbinary femme disabled writer and disability and transformative justice movement worker of Burgher and Tamil Sri Lankan, Irish, and Galician/Roma ascent. They are the author or coeditor of ten books, including *The Future Is Disabled: Prophecies, Love Notes, and Mourning Songs*; *Beyond Survival: Strategies and Stories from the Transformative Justice Movement* (coedited with Ejeris Dixon); *Tonguebreaker*; and *Care Work: Dreaming Disability Justice*. A 2020–2021 Disability Futures Fellow, Lambda Award–winner, and longtime disabled BIPOC space maker, they are currently building the Stacey Park Milbern Liberation Arts Center, an accessible residency for disabled 2QTBIPOC writers.

Maria Town is the president and CEO of the American Association of People with Disabilities, a national cross-disability civil rights organization working to increase the political and economic power of disabled people. Town previously worked for a decade in government, serving as the director of the Houston Mayor's Office for People with Disabilities, as a senior associate director in the Obama White House Office of Public Engagement, and as a policy adviser at the Department of Labor's Office of Disability Employment Policy. She is a red lipstick connoisseur and lives in Washington, DC, with her wife and two cats.

Dr. Marie E. S. Flores (she/her/*ella*/*suya*) is a family medicine physician at AltaMed and an assistant researcher in the Department of Epidemiology at UCLA Fielding School of Public Health. She was an undergraduate at Davidson College majoring in Spanish, got her masters and PhD in epidemiology at UCLA, and went to medical school at the University of Utah. She completed her residency at the social medicine program at Montefiore Medical Center in the Bronx, New York. Her professional interests include primary care in medically underserved communities, reproductive health and justice, transgender health, public health research in Latino populations, and environmental issues. She currently lives in the Los Angeles area with her husband, son, and two dogs and was featured in the 2021 *LA Times* article about pregnancy and disability that appeared on the front page of the Sunday paper: https://www.latimes.com/california/story/2021 -09-30/how-modern-medicine-neglects-disabled-mothers.

Marieke Nijkamp (she/they) is a #1 *New York Times* bestselling author whose work includes *This Is Where It Ends*; *Even If We Break*, a cabin-in-the-woods thriller with RPG nerds and a majority disabled cast; *Ink Girls*, a graphic novel with Sylvia Bi, in which two disabled girls take on the patriarchy by means of found family and free press; and *Unbroken: 13 Stories Starring Disabled Teens*. Marieke worked on *The Oracle Code* with Manuel Preitano, which gave Barbara Gordon a new origin story as Oracle; *Goosebumps: Secrets of the Swamp* with Yasmín Flores Montañez, which introduced one of the first disabled leads in a Goosebumps tale; and stories set at the final frontier and in a galaxy far, far away.

Marley Molkentin (she/her) is a photographer, videographer, and digital media specialist from Cincinnati, Ohio. She received her BA in multimedia photojournalism as well as an MA in civic media from

Columbia College Chicago. She is most passionate about collaborative creative storytelling that helps educate and broaden perspectives on social justice issues. Most of all, she just loves people. You can see more of her work on her website, marleymolkentin.com, or follow her on Instagram at @marleymultimedia.

Melissa Hung is a writer and journalist. She is the founding editor of *Hyphen*, an independent Asian American magazine. Her essays and reported stories have appeared on NPR, in *Vogue*, in *Jellyfish Review*, at LongReads, and in *Catapult*, where she wrote a column about living with a chronic migraine called "Pain in the Brain." She grew up in Texas, the eldest child of immigrants, and now lives in New York City.

Mia Mingus is a writer and educator for transformative justice and disability justice. Mia helped to create and forward the disability justice framework. Her writings on disability have been used around the world and are a regular part of college and university curricula. Mia has played a key role in connecting disability justice with other movements and communities. Her writings can be found on her blog, *Leaving Evidence.* Mia founded and currently leads SOIL: A Transformative Justice Project, which builds the conditions for transformative justice to grow and thrive.

Moya Bailey is an associate professor at Northwestern University and the founder of the Digital Apothecary and cofounder of the Black Feminist Health Science Studies Collective. Her work focuses on marginalized groups' use of digital media to promote social justice, and she is interested in how race, gender, and sexuality are represented in media and medicine. She is the digital alchemist for the Octavia E. Butler Legacy Network and the board president of Allied Media Projects. She is a coauthor of *#HashtagActivism: Networks of Race and Gender Justice* and is the author of *Misogynoir Transformed: Black Women's Digital Resistance.*

Naomi Ortiz (they/she) explores cultivating care and connection within states of stress. Reimagining our relationship with the US/Mexico borderlands and challenging who is an environmentalist is investigated in their new collection, *Rituals for Climate Change: A Crip Struggle for Ecojustice.* Their nonfiction book, *Sustaining Spirit: Self-Care for Social Justice,* provides informative tools and insightful strategies for diverse communities on addressing burnout. Ortiz is also a coeditor of the forthcoming anthology *Every Place on the Map Is Disabled: Poems and Essays on Disability.* As a 2022 US Artist Disability Futures Fellow and a Reclaiming the Border Narrative Project awardee, they emphasize interdependence and spiritual growth through their poetry, writing, facilitation, and visual art. Ortiz is a Disabled Mestize living with their partner and cats in the Arizona US/Mexico borderlands. For more: naomiortiz.com.

Nicole Lee Schroeder is a historian, educator, and a disabled activist in higher education. She writes about how disabled people have resisted medicalization, advocated against ableist structures, and leveraged power wherever possible. In her spare time, Nicole enjoys video games, fiber arts of all kinds, and iced coffee.

Pelenakeke Brown is a Sāmoan, queer, disabled artist and writer. Her practice explores the intersections between disability theory and indigenous Sāmoan concepts. She has presented performances and had exhibitions and residencies in New York, California, Berlin, Hamburg, London, and Aotearoa (New Zealand). She has published essays and poetry in *Apogee*, the *Movement Research Performance Journal*, the *Hawai'i Review*, and in various forthcoming books. She has been profiled in *Art in America* and recognized with a Creative New Zealand Pacific Toa Award. She is a cofounder of Rotations, a digital platform and collaborative movement practice for and with disabled artists.

Robin Wilson-Beattie (she/her) is a speaker, writer, and advocate for disability and sexuality and one of the first people to talk about disability, sexuality, and marketing to adult product retailers and manufacturers. She combines years of personal experience with medically sound research to provide a unique perspective on how life and identity impact one's sexual expression. Her speaking engagements include multiple keynotes and panels, including the Office of the Vice President of the United States, and three consecutive years of speaking at the Adult Video News convention in Las Vegas.

Her work has not only helped tens of thousands of disabled people but also inspired many others to become advocates for sexuality and disability education, an incredibly underserved area.

Robin is a certified sexual health educator with the American Board of Sexology and the City College of San Francisco. She is a member of the Association of American Sexual Educators, Counselors, and Therapists (AASECT) and the Women of Color Sexual Health Network (WOCSHN). A self-identified deep-fried Southern Inclusionista, she enjoys making delicious messes in the kitchen and exploring and adventuring with her family.

Ryan J. Haddad is an actor, playwright, and autobiographical performer based in New York. His acclaimed solo play *Hi, Are You Single?* was presented in the Public Theater's Under the Radar Festival and continues to tour the country. Other New York credits include

My Straighties (Ars Nova/ANT Fest), *Noor and Hadi Go to Hogwarts* (Theater Breaking Through Barriers), and the cabaret *Falling for Make Believe* (Joe's Pub/Under the Radar). Regional theatre: *The Maids, Lucy Thurber's Orpheus in the Berkshires* (Williamstown Theatre Festival), and *Hi, Are You Single?* (Guthrie Theater, Cleveland Play House, Williamstown Theatre Festival). He has a recurring role on the Netflix series *The Politician*. Additional television: *Bull, Madam Secretary*, and *Unbreakable Kimmy Schmidt*. Haddad is a recipient of IAMA Theatre Company's Shonda Rhimes Unsung Voices Playwriting Commission and Rising Phoenix Repertory's Cornelia Street American Playwriting Award. His work has been developed with the Public Theater, Manhattan Theatre Club, New York Theatre Workshop, Berkeley Repertory Theatre, Noor Theatre, Rattlestick Playwrights Theater, Primary Stages, and Pride Plays. His writing has been published in the *New York Times, Out* magazine, and *American Theatre*. Ryan is an alum of the Public Theater's Emerging Writers Group and a former Queer|Art Performance and Playwriting Fellow under the mentorship of Moe Angelos. Find him online @ryanjhaddad and at ryanjhaddad.com.

Sami Schalk is an associate professor of gender and women's studies at the University of Wisconsin-Madison. She is the author of *Bodyminds Reimagined* and *Black Disability Politics*. Schalk identifies as a fat, Black, queer, disabled femme and a pleasure activist.

Hoat! **Sarah Young Bear-Brown/tti-ka-mi-ge-a** is a member of the Sac & Fox Tribe of the Mississippi in Iowa—the Meskwaki Nation. She currently resides in Council Bluffs, Iowa. Sarah is a mother of two young children. She went to Iowa School for the Deaf and attended United Tribes Technical College in Bismarck, North Dakota. She walks in two different worlds; as a Meskwaki and as a Deaf woman.

Sarah is currently the chair for the Native American Caucus of the Iowa Democratic Party and from 2020 to 2022 was vice chair for NAC for IDP. She was formerly a member of the Deaf Poor People's Campaign. She believes in Human Rights. Sarah has been an activist/advocate for the Indigenous Deaf community since 2014 and founded "Gathering of Deafatives" for the community. She also advocated and protested with the No DAPL (Dakota Access Pipeline) at Standing Rock, Line 3 in Minnesota and supports the MMIW (Missing and Murdered Indigenous Women) movement. She works as an ASL story-teller, Deaf interpreter, and motivational speaker. Sarah was invited to the White House's roundtable for Native Disabled in September 2021. She was awarded for her leadership by Hamilton Relay and was a Native American Forty Under Forty honoree for the National Center for American Indian Enterprise Development for 2021. On March 18, 2022, Sarah was invited to the White House for Women's History Month and invited again on September 28, 2022, for the thirty-two-year anniversary of the ADA. She owns a small business called SAYBB Creations Beadwork and has been creating beadwork for twenty-three years, starting at age fifteen. Sarah is a fifth-generation beadworker, following her mother's, Mary Young Bear's, path as a beadwork art-ist; Mary was inducted into the Iowa Women's Hall of Fame in 2020. *Ketebi.*

s.e. smith is a National Magazine Award–winning Northern California–based writer who has appeared in *The Guardian*, *Rolling Stone*, *Esquire*, *Bitch Magazine*, and numerous other fine publications.

Sejal A. Shah is a queer, brown, neurodivergent writer of Kenyan, Ugandan, Indian, Gujarati background, born and raised in Rochester, New York. She is the author of the debut story collection *How to Make*

Your Mother Cry: Fictions and *This Is One Way to Dance: Essays.* Her viral essay, "Even If You Can't See It: Invisible Disability & Neurodiversity" (*Kenyon Review*), became part of a larger conversation about academia, accommodations, and disclosure. She is grateful to Alice for inviting her to contribute to this anthology/community. Sejal lives in western New York.

•

Dr. Syrus Marcus Ware is a Vanier Scholar, visual artist, activist, curator, and educator. Syrus is an assistant professor at the School of the Arts, McMaster University. Using painting, installation, and performance, Syrus works with and explores social justice frameworks and Black activist culture. His work has been shown widely. He is part of the PDA (Performance Disability Art) Collective and co-programmed Crip Your World: An Intergalactic Queer/POC Sick and Disabled Extravaganza as part of Mayworks 2014. Syrus is also a cocurator of The Cycle, a two-year disability arts performance initiative of the National Arts Centre. Syrus is a cofounder of Black Lives Matter Canada and the Wildseed Centre for Art & Activism and a cocurator of Blackness Yes!/Blockorama and the Wildseed Black Arts Fellowship. Syrus holds a doctorate from York University in the faculty of environmental studies. He is a coeditor of the bestselling *Until We Are Free: Reflections on Black Lives Matter in Canada.*

Tee Franklin (they/she) is a Black, queer, disabled, autistic, award-winning comic creator, screenwriter, keynote speaker, and veteran sex worker. Franklin has created new disabled characters for DC, Marvel, Archie, and My Little Pony and is the first Black woman to write Harley Quinn and Poison Ivy. Tee's debut graphic novella, *BINGO LOVE*, was nominated for a GLAAD award. When she's not writing—or tweeting (@MizTeeFranklin)—Franklin is watching anime, while eating lemon pepper wings with curly fries, and always gushing over her first grandchild. Tee resides in New Jersey with her adult children.

The Redwoods are writers, speakers, and activists in the San Francisco Bay Area. A decade into their liberation work for plurals, those who are many in one body, they give workshops and keynotes educating thousands at venues like UCLA School of Medicine and the Philadelphia Trans Wellness Conference, and millions more via media like BBC Radio and KQED News. The Redwoods founded and have led the mutual aid organization Mask Oakland since 2017, focused on protecting disabled and unhoused people's lungs in California's worsening wildfires and a pandemic. They love to cook, watch sci-fi, and improvise on piano. For more: redwoodscircle.com.

Travis Chi Wing Lau (he/him) is assistant professor of English at Kenyon College. His research and teaching focus on eighteenth- and nineteenth-century British literature and culture, health humanities, and disability studies. Alongside his scholarship, Lau frequently writes for venues of public scholarship like *Synapsis: A Journal of Health Humanities*, *Public Books*, *Lapham's Quarterly*, and the *Los Angeles Review of Books*. His poetry has appeared in *Wordgathering*, *Glass*, *South Carolina Review*, *Foglifter*, and *Hypertext*, as well as in three chapbooks: *The Bone Setter*, *Paring*, and *Vagaries*. Find him at travisclau.com.

Yomi Sachiko Wrong, a native of the Bronx, New York, is a Black disabled parent, activist, social justice strategist, and disability justice dreamer living on unceded Ohlone land (aka Oakland, California).

Permissions Acknowledgments